CROSSCURRENTS
PURSUING SOCIAL JUSTICE AND INTERRELIGIOUS WORK
SINCE 1950

CrossCurrents (ISSN 0011-1953; online ISSN 1939-3881) connects the wisdom of the heart with the life of the mind and the experiences of the body. The journal is operated through its parent organization, the Association for Public Religion and Intellectual Life (APRIL), an interreligious network of academics, activists, artists, and community leaders seeking to engage the many ways religion meets the public. Contributions to the journal exist at the nexus of religion, education, the arts, and social justice. The journal is published quarterly on behalf of the Association for Public Religion and Intellectual Life by the University of North Carolina Press.

The Association for Public Religion and Intellectual Life (formerly ARIL) is a global network of leaders, scholars, and social change agents who explore religious life, engage in intellectual inquiry, and lead ethical action in the world today. Their primary objective, especially through annual summer colloquia and *CrossCurrents*, is to bring together leading voices of our time to advocate for justice and to examine global spiritual and interreligious currents in both historical and contemporary perspectives.

A membership to APRIL includes access to *CrossCurrents* starting with Volume 58, 2008, though our partners at Project MUSE, monthly newsletters, early access to summer colloquium themes, a 40% on UNC Press books, and more. For more information, including membership and subscription rates, visit www.aprilonline.org.

This reissue of *CrossCurrents* was one of four issues published in 2018 as part of Volume 68. For a current masthead visit www.aprilonline.org.

© 2018 Association for Public Religion and Intellectual Life. All rights reserved.

ISBN 978-1-4696-6701-0 (Print)

CROSSCURRENTS

RELIGION, POLITICAL DEMOCRACY, AND SPECTERS OF RACE

5
Religion, Political Democracy, and Specters of Race: Introduction
James Logan

21
The Future of Sexual Inclusion: Anti-Black Racism, Black Patriarchy and Prospects for Political Democracy
Keri Day

38
Race: Fifty Years Later
Stanley Hauerwas

54
The Backlash This Time: Obama, Trump, and the American Trauma
Gary Dorrien

73
Black Dignity
Vincent Lloyd

93
A World on Fire and Whiteness at the Core
Jennifer Harvey

112
Do Black Lives Matter to White Chistians?
A Theological Reflection in Three Movements
Rubén Rosario Rodríguez

135
Can Theses Black Bones Live? Addressing the Necrotic in Us Theo-Politics
Antonia Michelle Daymond

159
When Hope Appeared in Flesh: From Black Power to Barak Obama and the Spirit of the American Jeremiad
Terrence L. Johnson

179
To Instill Love for My People: Reassembling the Social in a Time of Mass Criminalization
Laura McTighe, with Reverend Doris J. Green

201
Notes on Contributors

About the Cover: Washington DC, USA-December 13, 2014: Black couple protesting police brutality at a protest led by Reverend Al Sharpton on Pennsylvania Avenue in Washington DC. They bear a sign with the message Black Lives Matter. The deaths of Michael Brown, Eric Garner and Tamir Rice galvanized the Black community.

CROSSCURRENTS

RELIGION, POLITICAL DEMOCRACY, AND SPECTERS OF RACE
Introduction

James Logan

Since the election of America's first Black president-elect, Barak Obama, in the fall of 2007, the nation's political democracy has featured (and been shaken by) a heighted focus on race in America. From the beating and killing of Black bodies by law enforcement officers and vigilantes to the Cain-on-Abel (brother-on-brother) violence in the streets, to the xenophobic demagoguery against certain more darkly hued Latinx, Arabs (Muslim or otherwise), "Indigenous Peoples," and other "subaltern" residents of the nation; to the persistent poverty expressed via high joblessness rates, substandard education, and medical care in population centers of color; to the massification of incarceration; to the realities of trans-terror; to the all too routine misogynistic violence against women and girls; to the significant deficits of common civic virtues and values based in faith, hope, justice, and love; to the private plutocratic marketization of human life over social justice and human flourishing which exasperate the nation's racial divide, social and civic alienation in America is as pronounced as ever. And, indeed, our human divides have widened even further in this political (and cultural) age of Donald Trump.

Certainly, as the historic conclusion of the Obama administration came to a close at the start of 2017, the seeds of this volume of *CrossCurrents*, entitled "Religion, Political Democracy, & the Specters of Race in America," found fertile ground. This special volume offers nine eclectic perspectives by religious scholars on the relationship between religion and U.S. political democracy as these relate to the complex and subtle specter of race in America—that is, the racialized dimensions that animate and haunt so much of American life, a national life rooted in powerful religious currents and sensibilities from the theistic/confessional to the civil/patriotic and all complex and subtle admixtures therein.

Indeed, the national struggle with race has been wholly baked into the genetic code of U.S. political life, which harbors astounding measures of religious zeal for better or worse, since before the inception of the republic. Indeed, race and religion continue to mark distinctive central features of American life. This reality notwithstanding, national discussions and debates around the intersections of religion, political democracy, and race ought not, and do not, preclude concomitant intersectional and transnational complexities and subtleties, which include inextricably tied considerations of sexuality/gender, class, ethnicity, and geography. It is with such truth in mind that this volume aims, in the words of Muhammad Ali addressing the nation, to be (at least a small) "disturbance in the sea of your complacency," after the "post-racial" democratic disappointments, hopes, and promises that imbued the, now gone, Obama presidency. In this spirit, this issue of CrossCurrents is dedicated in celebratory remembrance of James Hal Cone, Katie Geneva Cannon, Aretha Franklin, and all others, passed on now, who exemplified the liberating intellectual and faith-filled rhythm, blues, and soul of life and history.

This volume begins with one of the most important emerging national voices, the constructive political theologian and scholar of Black religion, Keri Day. Day's contribution to this volume offers a compelling voicing of the intersections between anti-black racism, black patriarchy, and the prospects for political democracy as these are interrogated from the standpoint of sexual inclusion.

Day recounts Barack Obama's personal moral evolving in support of LGBTQ persons and communities during the period leading up to the legal 2015 Supreme Court decision to reject the Defense of Marriage Act (DOMA). With clarity, she notes the contrasting moral conundrum between Obama's eventual support of sexual justice over against the opposition to such justice, especially with respect to support for same-sex marriage, by both white and black Christian conservatives alike.

Day details critically important contours associated with the realities of black disenfranchisement, which, along with often-cited concerns related to housing, unemployment, education, and other social challenges, compel us to give serious moral and political attention to marriage equality. Indeed, not only does Day offer a sound accounting of the Trump administration's introduction of executive orders aimed at undermining sexual equality, she demonstrates well why and how Obama's moral and political evolution caused black clergy to withdraw their support from him. Highlighting many of the political and religious culture wars that reign over feuding interpretations of sexual freedom throughout society, Day ponders the provocative, paradoxical, and new conversations, which, she rightly contends, "raise different kinds of concerns in relation to LGBTQ enfranchisement and inclusion as well as the future of political democracy."

Undeniably, Day's intersectional perspective on justice in a nation both racist and hyper-heteropatriarchal deftly alerts readers to the contemporary religious and political arguments mounted by the Christian right to combat LGBTQ inclusion under the banner and mantra of "religious liberty" or "religious freedom." In particular, this conservative combat against inclusion misappropriates the moral righteousness of the Civil Rights Movement (Martin Luther King, Jr., in particular) as a religious and political guide. As Day mounts a case study against such a misappropriation, she also speaks of a "more mitigated position" which has emerged among Christian conservatives in their discourse and civil battles over religious liberty. Highlighted here is the interesting, constitutionally inspired, and pluralistically empathetic, "fairness for all" approach of the Mormon Church, which grants the freedom to marry for same-sex couples while preserving the right of conservative Christians to publicly hold (without "reprimand or lawsuits") their traditional views of marriage. Day notes that this Mormon approach to religious freedom (even beyond the issue of marriage equality) has found a hearing within a "vast number" of other white and black churches.

Perhaps most provocative about Day's essay is her query to readers regarding how our political democracy—which "involves *thinking [and deep listening] through the quality of our political culture*"—might assess "this turn in conservative churches' rethinking concerning religious freedom and LGBTQ concerns."

Indeed, Day's final musing understands that while the fairness for all approach advocated by some conservative Christians might entail good political and moral possibilities for charitable citizenship, serious difficulties remain. She knows well that such possibilities continue to ring hollow as conservative Christians continue to employ the central message that LGBTQ identities (along with other subaltern persons) are morally pathological, abnormal, deviant, and thus socially unfit for the political, economic, and other material riches of true, life-affirming, liberty. Even the liberty of life itself.

Next we find a contribution from one of the English-speaking world's most highly esteemed theological ethicists, Stanley Hauerwas. Hauerwas offers to a provocative reflection on the subject of race a half-century after his first published essay was penned for the Augustana College student newspaper in 1969; he began teaching at Augustana in 1968. Hauerwas offers here a "reproducing" of that very first paper, "An Ethical Appraisal of Black Power," as both a positive and negative marker, "indicating where I (we) have been, where I (we) still may be, and how I now think I (we) need to think about race," fifty years past his first attempt to defend black power.

To be candid though, Hauerwas admits to penning his piece in response to criticism this editor laid out twelve years ago in the Winter 2006 volume of *CrossCurrents* in an essay titled "Liberalism, Race, and Stanley Hauerwas." Be this as it may, Hauerwas offers readers here a valuable window into his often unseen views concerning race in America, including some accounting of his (alleged) past silence on the matter. Very briefly addressing the editor's past essay notwithstanding, Hauerwas moves on to offer a constructive view of race. With some stated concerns about the submersion of class, Hauerwas outlines the challenge and promise of black power (i.e., the new racial freedom) within a democratic society committed to extending participation to all who dwell within it.

Noting that "I got some things right in 1969," and adding that "even some of the things I wrote remain relevant," Hauerwas goes on to link Black Lives Matter to the story and memory of "what it means to be part of a people who have suffered a terrible injustice"; indeed, he understands that "the reality of slavery cannot be lost." It is wonderful to see Hauerwas tie the call of Black Lives Matter to many of the same presumptions that gave birth to the Black Power Movement, namely that African Americans resist white supremacy as we recognize and share a common story of survival, care, and enemy identification. Indeed, it is commendable that Hauerwas confesses that, at root, America is a *slave nation*, a notion that is anathema to many of even the most well-meaning white people. Drawing on the primary and secondary voices of numerous Black religious (and political) leaders and scholars—James Cone, Martin Luther King, Jr., Joe Winters, W. E. B. Dubois, Barak Obama, Jeremiah Wright, and Reggie Williams (all males)—Hauerwas' contribution is a challenge to offended white people, even those white people who claim to be very sympathetic to the cause of African Americans while insisting on a broader recognition of "all lives matter."

Winner of the 2017 Grawemeyer Award for *The New Abolition: W. E. B. Du Bois and the Black Social Gospel*, and among the most lucid and lauded American social ethicists and theologians of his generation, Episcopal priest Gary Dorrien's "The Backlash this Time" brings to mind the title given by the great Black literary social genius James Baldwin to his epic 1963 classic *The Fire Next Time*.

Offering outstanding thick and clear description of the political scope and depth of working-class white resentment, Dorrien reflects on, and past, the historical presidency of Barak Obama. In particular, he traces the now mainstream outrage against the rainbow coalition that propelled Obama's rise to the White House, an outrage which now powers a hellishly resilient political and cultural indignation in the post-Obama age of Trump.

Jumping off the page to grab the reader by the eyes is Dorrien's recounting of the false descriptions of Obama penned and spoken by conservative authors and politicians, which then fueled and refueled the worse of nationalistic-tribal rage against Obama among a vast majority of whites who make up the Trumpian cultural-political base. False descriptions include Obama as illegitimate socialist born in Kenya; Obama as a fraud of the highest Black order set to destroy Western Civilization as an expression of racial revenge and vengeful arrogance; and Obama as harbinger of authentic dishonesty. All of this and more are laid out by Dorrien as the cultural roots from which sprang the rise of Trump—and the subsequent demonization of immigrants, dark-hued urban dwellers, traditional international trade partners, Muslims, Mexicans, Haitians, and Africans in general.

Offering waves of examples that channel the awesome force of rage-filled backlash against everything thought to be tainted by the triumph of Obama, Dorrien paints for us a painfully bleak political portfolio that belies his ultimately, and still substantial, grasp on audacious hope. And this is despite his contention that "I fully expect that Trump will always outperform his poll numbers."

The hope Dorrien sees lies (only partially) in the demographic fact that Trump's base (old, white, and shrinking) offers potential for a political "seesaw" correction that he finds likely. Yet, Dorrien quite wisely does not count on political "a seesaw correction" as the wellspring of hope. Indeed, in the context of presenting Obama as "a liberal-leaning liberal" in 2008 whose "only radical position was that he could be elected president," Dorrien muses on the colossal difference Obama could have made, but did not, on issues of such magnitude as braking up big banks, agitating for a public health option in the Senate, immigration reform (where he broke George W. Bush's record for deportations), and a second stimulus for job creation and clean energy. And in relation to all of this, Dorrien wants readers to truly consider the problem of the white working class, which "looms large in our national trauma." This class of persons (into which Dorrien himself was born as white and part Cree) populate neighborhoods across the country that are "convinced that America society confers blessings on everyone except them," that eight years of Obama speeches about "economic progress" (for the wealthy donor class) failed to see and acknowledge their pervasive and ongoing suffering.

In the end, Dorrien places considerable hope in the political disposition of a person like Bernie Sanders with his single-payer-rebuilding-the-country-curbing-Wall-Street kind of progressive politics on behalf of persons who, like Trump supports though aimed differently, share political outrage against both Democrats and Republicans. Concomitant with a progressive politics, and in view of the guiding title of his contribution to this volume, Dorrien reminds us of Martin Luther King, Jr.'s admonition to justice seekers against the employment of "backlash talk." Expecting the worse of Trump's narcissistic disrespect for democracy to lie ahead, Dorrien's political hope for racial, sexual, and economic justice lies in the advancement of the none-pessimistic moral example of King, who saw the social grammar of "backlash" (even in an era of fiercely bitter backlash) to be a "species of denial" and wholly superficial in the face of persistent racial hostility.

Indeed, Dorrien's contribution, beyond any "backlash talk" in the service of progressive politics, remembers and follows King to that something-more place of risky, controversial, chaotic, life-affirming, and spirit-inspired hope and love. Which was the very place King found himself against the odds toward the end of his life while fronting a mass Poor People's Campaign, a Campaign which Dorrien rightly understands was embraced by King and waged in companionship with the "poorest of the poor and afflicted"—and compelled as a follower of Jesus Christ.

Undergirding so much of what is written in this volume is the question of, and quest for, emancipatory dignity. This is to say that human worth and value ought to be, and ought to have been, the inherent right of every human being there ever was. Indeed, Vincent Lloyd turns us to a call toward the democratization of dignity, that is, "the inherent, incalculable worth," of every human being, in particular and in this instance, African Americans.

Writing as one of the most preeminent scholars of Black political theology and religion alive today, the real force of Lloyd's vision of "Black Dignity" lies in his constructive hypothesis, and proposal, that if dignity took center stage as the common sense language of collective (though varied) black struggle, then black political movements seemingly at odds with one another might better collaborate and agitate for justice animated by "the same fundamental impulse," namely the quest for dignity. Embedded in Lloyd's proposal is an insistence that dignity be examined from the vantage points of marginalized communities as they correct and dispense with the errors found in European Christian and post-Christian sources that have been concerned with the language of dignity in human life and history. To put things more bluntly with respect to Lloyd's advocacy for the vantage point of marginalized communities' approach to dignity, he boldly asserts that "The black perspective of dignity is not just one more perspective, it is better." In building a case for this better black perspective, Lloyd seeks to bridge our understanding of Christian theological reflections on dignity in contradistinction to that of secular political theorists and intellectual historians as they now more readily engage (beyond Christian theology) "Jewish, Islamic, and other religious thought." Here, Lloyd reminds us of the common frustrations with the language of "human rights," which tend to advance the interests of the powerful and ebb and flow depending on the fleeting concerns of the day. In short, Lloyd presses to ground the language of "human rights" under a clearer moral language and promise of dignity.

The reader of Lloyd's very well-crafted work will be reminded of a number of important representative primary and secondary sources, which animate and inspire both intellectual and on-the-ground life-affirming expressions of black dignity: #BlackLivesMatter and its founding black female organizers (Alicia Garza, who first put the famous words into circulation, along with Patrisse Cullors and Opal Tometi), Nelson Mandela, Langston Hughes, Martin Luther King, Jr., Marcus Garvey, Malcolm X, Stokely Carmichael, Ida B. Wells, Anna Julia Cooper, Audre Lorde, Angela Davis, Alice Walker, Michelle Obama, and Brittney Cooper). That Lloyd's work on black dignity prominently evokes the critical power of black women's voices makes it a contribution to a critical black-truth that upends the misogynistic disparagement of women's dignity in the present age of Trump. And as important, Lloyd's work also upends the narratives of American and world history where men (yes, black men too) continue to wantonly and routinely terrorize and neglect embodiments and practices of dignity where women (and I would add, other than cis-gendered) persons are concerned.

Another compelling (and highly provocative) impulse presented in Lloyd's clarion call to *democratize dignity* is his insistence that the political language of dignity is to be "ascribed [as an attribute of *performance*, only] to those who struggle against domination." With respect to African Americans, this means thusly for Lloyd that "…dignity is properly ascribed to black artists and entertainers, black religious practitioners, black dancers, and ordinary black folks who subtly commit to resisting white supremacy." Indeed, one does not embody the virtue of dignity absent the character of their performance.

Lloyd ends up understandably cautious about "dignity's status as a common denominator of black political movements, from Frederick Douglas to Black Lives Matter." He understands clearly (offering compelling evidence from black life and history) that the language of "black dignity" can be (and has been) employed to denote a range of ideas from high rank to inherent worth to elite status, to black acquiescence to white culture's repressive insistence on "respectably politics." Cultural insistence on respectability politics in particular, as noted by Lloyd, is opposed by today's young black activists who reject internalized and overt consent to white supremacy.

So a supreme question (inspired by Lloyd and more than touched upon by all the contributions presented within this volume) is: What are the possibilities for a performative and democratizing language of dignity sufficient to truly realize the (always in a state of becoming) liberation of black folks (*and not just men*) against the complex and subtle tentacles of white supremacy?

Intersecting firsthand accounts, memories, and racialized symmetries between her extended southern family, white churches, and the fiery challenge of whiteness in America, Jennifer Harvey offers a superb account of self-interested white complicity in the political subjugation of Black (and other) minoritized populations.

Indeed, Harvey offers a white woman's view into the willful passivity and duplicity of even the most well-meaning white folks as the conditions that led to the election of a white supremacist president emerged and gripped the nation. In the whiplash of the Obama presidency which has given way to Trump, Harvey (with outstanding perception and insight) sees the deep betrayal of Black, Latino/a, Native America, and LGBTQ persons, indeed betrayal of the most sacred values of humanity and dignity—including white humanity.

Against such a violence, which includes the flesh-and-blood personal violence of a devastating white apathy as well as the systemic political violence of white political self-interest, Harvey wholly seeks to explicitly *not* come to terms with, and set a clarion fire upon, well-meaning White churches' too often "fleeting impulse toward humanity." On Harvey's account, this highly problematic fleeting white impulse makes white supremacy overtly consistent with the Christian gospel.

Of particular force is Harvey's spirit of "truth-telling lament-filled rage," which draws on Emilie M. Townes' articulation of the formative nature of lament, as well as William Stringfellow's brutally honest polemic that "My people is the enemy." It is in the context of such forthrightness that Harvey offers a compellingly robust survey of white women's political, psychic, and self-absorbed collusion in the election of Trump, the anti-Black president. Of particular note in this regard is Harvey's highly adept deconstruction of white women's claims of righteous "intersectionality" as shield from charges of collective white blame and ill-gotten racial privilege. Harvey tells the ugly truth that even the most liberal white women's relationships with women of color (relationships that have never been all that robust to begin with) have been obliterated with their too-silent opposition (thus, complicity) in the election of Trump. Therefore, on Harvey's account, any hope for a "post-white supremist nation" will require a tenaciously focused commitment on the parts of white women to "pull the support of other white people away from white supremacy." Nor are white Christian churches, in particular white evangelicals who are willing to support racist and sexually predatory politicians like Roy Moore of Alabama, spared from Harvey's indictment and charge to white folk.

Lamenting that "racist violence against communities of color and religious minorities has intensified since Trump took office" (think Charlottesville and DACA), what Harvey wants to know is this: Will white Christians forthrightly confront and deal with the many open questions concerning various dimensions of white supremacist complicity that "sit squarely in the center of the sanctuary?"

Citing the political realism inside Barack Obama's own musings on race relations, and notwithstanding a Black man having been elected president of the United States, Rubén Rosario Rodríguez presents a sobering legal, social, and intimately personal view into the limitations of the Obama presidency with respect to substantially advancing racial justice as a core aim of American Democracy. It is no surprise then, on Rodríguez's account, that Black Lives Matter "was born during his presidency."

Offering a sketch of that fateful day in Charlottesville, Virginia, when a mass "Unite the Right" rally ignited brutal, deadly, conflict with progressive justice seekers, including many of peaceable Christians, Rodríguez implores "the nation's progressive white Christians" to "deal more frankly and openly with realities of racism in the post-Obama America after the election of Donald Trump."

It is in the aftermath of tragedy at Charlottesville that Rodríguez ponders if he might develop a "spiritual Turing test" (inspired by the artificial intelligence work of English philosopher and mathematician Alan Turing) to determine if any spark of humanity dwells within "the hateful bigots" who fight for white supremacy on the one hand, and yet possess some deeper humanity amenable to a conversion capable of exercising their racial hatred. Indeed, a central concern of Rodríguez's musings is the extent to which racial bigots are capable of becoming better twenty-first-century humans. Rodríguez wisely dispenses with the idea of an "imitation game" consisting of a variety of theological and moral questions for white supremacists, understanding that such thinking, "however tempting," is a shibboleth down a slippery slope demonizing, objectifying, controlling, manipulating, and/or eliminating "outsiders." Instead, Rodríguez ultimately argues for a well-informed "dialogic approach" to engaging, even befriending, the enemy. Such an effort is to be rooted in the ongoing cultivation of trust-building among racial adversaries within the intersecting domains of community life: for example, between the personal, local governmental, law enforcement, civic-organizational, and religious spheres of St. Louis County, MO, where Rodríguez lives and teaches as a liberation theologian.

Applying his message and pedagogy of progressive and risky justice work to the teaching of nineteen-year-olds at the Catholic St. Louis University, Rodríguez affirms the rugged truth that Black Lives Matter as he centers Martin Luther King, Jr.'s 1963 *Letter From a Birmingham City Jail* among other "other perennial favorites"—Augustine, Anselm, Bonhoeffer. And understanding correctly that it was foolish to expect the election of Barack Obama to solve all the persistent racial and ethnic frustrations facing the United States, Rodríguez's contribution calls forth the Apostle Paul's vision of the Christian churches, holding together both an affirmation of racial and ethnic particularity and a holistic embrace of a spiritually inclusive vision that challenges and implores white Christians to actively and collectively confess that Black Lives Matter. As a Latino/a theologian living in this particular time and place in history, Rodríguez's voice offers a strong personal testimony to the truth that Black Lives Matter. A truth, which he confesses, "deserves the support of brown, yellow, red, white, straight, gay, trans, poor, rich, working class, and all other lives" on the way to building the ever-elusive "more perfect union."

Focusing the pervasive presence of black death, the gifted constructive theologian, Antonia Daymond, offers a view into literal, figurative, and social specters of Black life. Daymond haunting yet sublime rendering speaks of the vexing and ever-evolving archive of American democracy as it grapples with the ways the nation continues to rely upon Christian claims, logics, and myths to support its tragic rationalization of black death. Drawing from black liberationist and feminist thought, she positions blackness as unique and singular resulting from the historical continuity of slavery and its afterlife. Daymond suggests that black bodies remain bound within the violent, necrotic precincts of anti-black racism and white supremacy despite the multifarious differences in black subjectivity, despite the alternative ways black people have embraced life in the midst of pain, and despite as the vague progress made in American public and political life. At core, she advances a thesis which suggests that *both* exclusionary and so-called progressive sociopolitical discourses in our contemporary society depend upon racist deities (that are often informed by the Christian social imaginary) to romanticize, normalize, and neutralize black suffering and death. This, in turn, sustains America's racial and gender hierarchies disallowing any instance of equilibrium or just liberation for black folk. By grounding the violence levied onto black bodies and bringing the theodicy concern of black suffering to the fore, Daymond aims to provide theological redress by proposing a Christology and Soteriology of praxis as that which calls for a temperament of refusal that defies any attempt to rationalize black death. Against such a rationalization in the profound theological context of theodicy and the on-the-ground horror of black execution at Mother Emmanuel, Daymond draws upon a wide range of interlocutor voices to cement the thesis of her convictions: Achille Mbembe, Hortense Spillers, Jared Sexton, "Duboisian peculiarity," Frantz Fanon, Saidiya Hartman, Sylvia Wynter, David Marriot, Harriet Jacobs, etc. Certainly, Daymond's contribution offers an important theo-political view into the necrotic terror that U.S. democracy, as an expression of diasporic white supremacy and brutal female subjectivity, inflicts on black bones.

As the forces of Black death (bodily, civil, economic) reigned during the height of the Civil Rights Movement, a collision of political style and substance emerged in the struggle for Black survival and flourishing. Represented by the nonviolent Christian racial egalitarianism of Martin Luther King, Jr. on one end of the intergenerational divide, and by Stokely Carmichael's emerging and fervent cry of "Black Power" on the other, the highly gifted scholar of religion Terrance Johnson brings a substantial clarity of intellect to Barack Obama's political inheritance and refashioning of the spirit of the American Jeremiad.

Understanding Obama's rise to the American presidency as a potent political embrace of a new theo-political vision, hope, optimism, and lamentation, Johnson brings the debate between "Black liberalism (traditional civil rights voting rights strategy) and Black leftist politics (the inheritors of Black Power)" into present-day political focus.

Noting Obama's potent-yet-distinctive retrieval of the American jeremiad—one soaked in the lyrical style and narrative testimony of Black preaching—Johnson really captures the specter, the sublimely brilliant-yet-haunting essence, of Obama's ability to seize the public imagination and revitalize national conversations around politically charged race relations. Johnson rightly sees the power and ironies of Obama's "striking theological and political reorientation of the jeremiad," a reorientation where inspirational lamentation and "an unyielding faith" would promote social change in the service of justice that corrects social harms rather than tout American exceptionalism.

Indeed, Johnson's contribution to this volume does great service to the notion that Obama's distinctive American jeremiad was a rebuke of the nation's commonplace and widespread moral complacency and complicity in the neglectful oppression of neighbors, strangers, and foreigners. And within the political reading of this new jeremiad, Johnson flags (in particular) what some found in Obama to be a problematic "rejection of representational leadership and possibly…a sign of his dubious relationship to Black male leadership."

Whatever discussions and debates might emerge from Johnson's writing here, his is without question a fascinating exploration and commentary on the moral imagination of Barack Obama. Such imagination was a recasting (or "reconfiguration"), so Johnson argues, that signaled a new American Jeremiad that disrupted political affiliations and corrupt institutions, and was an indictment of both representational racial politics and conservative ideologies of antiblackness, xenophobia, bigotry, and sexism. Indeed, we have here a brilliant laying out of the political jeremiad of the Obama's years, years influenced and informed not only by the Black church and its homiletical social cadence, but also formed and fashioned by an earlier colonial Puritan jeremiad tied to conceptions of America's sacred history. And, not to be overlooked is Johnson's profound understanding that the contours of the American political jeremiad dwells within the hires of competing Black liberals and Black leftists, symbolically and respectively represented by two Black men, King and Carmichael.

Perhaps the greatest import of Johnson's voice concerning that Black presidential hope that, in 2008, appeared in the flesh, is the reminder that by reinvigorating the Black sermon motif in public life, Obama set front and center a dynamic appeal for collective responsibility in concert with individual transformation throughout this political democracy. Indeed, with the election of Donald Trump Johnson embraces the moral responsibility to remind us that post-Obama America is one where the demons have been unleashed. And not only with a realization that the Empire will strike back, but also with the difficult truth that Black people are as "human, normal, and fragile," as any people striving for hope, enfleshed.

And speaking of enfleshed hope, a hope that inspires and instills concrete everyday intimate love for those marked as the pariahs among us, Laura McTighe together with the Reverend Doris Green, who founded Men & Women In Prison Ministries (MWIPM) more than three decades ago in Chicago, offers an important contribution to *CrossCurrents* focused on the intimacy of "reassembling the social in a time of mass criminalization."

McTighe sets out to tell a story of the "the raced and religious underpinnings of our nation's collective obsession with punishment" while also excavating the religious ideas and practices of MWIPM as a counter imagining and generating concerning the love-soaked justice in family and communities hardest hit by mass criminalization. This contribution invites us to jettison many of the commonsense ideas concerning "religion" and "criminalization" that focused on an alienating, socially atomized, exclusionary, and terrorizing spirit of punishment against the hope of Black freedom. Of significant import here is the authors' rendering of mass criminalization as a system of forced migration as inmates, families, and communities must routinely move (psychically, emotionally, and bodily) "across lockups." Counter to such migratory forces, we learn here of MWIPM's "reimagining of the social" grounded by a love which binds and holds together that which mass criminalization severs: families and whole communities yearning for care, service, healing, and restoration. In short, we are summoned to consider and heed the intimacies of relationships, which are central to the idea of instilling "love for our people." Such a love cast over the spirit of in which McTighe and Green write ends the scourge of mass criminalization rooted in the entrenchment of something "worse than slavery," and theologically grounded in the Christo-religious mis-logic of white supremacy.

Indeed, one might experience a deep sense of Toni Morrison's seminal novel *Beloved*, as this contribution takes readers through the trapdoor of religiously justified racial expulsion, recounted here by way of Ida B. Wells' documentation of American lynching and other racially ritualized "terror, murder and expulsion," all wicked testimony to the rendering of Black people as "...trespassers among the human race."[1]

Ultimately, this contribution (not unlike other contributions to this volume) lifts up "the spirit of struggle." In this most profound instance, it is the work of Rev. Green and MWIPW rooted in the spirit of Wells and in what Wallace Best understood of the earlier migration period to be the creation of "a new, and especially *female*, sacred order in Chicago" (as paraphrased by McTighe). Indeed, McTighe grounds her work here in a long and sustained friendship of collaboration with Rev. Green, whose inspired work in the city of Chicago calls forth a reassembling of the social in a particular geopolitical context that houses one of the nation's largest jails alongside, "a soaring murder rate, gun violence, over medication, unsupported trauma, [and] overdose deaths." In fact, Green's journey to the work of MWIPM's work of intimate communal love is a personal story of ministry to people in prison as a path to saving her own life.

The collaborative Black-White female voice rendered here is profoundly suggestive of the ongoing active, and so often *invisible and unsung*, detailed attention that must be paid the daily social operations of organizing labor. For hidden and active behind the veil of many public intellectuals are innumerable persons working against the tragic and exclusionary migrations of mass criminalization and its consequences for Black families and communities.

People of faith, in particular, ought to embrace the story of MWIPM as a model of daily activism and religious witness, for the intimacy of its world-work teaches us, as McTighe so profoundly notes, that religion in a time of mass criminalization means being and staying on the move "to churches, to community centers, to food pantries, and to a longstanding black radical basement meeting on Chicago's South Side."

Certainly, this final contribution to this volume demonstrates the life-affirming truth that "instilling love for our people" means a day-to-day religious thereness of mutual ties in family and community. Such everyday thereness is embodied by the faith-work of Reverend Green, MWIPM, and the multitudes of unsung and unrecognized others "whose enduring work [stretches] across prison walls and keep people connected when they come home." Indeed, this final contribution to the volume (a contribution that makes no mention of the term "political democracy," or Barak Obama, or Donald Trump) is a tour de force in support of "re-assembling the social" against the forced migration of mass criminalization no matter the reigning political order of things. Although contextualized to a particular deleterious social issue, time, and place, McTighe and Green do offer with this writing both a specific and general witness against "the disruption—the *severing*—of social ties" and the death of whole communities, including the attempted destruction of Black humanity through the "brutal 'magic of the state' ritualized through expulsion."

As one comes to this fitting conclusion of this volume focused on religion, political democracy, and specters of race, recall the words of the great Black literacy genius Ralph Ellison in his seminal novel *Invisible Man*:

"... the end is in the beginning and lies far ahead."[2]

Notes
1. Toni Morrison, *Beloved* (New York: Alfred A. Knopf, 1987), 125.
2. Ralph Ellison, Invisible Man (New York: Random House, 1952), 5.

CROSSCURRENTS

THE FUTURE OF SEXUAL INCLUSION
Anti-Black Racism, Black Patriarchy, and Prospects for Political Democracy

Keri Day

Under the Obama administration, sexual justice was seen as a legal and moral priority. The historic decision in 2015 by the Supreme Court to reject the Defense of Marriage Act (DOMA) was fueled, in part, by Obama's personal reflections on his own moral evolving in support of LGBTQ persons and communities. Of great importance was the way in which Obama used his presidential office to affirm the rights, liberties, and human dignities of same-gender loving people. His public reflections in support of marriage and sexual equality also raised questions about the intersections between race and sexuality. Obama demonstrated that a cis-gendered black man could be in solidarity with individuals that span the spectrum of sexual identities. Room can be made for those who do not fit into the hetero-norm of marriage and love.

Upon Obama's publicly sharing of his personal reflections in support of sexual justice, white and black conservative Christian leaders protested. White conservative Christian leaders came together and argued that supporting LGBTQ marriage broke faith with biblical injunctions related to marriage and divine ordering, commands marked by hetero-patriarchal gender roles (i.e., one man and one woman). These white leaders see sexual inclusion as an attack on Judeo-Christian values, what critical race theorists might refer to as "white values." However, white leaders were not the only group that protested Obama. Numerous black clergy leaders assembled together and decried Obama's moral stance as unnatural and sinful. These black clergy, mostly men, expressed their disappointment with Obama for acquiescing to liberal white progressive values on sexuality, wondering why the first black president would use his platform to compare the struggle for racial justice with the quest for sexual equality. These black clergy people categorically rejected this comparison, feeling like such a comparison was a false equivalency. On one level, one could reasonably agree with these black clergy people that white gay men experience structural oppression in qualitatively different ways than black men or black women.

However, the gay community is not singularly constituted by white people—black people also constitute the LBGTQ community. To speak about black disenfranchisement is to also discuss how *black* LGBTQ persons are disenfranchised in housing, employment, education, and other institutions. Moral and political issues such as marriage equality are not about white progressive issues but deep questions about the cultural, political, and economic destinies of black people. Obama's shift on the issue of marriage equality forever changed his position in the black community. Clergy folks broke with their historic support of Obama, creating an ongoing feud between the President and many black church leaders deeply troubled by his stance on this seminal moral issue.

Obama's affirmation of same-sex marriage colored the 2016 US Presidential election. Although just a small percentage of black people voted for Donald Trump (4%), the majority of this small percentage were conservative leaning black men. These black men's support of Trump revolved precisely around this very issue of marriage equality (alongside abortion). Because Trump promised to roll back historic legal gains such as the Supreme Court's rejection of DOMA, these black male leaders sought to gather black social and cultural capital around Trump. Although this was not a successful plan (blacks overwhelmingly critiqued other blacks who voted for Trump), it raises questions about the actualization of sexual justice in this post-Obama/Trump era. As one might have anticipated from all this, the pushback against sexual inclusion is not just an issue of anti-black racism, but also of black patriarchy.

Although Trump's administration has introduced executive orders that seek to undermine measures geared toward sexual equality, new directions are being forged by conservative white and black Christian groups on LGBTQ questions such as marriage equality. I believe these new strategies need to be discussed and assessed by radical communities that support LGBTQ inclusion. This essay will highlight new conversations that are emerging in relation to marriage equality among white and black Christian conservatives, conversations which raise different kinds of concerns in relation to LGBTQ enfranchisement and inclusion as well as the future of political democracy. Before discussing and morally evaluating these new directions, I want to briefly review the deep intersections between sexual oppression, anti-black racism, and black patriarchy. The quest for sexual inclusion (such as marriage equality) reveals the need for *intersectional* perspectives on justice in this racist, hyper-hetero-patriarchal moment.

Sexual justice: a problem of structural racism and black patriarchy
Making connections between structural racism and black patriarchy is paramount in discussing "traditional values" related to sexuality. There are extreme expressions in support of structural racism, often demonstrated through white supremacist groups. There are also more politically correct practices of racially based forms of sexual exclusion such as when white Christian conservative groups appeal to the American founder's Judeo-Christian values, although they fail to mention that these values were grounded in white colonial order and rule.

What is often under-articulated in wider popular culture is the hyper-masculinity that grounds white supremacist views such as those of the Alt-Right and which also shows up in the hetero-patriarchal pronouncements of mainstream white conservative denominations and churches. White supremacist groups such as the Alt-Right believe that the liberation of white people can only come through "race men" or the Aryan man. Aryan men are characterized by a virulent, aggressive personality, a "man's man" who is willing to violently take back a country that belongs to him. The position of the Aryan man is in direct relationship to the role of the Aryan woman. White supremacy is rooted in a strict gender hierarchy. White women are imagined as the holders of white values espoused within society, while white men are seen as the "protectors" of this society. The image often employed by white supremacist men is a militarized image. These white men imagine themselves as protecting home and country from "foreign" threats. These foreign threats are not just people of other racial and/or ethnic identities; these foreign threats are also individuals and groups that express alternate sexual identities. This hypermasculine image of the military man within white supremacy is important to understand: white supremacists live in a world that cannot be shared with people of diverse religious, racial, ethnic, and sexual identities. These religious, racial, ethnic, or sexual "others" must convert or be punished.

Unfortunately, this is also the history of mainstream white Christianity in the United States (and the West more broadly). The view of religious, racial, ethnic, and sexual others as "threat" to the body politic has been a matter of Christian principle and truth. This legacy and heritage has not been wrestled with among white conservative Christians who equate Christian faith with hetero-normative social life. Denying this history keeps white conservative Christian groups from seeing how their hetero-perspective reinforces white supremacist views of strict gender hierarchy.

LGBTQ issues such as marriage equality are then not merely about sexuality alone. Marriage equality among LGBTQ persons is about the contamination of Aryan men and *the rupture of the gender hierarchy that sustains white power*. These men imagine themselves in a race and sexual war against those who want to pervert their world of moral purity (racial, gender, and sexual purity). Racial and sexual diversity complicate and frustrate the views and strategies of groups such as white Christian conservatives and more extreme groups like the Alt-Right. Seeing anti-LGBTQ rhetoric/practice as an instantiation of white supremacy is critically important. It discloses that measures to block or ban sexual justice are also about *race*, about issues of white identity and "white Christian values." It's about the need to assert a way of life that this nation was founded upon. It's about wanting to secure white privilege and power in the face of a growing moral center constituted by racially and sexually diverse people.

The preservation of whiteness sits at the center of questions of sexual justice in this political moment. And religion participates in this project of whiteness. Christian faith is employed as *the* source of anti-LGBTQ practice among white Christian groups and some black church communities. White conservative groups imagine themselves to be employing religious authority in naming same-gender loving relationships and policies as immoral. President Obama dealt with this project of whiteness and its homophobic sensibilities. Obama was called non-Christian, against family values, and a Muslim. All three charges are quite interesting. One is simply interpreted as non-Christian (even anti-Christian, persecuting Christians) if one chooses to be in solidarity with LGBTQ people with respect to marriage equality. Yet, note that this charge of being non-Christian is about being "savage," a threat to the nation, a betrayer of American values. This white supremacist sentiment is echoed in naming Obama as Muslim for being in support of LGBTQ inclusion. However, the term Muslim is a signification, pointing toward Obama as a terrorist or conspiring with terrorist elements. All of these charges reflect the need for powerful white communities to preserve their projects of whiteness. Obama becomes the receiver of white assault due to his moral and political stance on sexuality.

Understanding sexual oppression involves connecting it with the ideology and practice of white racism and white supremacy in this nation. Under the Obama administration, the battle for racial and sexual diversity was a deeper reflection of the problem of whiteness. Sponsored by Trump, the birther movement, which sought to discredit Obama as a citizen of the United States, was rooted in this larger narrative of white power. This birther movement was connected to a larger agenda to secure white male privilege as the primary authority in national political affairs and civil society. This larger movement to secure white male privilege and power is bound up with gender hierarchy and the rejection (even expulsion) of sexual diversity and inclusion. And white conservative Christian faith plays a central role in the narrative of whiteness.

Yet, black patriarchy also participates in the oppression of sexually different persons. Black patriarchy must be understood, in part, as an outgrowth of white racist culture. Within the United States, white culture has had a profound impact on black ideas of sexuality. Womanist scholar Kelly Brown Douglas has written at length about how black sexuality was deeply impacted by white Puritanical morality.[1] For blacks, a history of having their sexuality exploited along with debased stereotypes of black sexuality (black men as Bucks and black women as Jezebels) led to a politics of respectability—the need for blacks to prove their sexual purity and Christ-like moral agency.[2]

Of greatest concern was black men being able to lead within a society that denied them the practice of Victorian manhood (in which man is the "head" of his home). Since the founding of the United States, black men have been referred to and treated as "boys," which created a profound crisis of meaning within a patriarchally structured society. The need to "live into" one's manhood and masculinity meant being able to claim one's rightful position as head of household and leader of community. Being able to serve as patriarch also provided opportunities for black men to potentially receive respect and other cultural rewards within broader society. If manhood was grounded in a strict gender hierarchy, then black men needed to assert dominance over black women at cultural, social, and economic levels.[3]

Black churches have been instrumental to black men being able to carry out their role as patriarchs. With the establishment of black churches, especially black denominations, black men were able to realize the dream of being patriarchs. As I discuss in my book *Unfinished Business*, black men often exercised these patriarchal politics to the detriment of the black community. For instance, the black church was a site of deep critique for its misogyny as early as the Reconstruction era. Fannie Williams describes black male preachers as "corrupt" and "ignorant," often using their resources in ways that bolstered their one-sided leadership. During the Civil Rights Era, there are countless testimonies of women leaders who lament the black patriarchy that they experienced both within the churches and social activist movements. Black patriarchy relied upon strict ideas of gender, for example, who and what a woman was in contrast to who men were.[4]

This patriarchal politics of respectability then plays itself out when discussing LGBTQ matters. Black patriarchy is an internalization of white power, which included gender rigidity. I am not suggesting that non-white cultures across the board are welcoming to LGBTQ people. However, I am suggesting that other indigenous cultures, prior to colonization, had much greater tolerance and allowance for sexual diversity and diverse gender roles.[5] This diversity is loss within black communities that sought to live into black patriarchy as a form of white respectability. Black patriarchy, especially within black churches, continues to fuel anti-LGTBQ rhetoric and practice.

However, in this political moment, white and black conservative groups are retooling and proffering new directions on LGTBQ issues such as marriage equality. At first look, these views appear to be more tolerant and respectful. However, one might be left wondering if legal acceptance is enough without cultural transformation in relation to how LGBTQ people are morally assessed and valued. To these new directions, I now turn.

New directions

In order to understand the new directions, it is important to briefly review some of the old strategies white and black conservative groups employed in resisting LGBTQ issues such as marriage equality. Beginning under Obama's administration and continuing with Trump, the Christian political right crafted projects to combat LGBTQ inclusion such as marriage equality under the banner of "religious liberty." These conservative Christian political groups argued that their right to protest "marriage equality laws" should be protected under the language of religious freedom. In 2015, this argument came to full voice with the arrest of Kim Davis for refusing to issue a gay marriage license. Davis, at the time a 49-year-old county clerk for Rowan County, Kentucky, was pushed into the public eye when she refused, in defiance of multiple court orders, to grant a marriage license to a gay couple. She argued that as an Apostolic Christian, she could not perform this duty, as it contradicted her religious beliefs. Because Davis defied the 2015 Supreme Court decision to allow same-sex couples to marry, she was arrested and sent to jail. This inflamed the national debate. Many conservatives, and even moderates, were concerned that a woman was jailed for defending her beliefs. However, others who were dismayed with Davis' actions argued that a public servant must balance the constitutional rights of same-sex people to marry with one's own freedom to exercise their religion. As a county clerk, Davis was responsible for carrying out the law of the land related to marriage. The Supreme Court ruled in favor of same-sex couples legal access to marriage. Yet, conservatives retorted: but doesn't one have a right to refuse to carry out a public duty that is immoral and unjust, as Martin Luther King did?[6]

It is important to note that Christian conservatives used the protests of the Civil Rights Movement as a way to ground the morally appropriate character of Davis' action. However, these two cases (King and Davis) are far from similar. King, representing no official office, protested as a civilian and preacher. King was not a legally obligated public servant as was the case with Davis, and this distinction raises different kinds of questions and concerns. Davis certainly can practice religious freedom but what about the religious freedom of the gay couple coming to receive their license, a marriage license to which they have now been given legal access? In his protests, King was not depriving a particular group of a public good. Rather, he was illuminating the ways in which marginalized black communities were denied basic common goods. Davis denies a public good to this gay couple in an official political capacity as county clerk. At best, the drawing upon King to justify the religious right's support for Davis' "religious liberty" misrepresents the historical record as well as what's at stake for same-sex couples that have been granted legal access to basic common goods such as marriage. A number of white evangelical churches and black churches rallied behind Davis. This became fuel for fighting marriage equality, even to the extent of arguing that Christians were experiencing religious persecution for their beliefs in hetero-sexual marriage. Since 2015, there continues to be an attempt by the Christian right to deploy the language of religious liberty to deny basic legal protections and resources to LGBTQ people such as marriage equality, adoption rights, and worker/labor protections. This discourse on religious liberty in the United States continues to be a site of deep contestation, where the stakes are high for LGBTQ communities in particular.

However, a number of Christian churches (to the right and more moderate) are *shifting from this position to a more mitigated position in relation to discourse on religious liberty*. On one level, this mitigated position is theological; one another level, the changing position of a number of Christian churches is deeply pragmatic. I think more attention needs to be given to this mitigated position. This mitigated position is marked by contradictions, raising deep concerns as well as potential opportunities.

I am interested in addressing a growing movement of religious institutions, primarily conservative Christian churches, that are rethinking how they enter into questions of religious liberty. This approach differs in two respects from previous strategies. First, it makes room for legal protections among LGBTQ communities. Second, it seeks to protect religious language and speech associated with "biblical values" insofar as such language is not violent language, although how conservative Christians qualify theologically violent language is highly contestable. What is new about this approach is how conservative communities no longer attempt to deploy the language of religious liberty in order to legally disenfranchise LGBTQ persons. Rather than, for example, focusing on denying LGBTQ persons the right to marry or adopt, they focus on how to best protect their *own* religious liberties to publicly speak and act as they choose within their *own* institutional contexts without criminal reprimand. What is of greatest concern to these conservative, and some moderate, Christian churches is protection from legal incrimination when publicly voicing their faith commitments to biblical values surrounding sexuality.

Let me more thickly describe this new approach some conservative Christian groups are taking in relation to projects of religious freedom and the concerns that arise. The Mormon Church is one example of how churches with previously held fundamentalist beliefs and politics are discussing issues of religious liberty in relation to concerns such as marriage equality. The Mormon Church has recently announced their "fairness for all" approach. The Mormon Church, also traditionally known as the Church of Latter-day Saints, begins by noting that they cherish religious freedom as a civil right guaranteed by the U.S. Constitution. Notice that they do not first appeal to biblical texts in interpreting their position on social issues and civil rights within a pluralistic society (which has been the familiar strategy of conservative groups); they appeal to the Constitution. For them, pluralism is a deep moral question and the Constitution serves as the most appropriate resource for working out those questions within a society perpetually marked by conflicts over values and related claims of identity. The biblical text is important to the Mormon Church's religious self-assessment of its own ecclesial witness within our pluralistic society. However, the biblical text does not attempt to supplant the Constitution in deciding moral questions within broader society.[7]

The Mormon Church acknowledges that their own history of marginalization and persecution must make them more compassionate, open, and tolerant toward people who are different from them. They narrate the profound importance of appealing to the Constitution for religious liberty through their own history of religious persecution in the United States. Latter-day Saints remind their own communities of the bitter persecution and discrimination that once drove Mormons from their lands in the Midwest and, in some cases, into early graves along the western Plains. Their experience of being religiously different in mainstream Protestant America caused them great suffering and tragedy. Their experience of structural violence and cultural pain was directly related to how

Protestant Christians used the biblical text to deny them their basic freedoms. Foregrounding their own history is important in articulating their new position. As Mormons have experienced themselves, when freedoms and liberties are not properly valued or protected, an entire society becomes vulnerable to tyrannical governance. One might contend that this position reflects an ethics of empathy in which one agrees to protect the rights of the "other" as an expression of how they would want to be treated (i.e., with respect to the Golden Rule).

On their website, Mormon leaders remind their community and the broader public that the phrases "religious liberty" and "religious freedom" will stand for nothing except hypocrisy so long as they remain code words for discrimination, intolerance, racism, sexism, homophobia, Islamophobia, Christian supremacy, or any form of intolerance. They maintain that LGBTQ individuals absolutely deserve protections from discrimination, and all Americans should help advance this cause. The Mormon Church expresses the need to see religious liberty as something all should be able to exercise in private and in relation to accessing public goods such as marriage.

Yet, they intimate that LGBTQ protections need not come at the expense of religious liberties (in particular, the religious liberties of those who publicly disagree with the values of LGBTQ groups). The Mormon Church is concerned that churches who espouse marriage as "one woman and one man" are not subject to criminal reprimand or lawsuits for their beliefs spoken within the context of their community. The balanced fairness for all approach suggests that religious liberties for same-gender loving people to marry *and* religious freedom for conservative religious groups to publicly speak on their traditional ideas of marriage can be championed together. They conclude that what we need is "fairness for all."

On March 4, 2015, Utah Senator Jim Dabakis, LDS Elder D. Todd Christofferson, and Elder L. Tom Perry, members of the Quorum of the Twelve Apostles of The Church of Jesus Christ of Latter-day Saints, greeted one another before an announcement of a historic piece of legislation that will protect Utah's lesbian, gay, bisexual, and transgender community from discrimination in housing and employment while maintaining equal protection for the expression of religious beliefs at the Capitol in Salt Lake City.[8] These LDS leaders imagine that our robust pluralism to accommodate everyone's needs—religious protections for Christian communities and their religious beliefs as well as protections for LGBTQ communities—can be achieved. And most importantly, they believe we can *respectfully* share our diverse beliefs even in the midst of "disagreement."

What is intriguing to me is the vast number of conservative white and black churches that are coming into conversations with Mormon leaders on this question, seeking a different strategy on a series of LGBTQ-related questions (not just marriage equality). A number of black churches are currently engaging the Mormon Church as conversational partners on the issue of religious freedom. For example, during the summer of 2017, the Seymour Institute held a conference on religious freedom that sought to bring black clergy leaders into conversation on the efficacy of the "fairness for all approach," which involves no longer legally challenging LGBTQ persons in relation to marriage equality as well as legal protections in employment and housing for LGBTQ people. Some black clergy leaders see this "fairness for all approach" as a way to accommodate LGBTQ communities alongside other religious communities that hold "traditional values." One major point of anxiety for these black churches is to avoid facing lawsuits and/or criminal charges for expressing their traditional theological points of view on marriage in particular.

Some of the gathered black clergy expressed concern that criminal reprimand for publicly speaking their views of traditional marriage is racist. In this case, many of the black clergy see marriage equality as a progressive white agenda that holds potential for maligning black church communities who continue to be invested in helping their local neighborhoods on a range of social and economic issues such as poverty. Yet, the LGBTQ issue of marriage equality is hardly just or only (?) a progressive white agenda. There has been a long history of LGBTQ protest within black communities, and LGBTQ black persons continue to challenge same-gender communities to wrestle seriously with racism. For certain, marriage equality is not a "white" issue. In addition, the fear of being sued for hate speech does raise concerns for black churches. Yet, such a concern for being sued may misrepresent what is actually transpiring. For the most part, LGBTQ communities have been more interested in securing their right to have access to basic resources than being preoccupied with what's being spoken from pulpits. Despite considerable misgivings, black clergy are beginning to ask how they can support LGBTQ people's rights to marry while balancing their right to publicly speak their conscious on traditional marriage.

Enhancing political democracy?

So how do we assess this turn in conservative churches' rethinking concerning their politics surrounding religious freedom and LGBTQ concerns? One might argue that such a turn may enhance political democracy. On this account, such rethinking acknowledges the plurality of viewpoints individuals and group possess, admitting that this plurality deserves political recognition and even protection in the face of violence. What's at stake here is not whether the acceptance of LGBTQ identity by conservative groups is required. Indeed, moral agreement on this issue is not required. Instead, *social recognition* of LGBTQ rights and liberties is required within the practice of democratic political community. This kind of social recognition includes rejecting political and legal actions that deny LGBTQ groups political status as subjects and citizens of the *demos*. Because the "fairness for all" approach expands constitutional and religious liberties to LGBTQ communities, it could be seen as enhancing political democracy in the United States.

However, there is another account tied to (at least) the following three questions: Is political democracy just about representational politics and the constitutional context out of which citizens express their rights and liberties (in this case, a democratic process that affirms rights and liberties)? Or might political democracy also be concerned with the political culture of actions toward decision making? and How might we think about the political culture under which conservative groups now embrace the "fairness for all" approach? A larger discussion of enlarging political democracy involves *thinking through the quality of our political culture*. Under the Trump administration, political culture has moved from conflict to an almost complete atmosphere of intolerance. Trump's rhetoric intensifies the deep fissures and divisions in political culture today. I am interested in asking how certain forms of political culture can impede *or* enhance political democracy, even when more "accommodating" approaches (like "fairness for all") are present within the national political discourse.

Open political cultures contribute toward the stability of democratic institutions. The question seems to be whether the "fairness for all" approach points to an open political culture that also allows a *plurality of values* to frame the social meaning of "life-together." One could argue that while legal enfranchisement is supported by conservative groups that espouse the fairness for all approach, their moral view that LGBTQ identities are sinful will nevertheless affect how these groups are morally assessed by, and are able to socially navigate, the broader democratic culture. The conservative religious view that marks LGBTQ persons and identity groups as sinful reinforces a narrative of pathology. With their unyielding insistence that LGBTQ groups are pathological and morally deviant, Christian conservatives (and some moderates) seriously undermine the *cultural efficacy* of their fairness for all approach.

Even though conservative Christian communities are beginning to support the legal enfranchisement of marriage equality, one might ask whether their new approach answers the *cultural* question in relation to truly life-affirming religious liberty, even as such communities nevertheless practice cultural and social forms of exclusion in their ecclesial polity and work environments sponsored by their own churches. If we concede that civil institutions within society fashion the cultural ethos out of which legislation will be employed, clearly legal enfranchisement is one goal within a constellation of objectives LGBTQ communities hope to achieve. Yet another critical goal includes turning the tide on the symbolic and cultural violence that LGBTQ persons endure. But again, if *cultural* transformation is as essential as *legal* enfranchisement, how do LGBTQ communities and advocates hold these two together while noting the tension that the best we may be able to do is to secure legal protections and freedoms for these communities?

The tensions between legal objectives and larger cultural transformations related to how LGBTQ people are morally viewed and treated affects the kind of end goals LGBTQ communities and advocates articulate. A conversation on end goals within LGBTQ advocacy raises teleological questions about what LGBTQ communities want. What are the ultimate political, social, and cultural goals of movement building in response to the debates surrounding marriage equality and religious liberty? Are LGBTQ communities going after getting conservative groups to stay out of the way in terms of rights and legal protections for LGBTQ people, or are we after a more inclusive society on legal, social, and cultural levels? As one can see, answering this question on end goals may simply point to the complexities and ambiguities associated with our entire discussion surrounding religious liberty.

Within a pluralistic society where disagreement and conflict is a constant feature on a host of issues (race, class, gender, sexuality, and more), might we only be able to evoke, at best, tolerance?

Within discourses on moral philosophy and religious ethics, tolerance has not been described as a preferable norm or value toward which moral action ought to be directed. In fact, tolerance has been seen as antithetical to inclusion. However, a number of scholars in philosophy and religious studies are beginning to revisit this conversation surrounding tolerance, even intimating that tolerance may best be described as a virtue within a pluralistic society marked by agonistic political life. In fact, tolerance is understood as an important practice that enhances political democracy, where moral disagreement is an immutable feature.

For instance, in John Bowlin's book *Tolerance Among the Virtues*, he tries to narrate tolerance away from a kind of politically correct position that co-opts real meaningful inclusion. Instead, he argues that some acts of toleration are right and good, while others amount to indifference, complicity, or condescension. He provides criteria by which we might be able to draw these distinctions well and to act in accord with our better judgment. When we speak of tolerance as virtuous, we are commending a certain disposition in the face of *real* differences that may be irresolvable. I think it's worth asking how tolerance relates to this mitigated position conservative groups are embodying and if this is sufficient for LGBTQ communities (not sufficient morally and/or theologically, but sufficient socially within a pluralistic society)? Or perhaps not. Perhaps tolerance just doesn't offer a moral teleology in the quest and fight for gender and sexual justice. As stated, this mitigated position raises real concerns, although it could offer potential opportunities where complete impasses are persistently present.

Those who want to reclaim tolerance as a virtue within political life imagine that tolerance itself can be put in service of deep listening, a necessary political disposition to affirm among political communities. Conservative communities who embrace the fairness for all approach imagine themselves to be participating in charitable citizenship.

Charitable citizenship is about wanting to build a culture of political trust within an increasing polarized political discourse. Standards in support of a culture of political trust include practicing charity through civility, which leads to vulnerability across group differences. Such vulnerability may lead to thinking through alternate solutions that can appeal to groups who find themselves at an impasse. Charitable citizenship relies on democratic interaction where charitable listening and responding ground decision making between and among political communities. Tolerance functions as a precursor to deep listening, which encourages democratic participation in the broader goal of charitable citizenship.

However, should the fairness for all approach be considered an instantiation of charitable citizenship? It depends on whether legal objectives and/or cultural transformation constitute the end goals of LGBTQ advocacy. For certain, conservative groups such the Mormon Church are practicing tolerance. But their central message on LGBTQ identities nevertheless renders these groups as morally pathological. These groups continue to be interpreted and marked as morally abnormal in the eyes of the church. In fact, some of these church communities still support "recovery" therapy for people who identify as gay. In this case, why would LGBTQ groups feel compelled to enter a dialogue with groups that support such therapy when such views contribute to the physical and symbolic violence that LGBTQ persons routinely endure? How does the fairness for all approach extend human dignity to LGBTQ communities when they continue to describe the humanity of these persons in socially deviant ways? Couldn't charitable listening simply reinforce the tyranny of incivility, and worse? The tyranny of civility is a real problem throughout our political culture today. The call to be "civil" on a host of problematic issues misrepresents the fact that, for some marginalized populations, certain social issues are "life or death" problems.

Marriage equality is not only a moral issue, but a deeply economic one. Marriage accords all kinds of social *and* economic benefits for families. When LGBTQ persons are not given access to marriage, this affects them on economic levels ranging from modes of fiscal taxation to child adoption. Moreover, marriage equality is bound up with other political and socioeconomic issues such as employment, housing, and more. When LGBTQ persons are asked to "be civil" within a larger political culture that routinely debates their very humanity, such persons find themselves resisting and refusing to participate in the conversation altogether. For them, charitable listening feels more like hegemonic monologues because the conversations are pursued and set on the terms of hetero-normative religious discourse. The tyranny of civility then impedes political democracy for LGBTQ groups, reinforcing a political culture of skepticism and radical distrust.

The debate on marriage equality and the new directions that some conservative groups are taking raises profound concerns in this political moment. Perhaps this fairness for all approach entails both possibilities and deep limitations. Moreover, it occasions reflections on how to build a political culture of trust instead of skepticism. This is not only a question for LGBTQ communities. It remains important for LGBTQ communities to connect their fight in relation to conversations on religious liberty to how this struggle affects black women and those who are not Christians, such as Muslims. Certainly, conservative groups continue to employ the language of religious liberty when discussing and acting upon issues of reproductive justice, which disproportionately affects black women (i.e., just think about the landmark 2014 Supreme Court decision in Burwell v Hobby Lobby, which struck down the federal contraceptive mandate on behalf of for-profit corporations citing religiously held objections). Many corporations become profitable on the backs of working-class black women and other vulnerable workers but are able to employ the language of religious freedom in denying an array of resources on religious grounds such as birth control and abortions. Muslims also constantly face threats to their own religious freedom in light of Christian anxiety. All these intersecting issues must matter in moral and material discernments concerning how LGBTQ communities shape their own responses in the fight for their own freedoms and liberties. My hope is that the questions I have raised might foster dialogue and action within broader society.

Notes

1. Please refer to Kelly Brown Douglas' two texts, *Sexuality and the Black Church: A Womanist Perspective* (Maryknoll, NY: Orbis Books, 1995) and *What's Faith Got to Do With It: Black Bodies/Christian Souls* (Maryknoll, NY: Orbis Books, 2005).
2. Evelyn Higginbotham, *Righteous Discontent: The Women's Movement in the Black Baptist Church* (Cambridge: Harvard University Press, 1994) explores how black women employed a politics of respectability in contesting racism and sexism. She also discusses how this politics of respectability served as a response to the Victorian cult of social and sexual purity.

3. A plethora of books have been written on the history of black patriarchy in America. Three books that offer wonderful theological and religious analysis on this include the following: Delores Williams, *Sisters in the Wilderness: The Challenge of Womanist God-Talk* (Maryknoll, NY: Orbis Books, 1993); Marcia Riggs, *Awake, Arise, and Act: A Womanist Call for Black Liberation* (Cleveland: Pilgrim Press, 1994); and Riggs, *Plenty Good Room: Women Versus Male Power in the Black Church* (Eugene, OR: Wipf & Stock Publishers, 2008).

4. Barbara Savage, *Your Spirits Walk Beside Us: The Politics of Black Religion* (Cambridge: Belknap Press, 2008) and Keri Day, *Unfinished Business: Black Women, the Black Church and the Struggle to Thrive in America* (Maryknoll, NY: Orbis Books, 2012).

5. See Gloria Wekker, "Mati-ism and Black Lesbianism: Two Idealtypical Expressions of Female Homosexuality in Black Communities of the Diaspora," in *The Greatest Taboo: Homosexuality in Black Communities*, ed. Delroy Constantine Simms (New York: Routledge, 2004).

6. One article that discusses the Davis case and conservative Christian responses: Jack Jenkins, "The Religious Beliefs of Kim Davis, the Anti-Gay Clerk who Refuses to Do Her Job, Explained," in *Think Progress*, https://thinkprogress.org/the-religious-beliefs-of-kim-davis-the-anti-gay-clerk-who-refuses-to-do-her-job-explained-3b4462bec00d/, published September 2, 2015.

7. Jesus Christ of Latter–Day Saints, "Key Points From Church's Religious Freedom and Fairness Announcement," in *Newsroom*, https://www.lds.org/church/news/key-points-from-churchs-religious-freedom-and-fairness-announcement?lang=eng, published January 29, 2015.

8. Refer to this article which talks about this historic piece of legislation: Deseret News Editorial, "In Our Opinion: LDS Church's Call for "Fairness for All" Contrasts New Civil Rights' Report," in Deseret News, https://www.deseretnews.com/article/865662223/In-our-opinion-Fairness-for-all-must-guide-protection-of-religious-liberty-nondiscrimination.html, published September 12, 2016.

CROSSCURRENTS

RACE: FIFTY YEARS LATER

Stanley Hauerwas

Beginning with a beginning

I began teaching at Augustana College in Rock Island, Illinois, in 1968. My first published article was in the Augustana student newspaper. It was entitled "An Ethical Appraisal of Black Power." I do not remember what possessed me to write the paper, but the style of the paper betrays the arrogance of a young man who thought he knew more than he did. The writing moreover is embarrassingly bad. From time to time, I have been asked for a copy of the paper, but I had somehow lost it in the "mist of history." I do not remember who but someone found the damn thing and returned it to me. In preparation for writing this paper, I reread it and thought it an interesting historical document I might use to introduce this paper.

So I am going to begin by reproducing the paper "An Ethical Appraisal of Black Power" because I think both positively and negatively it is a marker indicating where I (we) have been, where I (we) still may be, and how I now think I (we) need to think about race.[1] For as I hope to show fifty years ago in my attempt to defend black power, there were present issues that continue to be important for our current thinking about race.

Yet I need to be candid, one of the reasons I begin with "An Ethical Appraisal of Black Power" is to respond to the criticism that I have not addressed the problem of race in my work. James Logan charges "that Hauerwas refuses to risk writing constructively about the problem of racism in society at large, or to face squarely and publicly the issue of racism in the White churches as a distortion in the grammar of the

Christian faith, is an example of the all-too-familiar silent narrative of collusion prevalent among Euro-American theologians and ethicists."[2] I have high regard for Logan and his work and I take seriously his charge.

I do not think, however, I have completely failed to address the issue of race.[3] I have always regarded race as the central challenge we face if America is to have a moral future. To be sure, I have worried that the dramatic character of the race question has meant questions of class do not receive their due attention. As someone who comes from a working class background, I continue to think race and class cannot be separated morally. But it is true I have not written extensively about race. The issue, however, is not whether I or anyone else has written about race, but rather how the profound racism that has shaped our lives should shape our most fundamental theological convictions. A paper or a book may not mention race, but it may nonetheless be significant for how we negotiate a world in which racism is deep.

Jonathan Tran has written a very interesting article that argues as a white theologian I have rightly been primarily silent "in the face of the normalizing powers of academic prolixity on issues of race."[4] I hope he is right but the truth of the matter is I have not been sure how I should write about race as a white person who has enjoyed a privileged place in that world called America and in particular the university. "An Ethical Appraisal of Black Power" I think is a good example of that difficulty because it reeks of the presumption that race is a problem that African Americans need to negotiate so they can join "our" social world. That said, however, I offer the paper—warts and all—as an introduction to where we were, or at least where I was, in the hope we may better understand where we are now on the question of race. So here it is:

An ethical appraisal of black power

The phrase "black power" and what it represents has come as a severe shock to many Christians who liked to think of themselves as liberal on the question of race. They feel as if the starved dog they tried to feed has suddenly bitten the hand of the benefactor. Moreover, it has made sentiments such as "All men are loved by God and should therefore be brothers" seem rather shallow, platitudinous, and logically doubtful.

Cherished strategies such as integration that were thought to be the only rational possibility for people who adhered to principles of equality and justice are now declared to be morally perverse. Instead of integration, the liberal seems to confront proposals that can only appear as reverse segregation. Thus, the white Christian liberal reaction to black power has been mainly one of some resentment and almost complete bewilderment. It has not only challenged their ethical stance, but suddenly all the avenues which relieve the guilt of being white have been cut off by the very people with which the liberal wished to identify.

As a result, the response to the black power movement from Christians has been almost completely negative as it is seen as the denial of the attempt to bring reconciliation between people; or it is totally embraced by some whites because they seem to assume that anything done by an African American today must be accepted simply on the grounds they are African American. In order to avoid these alternatives, I should like to try to evaluate in a discriminating way the ethical significance of the black power movement and in the process perhaps help clarify what place the white liberal might have in relationship to it.

The first difficulty one encounters in the attempt to do this is the ambiguity of the phrase "black power." It is apparent that many of the proponents of black power often understand the phrase in radically different ways. It would be impossible to try to analyze here all the emotive and substantive elements that are associated with the phrase in its public use. However, I think the phrase "black power" at least can be taken to represent appreciation of being black in America and the demand by African Americans for the right of self-determination.

So understood I think that the black power movement can be said to be a morally healthy development. This does not mean that I think reconciliation among people is a bad thing. Nor do I mean to imply thereby that I am denying such values as equality and justice for the ordering of society. Rather it is to indicate the complexity of how such values are institutionalized and made efficacious in our society.

The black power movement has again taught us that unless we realistically and honestly examine our assumptions in the light of the concrete situation, our highest values may become but a way of blinding us to the injustice that we are helping to perpetuate. People of good will who call for reconciliation today between whites and blacks in our society may be the black person's worst enemy as the result of such moral idealism may well be to placate the African American demands at a level that will not radically change their disadvantaged position in our society. Moreover, the black power movement has also reminded the white liberal that good intentions are seldom adequate in the face of complex social wrongs. Phrases such as "all people are brothers" do little to affect actual life in the city ghetto.

In order that this positive evaluation of the black power movement might be more intelligible, it is necessary to make clearer some of my normative commitments. Presupposed in my judgment is the whole history of racism in this country that has resulted in the African American being systematically denied their right to full participation in this society in a way no other group has experienced. I therefore assume that the African American has a prima facie claim that the injustices of the past be rectified and their rights fully acknowledged.

Secondly, I am committed to the continued need to extend the participation of all people in a democratic society. All that is involved in the phrase "democratic society" cannot be analyzed here, but I understand it least of all to imply the procedure by which pluralism of group self-interests are tolerated to a high level in order to provide the conditions for greater equality and to seek through a balancing of these self-interests the greatest possible common good. Democracy is the attempt to provide an avenue of change by which these interests can find possibilities for greater justice without resorting to anarchy or excessive violence. (For a much more extensive and adequate analysis of black power from this perspective, I highly recommend Joseph Hough's book, *Black Power and White Protestants*.)

In this context, I view the black power movement as a response by a minority to assure its participation in the society by organizing to protest its rights by power. It is a frank recognition that societies seldom respect the rights of the weak. Black power, as I understand it, is thus not a phrase that is calculated primarily to scare whites, but rather a call from one African American to another that the goods of this society are theirs, not as they become what the white man wishes them to be but only as they become black.

In this connection, it is genuinely a mass movement, as it aims at equality for all African Americans—not just the talented few. As such, it must be viewed as the real beginning of African American participation in our society. There is no doubt that this will cause extreme stresses in the established order of our society, but the development of justice seldom comes without tension. The moral substance of this development in this perspective in no way depends on the ethical goodness of the participants or their particular goals (just as the white participation does not), but rather should be regarded as an opportunity for the enrichment of our common social life.

Moreover, I think that the black power movement is morally sound as it perceives with greater clarity and honesty the role of power in group relations. No longer is the "good will" of whites depended on in their (African Americans') calculations. Rather they have discovered that such "good will" can be relied on only to the point that it affects white self-interest. In response, they have entered the arena of power by asserting their own voice(s) through candid and at times unrestrained speech. This seems to me to be a healthy reaction against some of the idealistic tone of the civil rights movement that was set by Martin Luther King.

The African American, in order to participate in our society and to assert their interests, is not required to have a higher moral excellence than the white; nor is her mission the attempt to save the white from the prison of their prejudice. The African American can and should take part in our society in the pursuit of her own self-interests and goals by trying to insure them through the same kind of power other groups in our society use.

Another aspect of the black power movement I find morally promising is the assertion of the right of participation in our society that envisages a way of life different from that of middle-class America. It is the claim that the African American has a special experience in America that they are intent on bringing into the future. This experience leaves them dissatisfied with the quality of life they see in wider society, and they are determined not to mimic it. I cannot help but think that the African American struggle to find a better way of life consistent with their experience will contribute immensely to the value of the American experience. It may even open for all of us further moral options that we had not before envisaged as possibilities for our lives.

Even though I have given a positive evaluation of the black power movement, there are some questions that I should like to raise concerning it in terms of its more specific manifestations and political strategies.

Approval of the general thrust of the black power movement does not necessarily imply approval of all that is done in the name of black power.

The first question is whether it can accomplish politically what is required of it. It used to be a maxim among liberals that the action necessary to meet the needs of the African American and the poor could only be accomplished by a coalition of African Americans, poor whites, unions, and white liberals. The black power movement has decisively and perhaps rightly called that strategy into question. It may be that the concentration of African Americans in American cities has provided the political opportunity for an African American declaration of independence. However, it is not clear to me whether black power alone is going to be able to provide the political leverage for the kind of help our cities currently need. Will it be necessary or possible for the African American to enter into coalitions with other groups in our society to work toward common political goals? Or will it be possible to determine "common political goals" from our mutual perspective?

This is not a question that is aimed at limiting the nature of the black power movement, but rather one that tries to ask: Where do we go from here in order to meet our immediate needs? It may be that the best thing for the African American child in the ghetto is not integrated education, but that does not solve the problem of how that child can be provided with the kind of education they will need to compete in the modern world as an African American.

My second question has to do with a broader concern. "Black power" is more than a political slogan. It is a phrase that denotes a search for identity with integrity on the part of the African American. This is an age in which all people are rather unsure as to who they are, and the African American search for identity is but a rather special case of this general problem. While I am in no way competent to judge how another can solve the question of their identity (if indeed such a problem can be said to have a solution), I am struck by a tendency that might prove dangerous in the long run for the black power movement; that is the assumption that to achieve political power can somehow satisfy the need for personal identity.

The political realm, while of utmost importance, has limits which make it a poor place to discover the ultimate significance of life. The achievements made in politics are put together by many compromises that simply cannot meet the criterion of ultimate legitimation and wholeness with which the question of personal identity seems to be so intimately connected. It may well be that as the black power movement develops it may find that its main contribution has been in the less sensational but perhaps more important areas of our lives together.

Where does this leave the white liberal? Does this mean that they simply become an anachronism in the light of these developments? While I think this need not necessarily be the case, I do think it means that white liberals must take this opportunity to seriously rethink their position. In a way, the white liberal is fortunate because the African American, by declaring independence, has created a new possibility of freedom for the white.

White liberals have had an almost morbid fascination with their own guilt. They have cherished it as a way of assuring their moral identity in a world where moral problems are so complex; questions of responsibility and guilt are impossible to determine. It is tempting for the African American to use this guilt to underwrite getting "theirs" as though they are but another interest group, but they have now rejected this temptation to get on with the business of being African American. (They may have done this partly because they found how unreliable the guilty are as their guilt can turn all too quickly to arrogant self-righteousness.)

Just as the African American cares not whether the white person feels guilty or not, so the white should quit worrying about the color of their skin. The African American has in fact said to white people, "Do not try to find out what it is to be a person by identifying with us for we will only be able to meet as people when you face honestly what being a person requires without me." As white people, we should accept this challenge to turn to the moral possibilities of our future which are far more interesting than the guilt of our past.

This new freedom however does increase the white persons responsibility. In a way, whites have been able, by their use of the "African American" problem to delay coming to grips with many of the hard moral questions facing them. Here, they were able to find an issue in which the good and the bad seemed to be drawn with unmistakable clarity. By identifying completely with the cause of the African American, the white was able to provide themselves with a feeling of righteousness. They therefore did not feel compelled to raise morally significant questions about the quality of life they were building for themselves in general. As Christians, we were able to assume that at least being Christian meant being for African Americans.

Now that the African American has refused to be the warrant for the white person's moral existence—now that they refuse to be our cause—we are forced to ask ourselves what kind of people we wish to be and in what kind of society do we wish to live. No longer can we assume that all that is morally significant in our life is how we feel about African Americans. If we seriously address ourselves to these questions of our future, we may find someday we are able to meet the African American as a brother or sister in a far more profound way than is now possible. For then, we will have found that we must both meet as people that share the struggle of what it means to be human.

So I wrote in 1969.[5] As I confessed above, some of what I wrote fifty years ago is embarrassing. There is, moreover, a presumptive air about the piece that is objectionable. An attitude of "I know better than you" pervades what I wrote. But write it I did and I should have known better. There are no excuses.

Black lives matter
I think, however, I got some things right in 1969 and even some of the things I wrote remain relevant. The most important move I made, I believe, was the suggestion that African Americans have a story to tell that is particular to their lives and cannot be lost. One must be careful how to say this, but the ambiguities surrounding "integration" come to a head when considering the importance of that particular story; that is, integration can threaten the story and memory of what it means to be part of a people who have suffered a terrible injustice which means the reality of slavery cannot be lost. Yet African Americans have refused to let their extraordinary mistreatment drive them to nihilism. In fact, they have done the impossible, that is, in the face of white arrogance and power they have had children.

In an interesting way, I think the call that "black lives matter" draws on many of the same presumptions that gave birth to the "black power movement." The cry "black lives matter" is meant to help African Americans recognize that they share a common story, that they need one another if they are going to survive, and they must always—with care—

identify who their real enemy is. Of course that is not a new reality, it just happens to have become a dramatic reality captured by incidence that make visible the everyday brutality African Americans have to endure.

Just as it was true of the black power movement, some whites, many who are very sympathetic with the cause of African Americans, find the mantra "black lives matter" offensive. They call for the recognition that "all lives matter." That is, of course, true; all lives do matter. But to pose these statements as contrasting statements implies white Americans feel threatened by the African American imperative to remember and tell their particular story.

"Black lives matter" is a cry that locates African American life in a history that is irreplaceable. In contrast, "all lives matter" fails to elicit the history that finds expression in the fear that fuels the white policeman's brutality toward African American males. At the heart of the problem of race in America, a problem I vaguely intimated in my essay on Black Power, is the inability of Americans to acknowledge that we are a slave nation. The civil war, which is often appealed to as the price needed to be paid to end slavery, is not sufficient to make slavery "an unfortunate period in American history that we are now long past."

The American attempt to relegate slavery to "history" is a correlative of the moral inability to deal with slavery and subsequent racism. In this respect, I think the civil rights campaign is now used by white people to justify our unwillingness to face morally what it means to be a slave nation. That failure results in what I call the failure of the success of the civil rights campaign. What could I possibly mean by that? I certainly do not mean that the gains made by Martin Luther King Jr. and those that followed him were not significant.[6] Without the civil rights struggle, one cannot imagine that Obama could have been elected president of the United States. Yet I think I am right to suggest that the continuing inability of Americans to confront this nation's slave history, as well as the subsequent racism, is at least in some sense due to the successful failure of the movement for civil rights for African Americans.

By suggesting that the success of the civil rights movement has become a failure is my way of calling attention to the presumption by many white people in America that racism, or at least the effects of racism, has been overcome—if not eliminated—by the civil rights movement and subsequent legislation. Many assume that Martin Luther King won. He got the vote for African Americans, he is a national hero with a day set aside to celebrate his life, and African Americans now have the same opportunities to a better life that white people have always had. Thus, the assumption that African Americans can move to the suburbs, have nice homes with four bedrooms, three TVs, two cars, and worry about Jews moving in. Thus, the presumption by white people in America that given the success of the civil rights movement, what could be the problem with a little slavery/racism between friends?

To call attention to the "failure" of the success of the civil rights struggle is my attempt to get at the mistaken presumption by many that the virulent racism in America is no longer a problem. The racism that dominates American life is all the more perverse because many now believe that America has come to terms with the reality that we are a slave nation. In short, the presumption that we have overcome slavery has now become part of the story of moral progress that shapes American self-understanding.

But slavery names a reality that is so wrong it feels as if there is nothing anyone can do to make it right. There is much to be said for reparations but no compensation can compensate for the terror that was slavery.[7] I do not want to be misunderstood. I am not suggesting that racism is less a wrong than slavery. Racism can in fact be more insidiously destructive than slavery. I live in wonder that African Americans are not more filled with rage than they are for the everyday slights they receive for no other reason than the color of their skin. Knowing how to resist racism, moreover, must take more energy and skill than most of us can muster on a daily basis.

Yet I think it true that slavery, the presumption that another human being can be "owned" by another human being, was and is a monstrous practice. It is also wise to remember that slavery and racism each have economic outcomes. The economic character of racism is obviously different than slavery but both entail forms of extraction of labor that results in keeping those who do the hard work poor. The economics of racism made racism a way of life that produced Jim Crow laws, justified white arrogance, and killed African Americans who were singled out for defying the system. It is probably true that racism is also an evil about which there is nothing that can be done to make it right.

There is a way to deal with a wrong that is so wrong there is nothing that can be done to make it right—it is called "forgetting." Perhaps the most effective form of forgetting is to regret that slavery ever existed but to celebrate that slavery was forever eliminated by the civil war. Both the civil war and the civil rights struggle are now seen as part of an ongoing story of progress that is thought to be the moral heart of America. I suspect there is no greater indication of the failed success of the civil rights struggle than how the results of the civil rights campaign are used as evidence against those who draw attention to the ongoing and pervasive racism that marks this country. The story of America's progress toward justice masks the reality that justice remains elusive for African Americans.

The crucial question, a question that I was close to asking in 1969, is: How do Americans come to terms with the reality that we were a slave nation without that telling of that story reproducing a progressive account of American history—that is, we once had slaves but we overcame that terrible institution? Joe Winters has recently written a book with the wonderful title, *Hope Draped in Black, Race, Melancholy, and the Agony of Progress*, in which he argues that progress, even when used to galvanize struggles for a more just world, harbors a pernicious side by downplaying the tensions, conflicts, and contradictions in the effort to sustain hope for a better future. Progress turns out to be a form of forgetting just to the extent it relies "on the denial or easy resolution of painful tensions and contradictions in past and present, those facets of life that remind us that the status quo is harsh and cruel for many people under its sway."[8]

Winters argues that is why melancholy is a necessary trope for how the African American story is told. That story cannot be told truthfully without the inclusion of the "somber stories and songs" produced by slaves and which remain the heart of African American life. In particular, Winters calls attention to Du Bois's use of the solemn songs in *The Souls of Black Folks* in an effort to resist having the striving of black people absorbed into a progressive account of history.[9] The problem, from Winters' perspective, is that progress has become the condition of hope in America which means there is no place for the melancholy that must suffuse the story of African American life if slavery is not to be forgotten.

Melancholy is the mood that names what it means to be unsettled and wounded by the unavoidable threats ever-present in human existence, that is, death, tragedy, and loss. Melancholy is a way of being in the world that does not attempt to wall the self from the everyday ways our life remains vulnerable and unsafe. Melancholy combines joy and sorrow, pleasure and pain, and in the process makes possible a hope that does not betray the reality that to be an African American means you inherit the sadness of a people who were enslaved.[10] Melancholy finds expression in the Psalms of lament.

Winters develops his argument by providing a painful account of President Obama's "A More Perfect Union" speech delivered in Philadelphia on March 18, 2008. Obama was responding to his former pastor, Jeremiah Wright, who had preached a sermon in which Wright called for God to damn America. Obama's speech, a remarkable speech in many ways, in a paradigmatic way is determined by the story of progress that Winters argues has become the basis for the hope for the end of racism in America. Thus, Obama urges African Americans "to embrace the burdens of our past without becoming victims of our past." To avoid being victims, Obama maintains that they "must always believe that they can write their own destiny."

According to Obama, Wright's mistake was to speak in a manner that assumes a static view of American society in which no progress has been made. But change has happened, Obama asserts, which indicates the true genius of America is the audacity to hope for what can be and must be achieved. Winters acknowledges that Obama indicates that his political status and success do not signify that racism has come to an end, so there is a mournful and tragic sensibility that the speech exhibits. At the same time, however, Winters contends that Obama's "reflections tend to rely on a familiar logic of progress and a semantics of national exceptionalism that diminish attunement to race-inflicted loss, suffering, and struggle."[11]

Winters concludes his account of Obama's speech with the harsh but I think true judgment that Obama adopted the grammar of American exceptionalism which has the effect of conflating hope and promise in a manner that assumes that the nation-state must be the agent of their realization. That mode of conflation, Winters argues, hides and minimizes the internal violence needed to secure the nation.[12] What is required according to Winters is a counter narrative that does not forget the solemn songs, the melancholic songs, that make possible the memory of slavery which renders the congratulatory progressive story of America problematic.

This account of the failure of the success of the civil rights movement may seem to continue the presumption that American politics will produce moderately progressive politicians that think it a "good thing" to find ways to continue to support the gains African American have made. But we know that assumption has now been decisively called into question by the election of Donald Trump to the presidency. Trump seems to have no understanding of what it means to be an African American in America. Nor does he seem to have any stake in the legal safe guards and social programs developed to help African Americans survive racism. Trump, moreover, has legitimated the return of a more overt racism that is as ugly as it is frightening. The gains made by the civil rights struggle cannot be lost.

Where has this gotten us

In his fine book, *Bonhoeffer's Black Jesus: Harlem Renaissance, Theology and an Ethic of Resistance*, Reggie Williams makes the judgment that Bonhoeffer "remains the only prominent white theologian of the twentieth century to speak of racism as a Christian problem."[13] The qualifier "prominent" makes his generalization true because Will Campbell, who spoke and wrote painful but true theological reflections on race, was not—nor did he wish to be—a prominent theologian.[14] But I believe it was from Campbell that I learned how to think about race theologically. For Campbell, racism is not just another sin; racism is a power that threatens our very existence as God's people.

The theology of my 1968 essay—to the extent it was theological—was basically that of Reinhold Niebuhr. I assumed some balance of power between groups was a given. But African Americans are not just another interest group. They are a people bound together by the story of their triumph over slavery and racism. That triumph I believe was made possible by the Christian faith African Americans received from slave owners which made possible the miracle of lives that were not to be consumed by hate.

Theologically, what is required is a determination by white people to remember the ugly history of slavery and racism. That is a story that can only be told as a confession of sin. But sin confessed makes possible a life no longer under the power of the dreadful need we have to justify the evil we do as good. Forms of penance offer ways that make kindness a possibility. For sure, one of the most destructive aspects of slavery is how slavery made kindness an anomaly.

I think that Williams' charge that white theologians have failed "to speak of racism as a Christian problem" is not just a suggestion that theologians ought to be against slavery and racism. That is a far too easy stance. Given Williams' account of Bonhoeffer, moreover, neither is his call to think theologically about race satisfied by taking a liberationist perspective. Rather I take Williams to be suggesting that a theology which may in every way be orthodox will be less than it should be if it is done ignoring how it may be implicated in racist practices. Put concretely, the "very man" of the incarnational claim that Jesus was very God and very man threatens to become a very *white* man if salvation does not entail liberation from the prison of race.

I confess that I may be guilty of doing theology in a manner that fails to struggle against the inherent racism that can be present, present because absent, in what appears to be straightforward theological claims. The repair of Christian theology will not be accomplished by some of the familiar forms of identity politics because that kind of theology is the attempt to avoid what is most needed, that is, the truth. Rather we must begin by acknowledging that racism is an ecclesia sin that can only be dealt with by the gifts of the Spirit. If slavery is a wrong so wrong there is nothing you can do to make it right, the only alternative is to be drafted into a history of God's redemption that makes confession and forgiveness a reality. Only those who are willing to be forgiven are those who can seek reconciliation with those they have harmed.

The church has been gifted by a story of a person whose death made possible the existence of a people that the world could not imagine. A church is made up of a people committed to sharing their stories, their lives, in the hope that through such sharing we might better understand who we are. To get our stories straight will require sharing our stories in a way that test their truthfulness. For if I have any comment about the continuing alienation between white and black people, it is that, finally, when all is said and done, the truth matters. That truth, a truth that is to be found hanging on a cross, makes hope possible even in the face of an ongoing injustice. Finally, the question must be: How are we to understand that in the years after the Civil War until our own day African Americans have most nearly been what we call "a Christian."

Notes

1. I am taking the liberty to edit the text in two ways—I have changed my use of the masculine pronoun and rather than "black" or "negro" I have used African American. There are some modes of writing that are too painful to repeat even if you can claim that you did not know better. I do not think I knew better but that may be self-deception.

2. James Logan, "Liberalism, Race, and Stanley Hauerwas" *Cross Currents* (January 1, 2006), online. I wrote this paper without having read Kristopher Norris's dissertation just written and defended in October 2017 at the University of Virginia entitled, *Witnessing Whiteness: Hauerwas and Cone and the Challenge of Black Theology for Postliberal Ecclesiology*. Norris's dissertation has a fair and quite critical account of my declaration that one of the reasons I have not written more on racial matters is because I have a different story than those stories that are determined by slavery and racism. Norris quotes Cone who quite rightly says that cannot be true because no white can fail to recognize our complicity with racism. I had disavowed writing on race because I worried to do so as a white man I would end up colonizing the African American story. But that does not mean that there were not ways I should have explored that made it possible to write on race. I highly commend Norris's work for no other reason he is able to identify conceptual moves Cone and I share though it remains the case that we have very different ways of doing theology.

3. See, for example, my "Remembering Martin Luther King Jr. Remembering," in *Wilderness Wanderings: Probing Twentieth-Century Theology and Philosophy* (Boulder: Westview Press, 1997), pp. 225–238 and my "Why Time Cannot and Should Not Heal the Wounds of History, But Time Has Been and Can be Redeemed," in *A Better Hope: Resources for a Church Confronting Capitalism, Democracy, and Postmodernity* (Grand Rapids: Brazos Press, 2000), pp. 139–154.

4. Jonathan Tran, "Time for Hauerwas's Racism," in *Unsettling Arguments: A Festschrift on the Occasion of Stanley Hauerwas's 70th Birthday*, edited by Charlie Collier, Charles Pinches, and Kelly Johnson. (Eugene, Oregon: 2010), p. 260.

5. I am indebted to Dr. Kristopher Norris for calling attention to my mistaken idea that I wrote the article in 1968. It was published on February 5, 1969, in the *Augustana Observer*. That I got the date wrong may not be all that important, but Kristopher Norris dissertation is an extremely important critical account of James Cone and my work on race. Norris argues that in fact Cone and I share some fundamental concepts that could make us more in agreement than either of us has thought. See Kristopher Norris, *Witnessing Whiteness: Hauerwas and Cone and the Challenge of Black Theology for Postliberal Ecclesiology* (Dissertation: University of Virginia, 2017).

6. For my account of King and his commitment to nonviolence, see my chapter, "Martin Luther King Jr. and Christian Nonviolence" in *War And the American Difference* (Grand Rapids: Baker, 2011), pp. 83–98.

7. For a strong defense of reparations, see Jennifer Harvey, *Dear White Christians: For Those Still Longing for Racial Reconciliation* (Grand Rapids: Eerdmans, 2014). I think Harvey makes a strong case for reparations but her account of reconciliation is far too shallow. Reparations and reconciliation are no necessarily in competition with one another.

8. Joseph Winters, *Hope Draped in Black: Race, Melancholy, and the Agony of Progress* (Durham: Duke University Press, 2017), p. 15.
9. Winters, p. 42.
10. Winters, pp. 210–21.
11. Winters, p. 190.
12. Winters, p. 191.
13. Reggie Williams, *Bonhoeffer's Black Jesus: Harlem Renaissance, Theology and an Ethic of Resistance* (Waco: Baylor University Press, 2014k), p. 139.
14. For my account of Campbell, see my "Race: The 'More' it is About: The Will Campbell Lecture," in my and Rom Coles, *Christianity, Democracy, and the Radical Ordinary* (Eugene, Oregon: Cascade, 2008), pp.87–102.

CROSSCURRENTS

THE BACKLASH THIS TIME
Obama, Trump, and the American Trauma

Gary Dorrien

Barack Obama's presidency fell short of what he promised to do in 2008 and should have tried to do, especially in his first two years. But he had a good presidency, he represented the nation with consummate dignity and intelligence, he finished with an outstanding approval rating of 56 percent, and he helped to sow a ferocious, titanic, vindictive backlash merely by living in the White House and doing his job. Every day that he served, President Obama made the nation look better than it was, something that Donald Trump keenly grasped while putting it differently. The United States has been caught in a perpetual backlash loop since Reconstruction in which the backlash is always bigger than whatever it reacted against. The election of 2008, it quickly turned out, was no different.

Trump caught the resentment against the rainbow coalition that carried Obama to the White House. He perceived, and evidently felt in himself, the outrage that a black liberal won the presidency. He realized that the backlash was sufficiently huge and seething to win the White House for somebody. It produced a bestselling conspiracy literature, an unhinged Right-blogosphere, and impassioned rallies demanding, "I want my country back," all within weeks of Obama's inauguration. The birther movement rang this alarm for two years before Trump joined it in 2011. It had no basis whatsoever besides racism and backlash hysteria, being too blatant to be called a dog whistle. Trump became a major political player by lauding the birther movement and stumping for it. He flirted with the idea of running for president, shooting to the top of the prospective Republican field, but wasn't ready to mount a campaign. He was impressed at how quickly he ascended and how easy it was. All he had to do was play to the rage and not get outflanked in doing so.

In 2011, more than one-fourth of the U.S. American population claimed to believe that President Obama was not born in the Unites States, was not a legitimate president, was a Muslim, and a Socialist, and either definitely or probably sympathized with the goals of Islamic fundamentalists wanting to impose Sharia law throughout the world. In some polling, up to a third of Americans tagged Obama as sympathetic with Islamic radicalism, and over half tagged him as a Socialist. Half of registered Republicans, that summer, agreed with Trump that Obama was not a legitimate president; another 20 percent said they weren't sure. Trump's presidency is a product of that period, when he realized how he would run, if he ran. When he ran, the culture war would be number one, not number two or three as usual. Facts would not matter, nor the voters who think that facts matter. Trump aimed at the millions of Americans who loathed Obama and were predisposed to love Trump. Any day that he won the news cycle with a story about immigration or anything racial would be a good day for him—and still is.[1]

Millions of Americans did not dream up, by themselves, their convictions that Obama was born in Kenya, his teenaged mother forged an American birth certificate so he could run for president, he imbibed radical Socialism from a father he never knew, or his real father was an American Communist poet, he wrote *Dreams from My Father* to hoodwink prospective voters, or he got a 1960s revolutionary to write the book for him, he exploited his friendships with devious white liberals and Communists to get him into Harvard Law School and the U.S. Senate, and his presidency was a conspiracy to destroy America. Bestselling books and the Right-blogosphere harped on these claims from his first presidential campaign to the end of his presidency. Jerome R. Corsi, Brad O'Leary, Orly Taitz, Aaron Klein, Jack Cashill, Michelle Malkin, Pamela Gellar, Robert Spencer, and Webster Griffin Tarpley were leading authorial players in this field when Trump flirted with running in 2011. They had sloppy lists of bad things that Obama supposedly believed, plus competing narratives about how Obama and his white lefty allies defrauded the nation. Always they claimed that most, or all, of Obama's inspiring life story is a fraud. In September 2010, popular conservative writer Dinesh

D'Souza got the cover of *Forbes* by cleaning up the argument and the narrative, claiming that the key to Obama is African anti-colonial rage.[2]

D'Souza said Obama was a seething anti-colonialist who viewed the world from the perspective of his bitter, defeated, deceased Kenyan father (never mind that he had almost no relationship with his father). According to D'Souza, Obama was determined to destroy Western civilization, which explained why he expanded the power of government in domestic affairs and diminished American power internationally. Obama yearned for the heroic grandeur of the black Africans who defied their white British oppressors. George Washington paled by comparison, as did the American civil rights movement. So did the dull global summits to which Obama dragged himself as President of the United States. D'Souza's book version, titled *The Roots of Obama's Rage*, soared to number four on the bestseller list in its first week. It seriously described Obama, of all people, as being consumed by racial revenge, plus bored by the presidency—a vengefully arrogant type determined to put down whitey and take whitey's money.[3]

D'Souza boasted that his book raised the anti-Obama literature to a new standard of sophistication and cleaned up its inconsistencies. Newt Gingrich, running for president in 2011-2012, said D'Souza's account was singularly profound and convincing. Gingrich sprinkled his speeches with conspiracy rot, declaring that unless one understood Obama's Kenyan anti-colonial mentality, he was "outside our comprehension," exactly as Obama liked it: "This is a person who is fundamentally out of touch with how the world works, who happened to have played a wonderful con, as a result of which he is now president." Obama, Gingrich declared, was "authentically dishonest," a mode of hypocrisy he learned as a Saul Alinsky organizer in Chicago.[4]

This is where the Trump campaign came from. The civil rights bills of 1964 and 1965 ostensibly committed the United States to racial democracy, white racial grievance realigned America's party politics in 1964, and the Obama phenomenon was an echo of Martin's Dream and the bridge to Selma. Trump exploited the same anti-Obama revulsion and paranoia that Gingrich tried to ride to the presidency in 2012. Gingrich blistered Mitt Romney as a vulture capitalist and establishment Republican, which Trump liked, but Gingrich had too much baggage to beat Romney, and normal politics prevailed. Gingrich accusing anyone of dishonesty was too rich in 2012. The backlash needed four more years of suffering under Obama's unbearable leadership to swell to game-changing proportions. Everything that Trump needed to know about how to run in 2015-2016, he learned in 2011-2012. He would run a better and meaner version of Gingrich's campaign, exceeding Gingrich's attacks on the news media. That put Trump ahead of the competition before he formally launched his campaign with a spectacularly vicious entry speech.

He demonized Mexican immigrants as rapists and murderers, which lifted him above all other Republican candidates. He conducted ugly rallies tinged with violence, inciting the violence. He lied constantly about urban crime rates, urban voter fraud, and NATO obsolescence. He demanded a thirty-foot wall along the entire U.S.-Mexican border and punitive treatment of undocumented workers and children. He bashed the news media, praised dictators, and promised to punish judges opposing his illegal and unconstitutional mandates. He bullied his competitors and hung degrading nicknames on them, mocking their physical characteristics. He charged that Ted Cruz's father killed President Kennedy, a whopper of stunning mendacity. He insisted that he saw "thousands and thousands" of Muslims cheer in Jersey City on September 11, 2001, a stupendously vicious and inflammatory lie ranking somewhere in his top five. He called for a ban on all Muslim immigrants, which made him unbeatable in Republican primaries. He branded as liars the many women who accused him of sexual abuse, never mind that he had boasted of abusing women. He told the Republican Convention that he alone could solve America's problems—in case anyone had missed the fascist overtones of everything else he said.

Trump's campaign for the presidency was straight out of the fascist playbook, with the single exception that he won a hostile takeover of the Republican Party instead of building his own party. Now, he governs as he campaigned, devoting his presidency to fear mongering, bullying, culture war, and completing his takeover of the Republican Party, with little actual governing. He caters to the white nationalists that his campaign brought to the front and center of Republican politics. His cabinet is filled with plutocrats, even as Trump boasts ludicrously of draining the Beltway swamp. He smears Haitians and Africans with racist obscenities, demanding that America needs white immigrants, not immigrants from "shithole" countries. He tore migrant children from their asylum-seeking parents at the Mexican border and consigned them to cages, until a public uproar forced him to back down. In the midst of the uproar, Trump recycled the Nazi imagery of vermin human infectors, warning that Central American children "infested" the United States—a vile contention marking a new low for Trump and the American presidency.

He is brilliantly demagogic, long on crude repetitions, loopy insults, and sneers that score with his base. Legislation is secondary, although Trump paid off the donor class by enacting yet another Republican tax cut for the rich and the corporations. He cannot be bothered to read policy briefs or to learn any specifics about health care, global trade, and the environment. Trump takes for granted that factual evidence matters only to losers and opponents lacking his skills of persuasion. He constantly wins the news cycle with race-baiting and other forms of culture war, cowing what used to be the Republican establishment. Republican legislators have capitulated to him, recognizing his hold over the Republican base. In Trump's telling, he is never wrong, and never stands in need of forgiveness, even by God. Thus, no factual correction breaks through his raging narcissism and shamelessness.

The reasonable decencies in American politics and society that Obama exemplified are under assault on Trump's watch. He derides the rule of law and America's democratic institutions, ridiculing even his Cabinet officials. He admires dictators, shamelessly fawns over them, and wants very much to be one. He praises Russia's dictator effusively, claiming that Vladimir Putin should not be blamed for annexing Crimea; that was Obama's fault for inviting Putin to disrespect him. Trump does not pretend to care that Russia tried to sabotage the 2016 election, because that benefited him. He cares only about whatever benefits him, which may have caused him to collude with Russia and launder Russian plutocrat money. Trump's egotism yields nothing to what is known about the perils of trade war, tweeting that "trade wars are great, and easy to win." He went straight from insulting and deriding European leaders at the G-7 conference of June 2018 to fawning over the mass-murdering Kim Jong Un of North Korea; *anything* that puts him in the spotlight can be justified. Then, he claimed in a press gathering that Kim has dismantled his nuclear arsenal and Paul Manafort had nothing to do with his 2016 campaign; the cascade of lies is torrential. Trump is set upon enormous harm on health care, climate change, fiscal policy, immigration, voting rights, and financial deregulation, and all of it is overshadowed by the obvious danger of putting the nuclear box in his hands.

I am more hopeful than this is sounding, but I fully expect that Trump will always outperform his poll numbers. He shrewdly understands what worked for him in 2016, knowing that he has an unshakeable base, plus a critical swath of supporters who do not admit supporting him. He understands that a determined minority of approximately 40 percent can hold power and subvert democratic institutions. Thus, he is persistently offensive, thrilling his base, and has benefited politically from the continuing decrease in unemployment that began in 2010, never mind that as a candidate he mocked the same unemployment statistics as fake. Trump's weekly spectacle of insulting the media, liberals, non-white voters, and global elites has swollen his favorability rating, reaching 45 percent. No candidate on the other side has any chance of winning similar devotion.

There are plenty of reasons for Democratic officials to count on a seesaw correction featuring vaguely anti-Trump campaign ads. The segment of the population to which Trump appeals is old, white, and shrinking. He is degrading the Republican brand and its future, as old-style Republicans recognize. The national majority that elected Obama twice and supported him to the end is still out there, suggesting that a blue wave is possible in 2018 and/or 2020. In 2020, the Democratic presidential candidate will not have a 56 percent negative rating, a significant advantage over the 2016 campaign. Some prospective Democratic candidates are willing to run yellow dog campaigns, talk out of both sides of their mouth, stand for as little as possible, shake down Wall Street money, and demoralize the party's progressive base once again. I am not for that.

I believe that President Obama was one of our better presidents of the past century, and I deeply regret that he squandered opportunities in his first two years to make historic gains for social justice. I never believed he was a lefty progressive or anything of the sort, so I was not surprised at how he governed. Obama campaigned as a liberal-leaning moderate in 2008, lacking a single risky position, although he briefly considered a gas tax. His only radical position was that he could be elected president. There were four issues, however, on which Obama could have made huge gains as president without breaking from his campaign platform. He could have broken up the big banks. He could have fought for a healthcare public option in the Senate. He could have achieved an immigration reform bill. Or he could have won a second stimulus for job creation and clean energy.

I do not mean that all four things together were achievable. Any two would have required all the political capital he possessed in 2009. But on no issue did Obama plant a flag, risk legislative defeat, and fight for the historic achievement that was within reach. Instead, he played for half of what he wanted and took whatever he could get from the 60th vote in the Senate without twisting anybody's arm. Then, Democrats lost the House and we got debt ceiling hostage politics. In both halves of his first term, the president demoralized his progressive base. I met progressives every week who said they would not work for him a second time; they were done with him, feeling betrayed. So I wrote a book in 2012, *The Obama Question,* about why progressives should not give up on Obama.[5]

One of the most telling and fateful moments of Obama's presidency occurred on March 27, 2009, when he met with the CEOs of the big banks. The mega-bankers were not so swaggering back then, having just gambled and swindled their way to the biggest financial meltdown since the Depression. They knew very well that if the new president cut them down to size, he would reap an enormous political windfall. People across the political spectrum would have welcomed it. The Tea Party might not have taken off. Any bank that is too big to fail holds the country hostage, and it's too big to be regulated.

Obama had two golden opportunities in this area. The first was in March 2009, when he told the mega-bankers, "My administration is the only thing between you and the pitchforks. We have to work together." The bankers nodded in fake agreement and *they* got together, forming the CDS Dealers Consortium, through which they fought every plank of the Dodd-Frank bill. The second opportunity was the Brown-Kaufman amendment to Dodd-Frank, which would have allowed no bank to risk more than 3 percent of the nation's GDP or hold more than 10 percent of the nation's total insured deposits. This amendment got thirty Democratic votes and three Republican votes in the Senate even though Obama and the Senate leadership opposed it.[6]

Brown-Kaufman would have passed had Obama supported it. He came out against it because he wanted to reinstate the wall between commercial and investment banking—the Volcker Rule. In 1999, the Clinton

Administration teamed with Texas Republican Senator Phil Gramm to tear down the Glass-Steagall wall between commercial and investment banking, which opened the door to the megabank empires and mergers of the George W. Bush years. The federal government provides deposit insurance and other safeguards to ensure that America has a stable banking system. These privileges were not created to give unfair advantages to banks operating hedge funds or private equity funds. Banks should not be allowed to speculate with cheap money that the government safety net provides. The system allows banks to make trades conflicting with the interests of their own customers, which fueled a riot of speculation.

The ostensible purpose of Wall Street is to raise money to finance making things in the real economy. But CDO deals are not investments. They do not create any actual bonds or mortgages, or add anything of value to society. They are pure gambling on whether somebody else's bonds will succeed. They are like side bets at a casino, except the Federal Reserve, implicitly, protects these bets. According to the SEC, Goldman Sachs, Citigroup, and other firms looted their own customers by creating derivatives that were designed to fail, and then bet against them.

The Volcker Rule was supposed to stop that. But to pass the Dodd-Frank bill, the Volcker Rule was gutted with exemptions for trading in Treasury bonds and bond issues by government-backed entities. As always, these exemptions led to others, and today the Volcker Rule is riddled with exemptions. Former Federal Reserve chair Paul Volcker's original proposal was three pages; in the Dodd-Frank bill, it was ten pages; today it is a four hundred-page monument to the lobbying power of Wall Street. The big banks have become giant hedge funds trading on their own accounts, run by people who think the public has no right to regulate them.

The second issue was the public option in health care. Here, one mistake led to another. I am a longtime advocate of single payer, and it was wrong to exclude us from the discussion. We were pushed aside as irrelevant, and many activists on this issue were so angry at being disregarded that they didn't get behind the public option. That was a mistake on their part, because the public option is a magic bullet, and the Congressional votes for single payer were not there in 2009. Health care is a fundamental human right that should be available to all people regardless of their economic resources. A decent society does not relegate the poor and underemployed to second-class status. When wealthy and middle-class people have to rely on the same healthcare system as the poor, they use their political power to make sure it's a good system. The public option became the acid test of whether we were going to structurally reform the system or just make the insurance companies take more customers. If people are allowed to choose a government plan, they will do so—which could lead to a universalized Medicare, with everybody in and nobody out.

A good public plan would be open to all individuals and employers who want to join. It would allow members to choose their own doctors, eliminate high deductibles, and allow members to negotiate reimbursement rates and drug prices. The government would run it. And it would be backed up by tough cost controls and a requirement that all Americans have health coverage.

When Obama took office, there was a serious momentum for a public option. He supported it, the House passed a weak version of it, and there was a majority for it in the Senate. This was the moment to take a stand, spend some political capital, and fight for something that made a huge difference. But when the president learned he was seven or eight votes short of beating a filibuster in the Senate, he bailed out, and he didn't bother to tell us, so many of us spent months pushing for something that was already dead. That made a lot of progressives very angry, and at that point, we were only seven months into Obama's presidency.

In the end, to his immense credit, Obama won an important half-victory in this area. He risked his presidency, knowing it would hurt him politically, to gain health coverage for millions of poor and vulnerable people. He abolished the worst abuses of the health insurance companies and made a significant gain toward universal coverage, albeit with a clunky bureaucratic plan that strengthened the health insurance industry. We don't need health insurance companies. We need universal Medicare, covering everyone with a public plan, like they have in decent societies with comparable economies. Now, we are faced with the outright elimination of Obama's half-victory.

On immigration, the president thought it would be a good third year issue. Then, he got the most obstructionist opposition ever faced by a president. Obama had barely been inaugurated when rally crowds began wailing about wanting their country back. He hadn't done anything yet, but they had already lost their country, which sparked the Tea Party. The American economy had lost three million jobs in the past year. The nation was freefalling into a Depression, yet somehow it was horribly wrong to inject a stimulus that spared the United States from reliving 1933. On the basis of that utterly absurd position the Tea Party became a powerful force in American politics, and immigration reform was no longer possible. Until Obama was elected, there were upwards of twenty-three Republican votes in the Senate for the Dream Act. That number swiftly fell to zero under Obama, and he went on to deport more than 2.5 million persons, breaking George W. Bush's record. The deportation numbers soared under Bush and Obama because so-called catch and release deportees had not been counted previously; the new policy put a formal charge on the record of every apprehended border crosser.

On number four, we will never know what political difference it might have made had the Obama Democrats pushed hard for infrastructure and clean energy investments when they had the chance. The United States has under-invested in infrastructure, education, and technology for decades. We need to renew the country by making massive investments in a healthy, educated, productive workforce and a clean energy economy. Labor costs, equipment costs, and the cost of capital have been at historic lows for the past decade, and the government has abjectly failed to take advantage of it for the sake of rebuilding the country. Here, the rage of the Trump base is fully merited, however misdirected. Investments that benefit society are more important than wedge issues and even tax policy, but we have idiotic politics in which distractions are easily manufactured and "build a Mexican wall" is considered a populist economic agenda.

The so-called Tea Party has now melted into Trumpism, helping to produce the Trump presidency. I got a strong dose of its worldview when I did hundreds of radio shows in 2012: Americans are overtaxed, the federal debt exploded because Democrats created too much government, somehow the federal government caused the financial crash, and cutting taxes is always in order. The Tea Party thrived, and still does as Trump's base, on a deeply felt dichotomy between the deserving and the undeserving. It is driven primarily by its rage against the supposedly undeserving and the liberal elites who are said to coddle the undeserving. At the grassroots level, much of the Tea Party was not hostile to Social Security or Medicare, unlike the professional ideologues that exploited it. Trump caught the difference. But Trump brilliantly appealed to the resentments that created the Tea Party: Undeserving people get benefits from the government, "illegal aliens" are stealing our jobs and money, and we white Americans are losing the privileges we had when America was Great.

In point of fact, the nation's total tax revenue was customarily 28 percent of GDP during the last three decades of the twentieth century, compared to the 35 percent average of comparable nations, and in 2012, the U.S. rate dipped to its lowest point since 1958, 23 percent. Today, it stands at 26 percent. Americans are not overtaxed; in fact, the historic lows of the past fifteen years are the cause of the escalating federal debt.[7]

In 1981, when Ronald Reagan took office, the national debt was $907 billion, approximately 26 percent of GDP. Eight years later the debt stood at $2.7 trillion, representing 40 percent of GDP. Reagan corrupted the Republican Party by persuading it that deficits don't matter and another tax cut is always in order. He tripled the nation's accumulated debt by cutting the marginal tax rate from 70 to 28 percent and cutting the top rate on capital gains from 49 percent to 20 percent—social engineering on a staggering scale that fueled a huge inequality surge. George H. W. Bush, frightened when the debt surged to $3.9 trillion on his watch, raised the marginal rate to 35 percent, demoralized his party, and lost a second term. Bill Clinton, finishing what the elder Bush began, raised the marginal rate to 39.6 percent and rang up budget surpluses of $70 billion in 1998, $124 billion in 1999, and $237 billion in 2000. If the United States had stuck with the Clinton tax rates, our national debt heading into the Obama years would have been minimal or non-existent. The debt exploded because George W. Bush blew a $2 trillion hole in the deficit by cutting the marginal rate and capital gains. He fought two wars that the nation didn't pay for, becoming the first president in U.S. history not to raise taxes to pay for an expensive war. He added a $1 trillion Medicare drug benefit without paying for it either, a windfall for the pharmaceutical industry that created the first entitlement in U.S. history lacking a revenue source.[8]

These expenditures doubled the nation's debt in seven years, and that record keeps mounting. Now, the debt is intractable, reaching $20 trillion in September 2017. The politics of this issue are especially perverse, because the party that stages debt ceiling dramas when a Democrat is in the White House is the one that mindlessly explodes the debt whenever it gains power. In December 2017, Trump and the Republicans cut the top tax rate to 37 percent and cut the corporate tax rate from 35 percent to 21 percent. We know only too vividly how this will play out, because it has happened twice before since 1980.

A morally decent tax system would have additional brackets for the highest incomes, as the United States once did. It would have a bracket for $1 million earners and a bracket for $10 million dollar earners and so on. It would lift the cap on the regressive Social Security tax, taxing salaries above $127,000 per year. It is absurd that someone making $1 million per year pays no more into Social Security than someone making $125,000. A decent tax and budget plan would tax capital gains as ordinary income. It would tax U.S. foreign income as it is earned. It would eliminate the subsidies for oil, gas, and coal companies. It would place a tax on credit default swaps and futures and charge a leverage tax on the megabanks. I stress that these are modest, prosaic, center-left proposals. The United States would still be far below European levels of taxation. But struggling for decency is a fighting matter in our context, not a matter of waiting for a seesaw political correction.

The problem of the white working class loomed overlarge in postelection commentary, obscuring that Trump won *every* sector of the white votes. Black Americans, though always treated badly by political elites, have never turned to fascistic candidates. Still, the elitism of the Democratic Party's professional class is terribly real to working class whites, so I will say a word about it. I grew up in a poor, semi-rural family in mid-Michigan. My parents moved there from Michigan's Upper Peninsula, where my father experienced discrimination for having a Cree mother. He moved to mid-Michigan to claim for himself and his children all the white privilege he could get, the most loving thing he could imagine doing as a parent. Today, my father is proudly, even aggressively, Native American, and I appreciate the changes in American society that made it possible for him to reclaim his racial identity. But I am a child of the white working class, having never experienced or claimed any other racial identity.

My childhood neighbors would have repudiated any suggestion that being white conferred any cultural privileges upon them. Today, they are convinced that American society confers blessings on everyone except them. They believe the game is rigged against them and the federal government is their enemy. For eight years, they heard Obama give sunny speeches about economic progress and they were infuriated, realizing that they were invisible to the neoliberal elites that run the Democratic Party. Trump routed Hillary Clinton in mid-Michigan, and nationally, he won the white working class by a staggering 39 percent. It did not matter that his hotels and lifestyle are flagrantly upper class and he had no basis whatsoever for making a moral appeal to evangelicals and conservative Catholics. At left-liberal gatherings today, one side of the room says, "The white working class is too big to write off," and the other side says, "The trend lines are hopeless, write them off." I am with the former group, but for moral reasons, plus personal history, not because I'm convinced that the second group is pragmatically wrong, and even the moral argument is a close call, because wooing the white working class runs the risk of selling out moral decency on racism, sexism, LGBTQ rights, and xenophobia.

A slightly modified take on the first choice recognizes that the white working class is not monolithically anti-government. According to Peter Hart Research Associates, a tiny sliver of the white working class is politically liberal, 35 percent is ideologically moderate, and the overwhelming majority is ideologically conservative. The moderate group represents 15 percent of the total electorate, approximately 23 million registered voters. Trump beat Clinton by eighty-five points among the conservatives and by twenty-six points among the moderates. However, this 26-point margin was exactly twice as big as Romney's margin over Obama with the same group in 2012. Had Clinton performed even slightly less badly among moderate white working class voters, she would have won Michigan, Wisconsin, Pennsylvania, and the election. The moderate group, which was open to being swayed, swung the election to Trump.[9]

Tim Kane on Clinton's ticket was supposed to play the role that Joe Biden played for Obama, helping to swing moderate working class whites to the Democratic side. The Democratic Party will play it that way again if the establishment professionals currently running the party get their way. The alternative is a democratic politics that changes the view of some white working class Americans about the role that government plays in their lives. Nothing less than *change* is necessary, because white working class Americans overwhelmingly despise the government.

Moderates and conservatives share this aversion. In 2015, 73 percent of white working class voters told pollsters that the federal government makes it harder, not easier, for them to achieve their goals. By a four-to-one ratio, they said the federal government's economic impact is negative. The difference between the moderate and conservative groups is that moderates say they would support progressive candidates and policies *if* they believed that doing so would help them achieve their goals. They don't believe it of the existing Democratic Party—even as polling consistently shows that voters support higher taxes on the wealthy, curbing the power of Wall Street, and ensuring paid leave for workers.

White working class voters would welcome government intervention that benefits them, and they emphatically believe that Democratic and Republican politicians are greedy, self-serving, and obsequious to the donor class. There is an opportunity here for progressives to run hard on single payer, rebuilding the country, and curbing Wall Street. But that would require some recognition that Bernie Sanders was right. Sanders spoke directly and powerfully to voters left behind by corporate capitalism and the power of Wall Street over both political parties. His message and motivation were perfectly clear, conveying, every day, his gut level passion about inequality, poverty, and injustice.

Sanders spoke about the economic pain ravaging American communities and the moral necessity of doing something about it. He fought for equality with a tenacity surpassing any elected official since the New Deal. Sanders hates that Wall Street owns both parties, that corporations get rewarded for shipping jobs overseas, and that everything public is under assault in contemporary politics. He is rightly outraged that the tax system is skewed to exacerbate inequality and that Republican leaders are bent on destroying Medicare and Social Security. Sanders is a symbol and a voice—a radical democrat who grasps why authoritarian nationalism is surging in American society. He shares, in opposite fashion, the anger of Trump voters against a system that does not work for the majority. He was a flawed candidate in some respects, radiating an Old Left economism that sang in one-key-only. Sanders never broke through to African American voters, which caused many of us to regret that he never had to try until he ran for president, representing very white Vermont in Congress. But being an Old Lefty is his strength in this wretched political context. Sanders reminds Democrats that they're supposed to care about ordinary wage earners and the vulnerable, not the interests of the donor class.[10]

In decent democracies, health care is a human right, laws curtail the power of private money in the political system, and nearly everyone recognizes that there is such a thing as an intolerable level of economic inequality. That describes every nation on the planet with a social democratic tradition. But the United States never achieved more than a modicum of social democratic decency, and now even the modicum is endangered. Here, health coverage depends on what you can afford, millions have no health coverage at all, private money dominates the political system, and nothing is done to stem enormous inequalities of income and wealth. No democracy can perpetually survive gross disparities in economic and social condition. The fascist movements of the 1930s soared by responding to the ravages of inequality and breakdown, speaking to the distress of hurting majority populations in ostensible democracies, pinning the blame on scapegoats. Trump has taken that path, betting everything on the politics of white grievance and the greed of the corporate class.

Democracy, the real thing, is the answer to the Trump trauma, but illiberal, nationalist, mean-spirited democracy can shred the real thing in a few months. I expect that the worst of Trump is still to come. Sooner or later, he will declare a state of emergency that nullifies democratic institutions, making a grab for as much power as he can get. Robert Mueller's investigation of the Trump campaign's possible collusion with Russia has slowed and distracted Trump, but it has the obvious potential of accelerating Trump's dictatorial impulse at any time. However, the Mueller investigation turns out, Trump's narcissistic disrespect for democracy poses a constant threat to democracy. He and his allies must be opposed at every step, assuming the worst without getting panicked or attributing to Trump more power than he possesses. Trump's ability to start a catastrophic war is by far the ultimate threat; here, the character of the military top brass might have to be counted upon. Everywhere else, the everyday imperative is to defend democratic institutions and refuse to normalize the way that Trump operates.

Steve Bannon offered a telling peek into the Trump White House just before he got bounced from it in August 2017. Bannon clashed with National Security Advisor H. R. McMaster over the Trump

Administration's nuclear brinkmanship with North Korea and its deference to China. Then, Bannon gave an out-of-the-blue telephone interview to *American Prospect* editor Robert Kuttner. Bannon apparently realized that Trump's "fire and fury" bombast about North Korea was just for show. The serious issue, he said, is America's economic war with China. China is bent on overtaking the United States as a global hegemon, and in ten years, if nothing changes, it will be too late to thwart China from succeeding. Meanwhile, the brinkmanship between North Korea and the United States was a boon for China: "On Korea, they're just tapping us along. It's just a sideshow." Bannon urged Trump to restrict technology transfers by American companies doing business in China and to formally accuse China of steel and aluminum dumping. He told Kuttner that he fought Treasury Secretary Gary Cohn and the Goldman Sachs lobbyists every day over China. He also boasted that he was purging the White House of soft-on-China diplomats—until the Wall Street powerbrokers pushed him out.[11]

Bannon made a plausible claim to understand Trump's game plan. He angered Trump by providing quotable zingers for Michael Wolff's book, *Fire and Fury,* though I would not bet against Bannon's ability to regain Trump's favor by 2020, since Bannon got him elected in the first place. Meanwhile, Bannon says that the political left has made itself irrelevant: "I want them to talk about racism every day. If the left is focused on race and identity, and we go with economic nationalism, we can crush the Democrats."[12]

Note the clever cynicism of this pitch. Bannon is famous for stoking and manipulating white nationalism as the Alt-right guru of Breitbart News. No one except Trump, in recent years, has made more political capital off racism and racial identity politics than Bannon. But according to Bannon, only the left makes an issue of race, except for the handful of "losers" and "clowns" who showed up at Charlottesville. Outright white nationalists are a "fringe element" with no power, he says. The serious version of American nationalism does not have to call itself "white" because it already has immense power, and is gaining more of it.

It's a much harder job in the political sphere to say that racial, sexual, gender, and economic justice go together and must do so. The difficulty compounds because progressives say what they believe and Trump nationalists lie about what they believe, reaping the advantages of doing so in the cutthroat sphere of politics. Some political moments are so grim that sustaining a glimmer of hope is extremely difficult. Thus, we are witnessing an upsurge of Afro-pessimism. The case for Afro-pessimism is powerful; Afro-pessimists rightly stress that "people of color" multicultural rhetoric obscures the specific anti-black animus of racism. Whiteness is the desire not to be black. But pessimism never saved anyone or inspired any great movement, a point that Martin Luther King Jr. pressed repeatedly in his last years. Anti-blackness is only one form of the racism assaulting American society, as dramatized by Trump's attacks on Latinx migrants and Muslims. Moreover, opposing anti-blackness should not *replace* the condemnation of white supremacism, as some are advocating, for that abandons the focus on structures of power based on privilege. We must not return to describing racism as mere personal bias, a convention that thwarted anti-racism work for decades.

Racism-as-bias obscures structural factors and thwarts political agency. No one admits to being racially biased, while the bias concept reinforces the "race blind" idea of racial justice. Racism-as-bias yielded generations of white liberals who claimed that giving no credence to racial anything was the most anti-racist thing they could do. Some of the white liberals who cofounded the NAACP held this view, galling W. E. B. Du Bois. Howard Thurman's spiritual mentor, Quaker theologian Rufus Jones, similarly believed that all talk about race is toxic and reactionary. Thus, he wrote nothing about racism, while writing constantly about peace and love. Race is a baleful category, Jones reasoned, so pay it no mind! We can end it by refusing to recognize it. My students cannot comprehend how this brand of white liberal might have been ethically sincere. They are very hard on ignore-it-away white liberals. But the bias view produces sincere reductionists who just want to be blameless by their lights.

King struggled mightily with the hope problem upon witnessing the backlash of the 1960s. He tried to buck up his allies after the civil rights bills passed and the backlash commenced. The election of November 1966 approached and King oscillated between saying what he really believed and trying not to hurt liberals running for office. He had not previously said that white Americans never intended to integrate their schools or neighborhoods. Then, he got pelted with rocks in Chicago and King said it bitterly to the Alabama Christian Movement.[13]

The election came and the backlash was fierce, though King spurned backlash talk, because that kind of language always blamed him for something. Calling it a backlash suggested that racism was increasing and he should do something different. Backlash talk was a species of denial. He convened a retreat at Frogmore, near Savannah, for the battered Southern Leadership Christian Conference (SCLC). He was bleak and grim, admitting he didn't know what to do next. American racism, King noted, was distinctly vicious: "The white man literally sought to annihilate the Indian. If you look through the history of the world this very seldom happened." This was what black Americans were up against—a genocidal impulse fueled by the pervasive white American belief in white superiority. By that optic, the current talk about a backlash was superficial.[14]

Then, King wrote his last book, *Where Do We Go From Here,* and he stopped imploring against backlash talk, because it named something terribly real. But what mattered, he said, was the cause, not the backlash loop. Racial hostility was always there, and it had never been otherwise. The civil rights movement merely brought this deep hostility to the surface. Coping with that reality was a spiritual discipline.[15]

In his last years, King grew accustomed to being more radical than everyone around him. He doubled down on the path of public sacrifice, dragging others along. He had never taken care of himself, and he was not going to change merely because he was ill and exhausted. The Poor People's Campaign, which King launched at the lowest point of his life, topped his previous forays into risky, controversial, chaotic protest. He would not be shamed into reverting to middle-class politics. Now, he outflanked even James Bevel, his usual barometer of too-far extremism. King wanted a housing bill and a minimum guaranteed income, but he did not claim to have the political angles figured. Perhaps his lieutenants were right that squatting in the nation's capital would hurt his reform proposals. He knew only that he had to stand with the poorest of the poor and afflicted. Otherwise, he said, he was not really a follower of Jesus.

Gary Dorrien teaches at Union Theological Seminary and Columbia University. His many books include *Kantian Reason and Hegelian Spirit,* which won the Association of American Publishers' PROSE Award in 2013, and *The New Abolition: W. E. B. Du Bois and the Black Social Gospel,* which won the Grawemeyer Award in 2017.

Notes

1. Dorrien, Gary, *The Obama Question: A Progressive Perspective* (Lanham, MD: Rowman & Littlefield, 2012), p. 4.
2. Corsi, Jerome R., *The Obama Nation: Leftist Politics and the Cult of Personality* (New York, NY: Threshold Editions, 2008); Corsi, *Where's the Birth Certificate? The Case that Barack Obama is Not Eligible to be President* (Washington, DC: WND Books, 2011); O'Leary, Brad, *The Audacity of Deceit: Barack Obama's War on American Values* (Los Angeles, CA: WND Books, 2008); Klein, Aaron, *The Manchurian President: Barack Obama's Ties to Communists, Socialists, and Other Anti-American Extremists* (Washington, DC: WND Books, 2010); Cashill, Jack, *Deconstructing Obama* (New York, NY: Threshold Editions, 2011); Cashill, "Is Khalid al-Mansour the Man Behind Obama Myth?" WorldNetDaily (August 28, 2008), www.wnd.com.; Malkin, Michelle, *Culture of Corruption: Obama and His Team of Tax Cheats, Crooks, and Cronies* (Washington, DC: Regnery, 2009); Geller, Pamela, *(with Robert Spencer) The Post-American Presidency: The Obama Administration's War on America* (New York, NY: Threshold Editions, 2010); Griffon Tarpley, Webster, *Obama: The Postmodern Coup* (Joshua Tree, CA: Progressive Press, 2008).
3. D'Souza, Dinesh, *"How Obama Thinks," Forbes* (September 27, 2010); D'Souza, *The Roots of Obama's Rage* (Washington, DC: Regnery Publishing, 2010).
4. Costa, Robert, "Gingrich: Obama's 'Kenyan, Anti-Colonial Worldview,'" National Review Online (September 11, 2010), www.nationalreview.com.
5. This section contains a capsule summary of arguments I made in The Obama Question.
6. Javers, Eamon, "Inside Obama's Bank CEO's Meeting," Politico (April 3, 2009), quote; "Banks Promise Obama They'll Cooperate," New York Times (March 27, 2009), http://www.nytimes.com/2009/03/28/business/economy/28bank.html.
7. Organization for Economic Cooperation and Development, "Revenue Statistics, OECD Countries, Comparative Tables, https://stats.oecd.org/Index.aspx?DataSetCode=REV; OECD, "Tax Revenue," https://data.oecd.org/tax/tax-revenue.htm.
8. Dorrien, Gary, *Economy, Difference, Empire: Social Ethics for Social Justice* (New York, NY: Columbia University Press, 2010), pp. 144-5.
9. Molyneux, Guy, "Mapping the White Working Class," American Prospect (December 20, 2016), http://prospect.org/article/mapping-white-working-class.
10. Dorrien, Gary, "Saving Democracy: How to Resist Tyranny," Christian Century (June 21, 2017), 20-5.
11. Robert Kuttner, "Steve Bannon, Unrepentant," American Prospect (August 16, 2007), quotes, http://prospect.org/article/steve-bannon-unrepentant.
12. Kuttner, "Steve Bannon, Unrepentant."
13. This section is a gloss on my book, *Breaking White Supremacy: Martin Luther King Jr. and the Black Social Gospel* (New Haven, CT: Yale University Press, 2018).
14. Luther King, Martin, Jr., "Dr. King's Speech—Frogmore—November 14, 1966," The King Center, www.thekingcenter.org/archive, quotes, 6, 7.
15. Luther King, Martin, Jr., *Where Do We Go From Here: Chaos or Community?* (New York: Harper & Row, 1967), pp. 86-7.

CROSSCURRENTS

BLACK DIGNITY

Vincent Lloyd

The language of dignity is a common denominator of the abolitionist movement, the civil rights movement, the black power movement, and black feminist organizing. In 2016, the Movement for Black Lives disseminated a platform that begins, "Black humanity and dignity require Black political will and power," and #BlackLivesMatter-associated preacher Osagyefo Sekou proclaimed, "I understand the gospel to affirm black dignity."[1] Yet black political struggles, and in the background black political theology, are more often identified with themes of love and justice than with dignity. I hypothesize that, if dignity takes center stage, forms of black political struggle seemingly at odds with each other—black nationalists and integrationists, black feminists and Afrocentrists, black writers and black community organizers—in fact appear to be animated by the same fundamental impulse. Before that hypothesis can be tested, it is necessary to reflect on what dignity means in black politics. This latter, preliminary task is the one I take up here, first by reviewing the use of dignity in recent black political organizing and its antecedents, then by positing three basic characteristics of dignity in black politics, and finally by responding to two worries about my account of dignity.

Attending to dignity in black politics allows for a dialogue with the large number of scholarly studies that have examined dignity over the last decade. Political theorists and intellectual historians have shown particular interest in the concept, developing a rapidly growing literature that stands at a distance from the steady stream of Christian theological reflections on dignity over the past half-century. Attempts are underway to bridge this divide, with secular political theorists taking a deeper interest in the role dignity plays in religious thought, not only Christian theology but also Jewish, Islamic, and other religious thought. I suspect frustration with the language of human rights partially motivates this turn to dignity. Over the last two decades, critics of human rights from the academy, from activist circles, and from global South political circles have pointed to ways in which human rights language and ideas are applied arbitrarily, often advancing the interests of the powerful rather than part of a consistent, systematic moral position. Moreover, the set of human rights seems to grow or shrink based on the interests of the day, with no agreement on how to determine what counts as a human right. Those theorists proposing a method for determining what counts have been charged with Western cultural imperialism, given the uncanny similarity between the set of rights their theories produce and the set of rights endorsed by Western political actors.

Dignity promises to ground human rights in a clear, relatively uncontroversial claim, one that is endorsed broadly by many religions and traditions of the world (or so its proponents insist), namely, that each human being has inherent, incalculable worth. Accounts of dignity along these lines clearly resonate with Christian theological accounts of dignity —where incalculable worth comes from humans' creation in the image of God—but there are also long lines of secular and non-Christian reflection on dignity. Most famously, this includes the ethical theory of Kant, but an alternative lineage of dignity following from Hegel's thought is attracting increasing attention as well.[2] At the level of political and legal practice, the intellectual foundations of dignity remain bracketed as the concept, enshrined in international and national legal norms—it is affirmed by the United Nations charter, the Universal Declaration of Human Rights, and the constitutions of 142 countries—is applied to specific circumstances in contexts ranging from bioethics to the laws of war to prisoners' rights.

Recent attempts to provide expansive, interdisciplinary overviews of the concept of dignity, including most notably the hefty edited volumes *Understanding Human Dignity*, published by Oxford University Press in 2013, and *The Cambridge Handbook of Human Dignity: Interdisciplinary Perspectives*, published by Cambridge University Press in 2014, have sought to pluralize the scholarly conversation about dignity. Am I attempting to add yet another perspective on dignity from a different cultural context, that of African Americans?³ In one sense, the sources I discuss here do this, but my interest in more fundamental; I wish to make a stronger claim. Dignity as it is found in black political thought is not an example of an important political-philosophical or political-theological concept applied to a specific context; rather, dignity is misunderstood by European Christian or post-Christian sources (or their pluralization).⁴ Put another way, making explicit my methodological commitments, examining dignity from the perspective of marginalized communities corrects errors that necessarily arise when a concept is examined from a perspective of privilege. The black perspective on dignity is not just one more perspective, it is better.

Circulation

According to the three women who coined the hashtag BlackLivesMatter, dignity has always been at the heart of their movement. It was labor organizer Alicia Garza who first put the now famous three words into circulation, in response to the acquittal of George Zimmerman for the killing of Trayvon Martin, and with the work of fellow organizers Patrisse Cullors and Opal Tometi a movement took shape, spreading on social media but grounded in local racial justice organizing collectives taking action in the streets. Amid multiple media narratives circulating around the origins of the movement, Garza told the story herself—a "herstory" of the movement, as she called it. After reflecting on the movement's origins, Garza asserts its core commitment: "When we say Black Lives Matter, we are talking about the ways in which Black people are deprived of our basic human rights and dignity."⁵ In the paragraph that follows, she lists some of what ails the black community: poverty, incarceration, economic exploitation, immigration issues, particular harms faced by blacks with disabilities and by black queers, and more. All of this, Garza asserts, is part of "White supremacy," a structure of domination that #BlackLivesMatter aims to challenge. The ultimate goal is not to benefit black people, but to benefit everyone: "When Black people get free, everybody gets free." What the movement calls for, Garza concludes, is "defense of our humanity"—that is what will restore dignity to blacks, and that is what will point us in the direction of a world without domination, a world where everybody is free.

Cullors, Garza's collaborator, similarly places dignity at the heart of her understanding of the movement. She reflects, "I come at all my work from a deep philosophical place that [asks], what does it take for humans to live in our full humanity and allow for others to live in their full dignity?"[6] Cullors founded Dignity and Power Now, a grassroots organizing collective based in Los Angeles that focuses on empowering those incarcerated and their loved ones. Using tactics that include coalition-building, art, research, and leadership development, Dignity and Power Now challenges mass incarceration by focusing locally, aware of both the effects of imprisonment on individuals and the broader systems—the prison industrial complex—of which the Los Angeles criminal justice system is a part. In her memoir, Cullors reflects on the origins of her organization's name. She remembers the arrest of her brother, and she remembers how, at the same time that mainstream America was ignoring the realities of police violence experienced by black communities like hers, Nelson Mandela had become an international icon of the struggle for justice. She recounts the words of Mandela's speech from his 1964 trial, "Our fight is against real, and not imaginary, hardships, poverty and lack of human dignity. The lack of human dignity experienced by Africans is the direct result of the policy of white supremacy."[7] Domination deprives individuals of dignity, and the call for dignity motivates the struggle against domination. That struggle takes place through art, activism, research, and other activities. If we take "now" seriously and equivocally in Dignity and Power Now, it becomes clear how dignity can both be the goal and, in another sense, the achievement entailed by the practices of organizing themselves.

Tometi is a Nigerian American who directs the Black Alliance for Just Immigration. She, too, describes #BlackLivesMatter in terms of dignity: It aims "to protect and affirm the beauty and dignity of all Black lives."[8] When speaking out on immigration, she also uses the language of dignity, decrying current immigration laws because they have "disregarded the dignity and human rights of millions of immigrants," with the struggle for the dignity of immigrants (including black immigrants) connected to the struggles for dignity of blacks in Africa and black Americans.[9] Tometi describes herself as "a believer and practitioner of liberation theology," and she links her commitment to dignity to her faith commitment. "We are all called," she asserts, "to our highest most dignified selves." Further, "one's spiritual practice and aspirations for dignity and self-actualization [are] what a rich faith life is about."[10] Note here how Tometi is not identifying faith with a commitment to dignity, for example, by saying that belief in God allows her to recognize the inherent worth and dignity of every human being. Rather, dignity appears in gradations, and becoming more dignified (which is "self-actualization") is something we can achieve through faith life. Tometi goes on assert that faith and justice are inextricably intertwined: A rich faith life means a life committed to the struggle for social justice.

While three women started the Black Lives Matter movement, it quickly took on a life of its own as individuals connected via social media or organizing meetings, creating new formations and energizing existing grassroots networks. With media narratives defining the movement, and limiting it, leaders decided to work together on a platform that could spell out in detail the shared values of movement participants and the injustices that the movement, in all its manifestations, targeted. Through a year-long consultative process creating dialogues between local racial justice groups, the Movement for Black Lives Platform began to take shape. This document includes a preamble and six demands, with each demand detailing a problem and solutions at the national and local level, together with further resources and information about groups organizing around this demand. The Platform's preamble describes the world desired by the Movement: "a world in which the full humanity and dignity of all people is recognized."[11] To achieve this "requires Black political will and power." Again there is a certain equivocation here. In one sense, dignity is the desired end state, likely never to be reached; in another sense, the more black organizing, the more black dignity. In other words, it seems as though there is an eschatological sense of dignity at work, present in the world of "full humanity" (in Christian terms, when the dead will rise), and also a worldly sense of dignity at work, where dignity is identified with struggle. In the demands themselves, a third sense of dignity is at work. This is dignity achieved when specific practices of domination end, not eschatologically and not in struggle. To take three examples, the Movement opposes the Trans-Pacific Partnership trade agreement so as to advance the dignity of black workers; it supports a constitutional right to education in order to advance the dignity of students; and it opposes the shackling of women during pregnancy and childbirth to advance women's dignity.

Many intellectual and organizing streams flow into the current movement for racial justice in the United States, and young organizers have been particularly effective at discerning which practices and ideas of earlier generations are most important to embrace. As Cullors's citation of Mandela on dignity suggests, organizers are well aware that dignity has long been a part of the vocabulary of black politics. In fact, it is astounding just how ubiquitous it is. Even militantly secularist youths rallying around the slogan "black power," who would discard as ineffective and old-fashioned many elements of civil rights movement Christianity, continued to talk about dignity. Even those black feminists who turn toward the language of love and self-care embraced the language of dignity. From poets to novelists to orators to elected politicians, dignity was widely discussed, though this has rarely been reflected on by political theorists.

I do not have space here to carry out an exhaustive survey and analysis of the concept of dignity in black politics, but I will offer a few samples. Langston Hughes develops the concept of dignity in two quite different contexts. In one poem from the 1930s about the ordeal of the Scottsboro boys, Hughes writes of how "A young black boy will die" yet "Judges in high places/Still preserve their dignity."[12] This suggests a sort of hollow dignity, dignity that is not dignity at all: the dignity supposed to attach to a judge that is given the lie when we see that judge as a child-killer. In a poem titled "Harlem Dance Hall" first published in 1947, Hughes describes the transformation of the eponymous building when music starts. "Suddenly the earth was there,/And flowers,/Trees,/And air."[13] The hall "had no dignity before," the poem begins and ends, but music gives it life, and with that dignity. In contrast to the hollow dignity of the judge, a band creates rich, thick dignity, dignity that includes individuals but is not reducible to the sum of individuals.

The concept of dignity was deeply baked into the vocabulary of Martin Luther King, Jr. Indeed, in a collection of his key writings, the word "dignity" appears more than one hundred times, and it occurs more than thirty times in King's account of the Montgomery bus boycott.[14] Sometimes, King uses dignity to suggest nobility ("the dignity of courtesy titles"), but more often dignity contrasts with life subject to domination ("it is ultimately more honorable to walk the streets in dignity than to ride the buses in humiliation").[15] Both senses of dignity touch on honor, but in the second sense honor is achieved under the shadow of segregation. Moreover, in the case of the bus boycotters, dignity was not only connected to personal honor, it was also connected to collective struggle. Walking the streets gave the boycotters dignity, deserved honor, because in this act they were challenging a system of domination. After the Montgomery protest had continued for eleven months, with its ups and downs, King told assembled protesters, "I want you to know that this struggle has not been in vain." He continued, "If it has done any one thing in this community it has given us a new sense of dignity and destiny. And I think that in itself is a victory for freedom and a victory for the cause of justice."[16] Dignity is achieved through struggle, King is asserting. Regardless of whether particular policies are changed, regardless of whether complete dignity beyond domination is achieved, dignity in a meaningful sense is found in a community working together to challenge white supremacy, to challenge domination.

Marcus Garvey frequently used the term dignity in the sense associated with nobility, but occasionally he used it in more expansive senses as well. Near the end of his life, in theological reflections, Garvey exhorts his audience to be sure they are clean before they approach God, not in bodies but in minds. "Your thoughts are the things that make you look like God ... It is our soul, our intelligence, that is in His lik[e]ness." Therefore, "We must live up to the dignity and honour of His intelligence by possessing our souls and using our minds."[17] Regardless of how wealthy or healthy someone is, she or he has the potential to participate in the dignity of God by using a mind creatively. Garvey takes his own life as an example, recalling how he was born black in a white-dominated world, in Jamaica, but he did not let himself be constrained by the ways of the world. "I looked at the system that man fixed up for me and I said it did not suit me." This is dignity: realizing that systems of domination constrain our humanity, stamp out the image of God, and then creatively rebelling. In later black nationalist writings, dignity would continue to play an important role, for example, with Malcolm X repeatedly naming "human dignity" as the goal of his struggle—and noting how collaboration with structures of domination through the welfare system is "robbing us of our dignity."[18] A few years later, Stokely Carmichael would repeatedly invoke the concept of dignity, for example, calling on black nationalists to "make alliances with people who are trying to rebuild their culture, trying to rebuild their history, trying to rebuild their dignity, with people who are fighting for their humanity."[19]

The concept of dignity is found in the classics of black feminism, from Ida B. Wells to Anna Julia Cooper, as well as the modern classics, from Audre Lorde to Angela Davis to Alice Walker. bell hooks is particularly instructive because she uses dignity not only to mark opposition to white supremacy but also to look at the differential impact of domination across gender lines. Black women, unlike black men, "were made to feel that when survival was the crucial issue, personal dignity should be sacrificed."[20] In other words, hooks suggests a way in which challenging domination is a privilege that not everyone in dominated communities can afford. Sexual and racial domination intersect, with the result that the possibility of dignity is taken away from black women. "Black women were told that we should find our dignity not in liberation from sexist oppression but in how well we could adjust, adapt, and cope."[21] Life bent into conformity with systems of domination, hooks suggests, is not dignity at all—practice oriented toward liberation is where dignity is to be found. In a quite different sort of political arena, Michelle Obama repeatedly invokes dignity in her speeches, and is described as embodying dignity. "America's greatness comes from recognizing the innate dignity and worth of all our people," she told a New Hampshire audience on the campaign trail for Hillary Clinton.[22] Having a president who does not respect the dignity of women cannot make America great. While the same word is used by Obama and by hooks, and by many other black feminists, in the realm of electoral politics dignity is reduced to a status, disconnected from a practice of liberation.

Characteristics
The standard history of dignity told by political theorists is based around a shift from one meaning of dignity before modernity to another meaning of dignity in modernity—with the earlier meaning persisting in a subordinate role in ordinary speech today. Before modernity, dignity suggested the honor and privileges associated with high rank or office. Dignity in this sense was attributed to kings and nobles, church officials and government officials. Dignity was an attribute of, as the word suggests, dignitaries. Among kings, all of the same rank, there is equality, and so among dukes, among bishops, and among judges. According to Jeremy Waldron, in the late eighteenth century, a "transvaluation of values" occurs: Now, it is ordinary people, rather than classes of elites, who have dignity, while the dignity previously ascribed to elites comes to be seen as "superficial or bogus."[23] Ordinary people all share in the same

rank, all share in humanity, and so all share in a basic type of equality. Dignity now, in modernity, is ascribed to each person by virtue of his or her humanity. We still talk of dignitaries, and about politicians or other elites sullying the dignity of their office, but in political and legal discourse dignity refers to the inherent worth of each human being. Dignity is democratized.

In contrast, the concept of dignity found in black political thought, at its best, is neither attributed to classes of individuals because of their rank nor is it ascribed to all individuals by virtue of their humanity.[24] Dignity is ascribed to those who struggle against domination. Those who dominate, or who participate in systems of domination, do not have dignity. Those who are entirely dominated, to the point that all of their speech and actions are determined by the dynamics of domination, do not have dignity. But those who are subjected to domination and challenge that domination in whatever way, from passive resistance to active political organizing to aesthetic imagining, those individuals are properly described as having dignity. In the US racial landscape simplified to black and white, this means whites who ignore their privilege lack dignity, blacks who follow the scripts given to them by white supremacy lack dignity, but all who challenge white supremacy have dignity. Obviously, these are ideal types, considered in laboratory conditions. In the real world, all people experience domination in some aspects of their lives and participate in systems of domination in other aspects of their lives. Nevertheless, ideal types illuminate, inviting us to consider a third sense of dignity that relates neither to nobility nor to shared humanity.

When white supremacy is nearly all-powerful and omnipresent—imagine the Jim Crow South—challenges to this form of domination will not look like community organizing meetings advertising "Challenge White Supremacy!" In a system meant to humiliate individuals and destroy sociality, resistance takes the form of any commitment to sociality (including family, religious community, dance, even funeral processions) as well as refusals to be humiliated (including pride, holding one's head up, literary or aesthetic production, even humor). Thus, dignity is properly ascribed to black artists and entertainers, black religious practitioners, black dancers, and ordinary black folks who subtly commit to resisting white supremacy. Not every black dancer or artist, joker or preacher counts as having dignity. Rather, dignity requires discernment.

Is the aesthetic production or humor or sermon, or whatever else, participating in or challenging the logic of domination? If the white powers that be become accustomed to a particular black man who holds his head high, refusing humiliation, and then decide to make use of him as a liaison with the rest of the black community, to keep that community in check, should this particular black man still be described as having dignity? These complexities require judgment and discussion rather than the application of clear rules to classes of individuals.[25]

Holding your head up high, looking others in the eye, when others around you are bowing their heads and averting their eyes—this looks like nobility.[26] The king or princess or bishop also carriers himself or herself in these ways in contrast to those individuals nearby who are not dignitaries. This dynamic occurs under the shadow of white supremacy in African America, where nobility and subtle resistance become identified: black dignity. Black dignity also includes a sense in which everyone, by virtue of our shared humanity, has dignity—resonating with the modern, European concept of dignity. If each of us is dominated in some ways, and everyone who is dominated resists in some ways, each of us has a degree of dignity. It is by virtue of our shared humanity that we all always, to some degree, resist being dominated, and it is also by virtue of our shared humanity that we are in some ways dominated. The dynamics of domination are all-pervasive and unavoidable, whether they be around gender, race, class, disability, nationality, or some other ideology. In Christian terms, we live in a fallen world. In equally Christian terms, we all have the capacity to accept redemption. In a world of domination, we all have the capacity and desire, latent or not, to challenge domination. Secular political theorists sometimes label this realizing our humanity: The more we struggle, the more human we become.[27]

In the concept of dignity I am outlining, dignity is not ascribed because of a status but because of a performance.[28] You have dignity because of something you do rather than because of who you are. Certainly, repeated performances suggest something about the character of the performer, leading to a person being ascribed with dignity independent of a specific performance, but the performances remain essential. What performance of dignity looks like can vary widely. Systems of domination are deep and insidious, dictating what can be said and done but also what can be felt and even habits of thought, so challenges to domination can take place in many domains, by many means. Performances of dignity can involve performance in the narrow sense, such as theater, music, or oratory, but also in the broader senses of writing, philosophizing, praying, hesitating, and, of course, organizing.

That black dignity is to be found in performance raises the worry that black dignity merely describes a social dynamic with no normative edge—and so lacks what political and legal practitioners find so valuable about the concept of dignity today. Of course, in the tradition of black political thought, there are clearly normative claims made for dignity: *we demand dignity*. In my account, such claims are performative: A woman achieves dignity by saying out loud (in the right sort of circumstances) that she demands dignity.[29] But this would seem to reduce the normative to the descriptive, and it does not seem to take the content of political speech seriously enough. Those struggling against domination seem to have a particular goal in mind: a world where domination is no more, where struggle is no longer necessary. In that world, everyone can hold their head up high and look everyone else in the eyes. This strikes me as an eschatological scene, much like those evoked when we are invited to imagine a world of peace, freedom, harmony, love, justice, or equality. Whenever we take these slogans as more than rhetoric, when we try to explicate their content and turn it into a plan for action in this world, things go wrong. (Political theorists, recognizing this, have finally become suspicious of "ideal theory."[30]) In contrast, at the eschaton, there will be a world of dignity in both the sense of rank and the sense of inherent worth: Without domination, all will hold their heads high.

The explications of slogans invoking the eschaton that are helpful, and that do pack a normative punch, focus on the negative. Civic republicans like Phillip Pettit explicate freedom as non-domination, some theorists have urged a focus on injustices rather than on theorizing justice, and I have argued that the language of love that Martin Luther King, Jr., so famously deploys is best understood as a criticism of what love is not.[31] The rhetorical power of such language, including the demand for dignity, certainly motivates, but it also contains a normative claim: Systems of domination are illicit and ought to be challenged. Put another way, performances of dignity of whatever sort contain implicit within them the call for others to join in. Black dignity is contagious, and it catalyzes community organizing against domination.

When dignity is invoked in black political practice, however, it seems to have a much more worldly focus. For example, consider the assertion, *segregated lunch counters are an insult to our dignity!* As a performance, dignity is always situated within a specific context. What amounts to a performance of dignity in one context will have nothing to do with dignity in another context. Rather than taking the anti-segregation activist's rallying cry as expressing an eternal truth about dignity, that it implies segregation is always wrong, I take the slogan as pointing to a particular manifestation of a specific system of domination.[32] In other words, what *segregated lunch counters are an insult to our dignity* means is that segregated lunch counters are part of a system of domination that we must oppose. The claim also conjures a world without domination, a world redeemed, that motivates action in the present. Segregation is a mark of the distance between that world and our world, and opposing segregation indicates our commitment to that other world. Through the performance of that commitment, in rhetoric and action, we see dignity as it appears in this world—not in some pure form imagined in a world redeemed but in its worldly form, as opposition to domination.

This brings us to the question of religion, and specifically political theology. The democratized account of dignity that circulates in modernity is often presented as a secularized theological concept. In Christian thought, humans are created in the image of God, guaranteeing our inherent worth. With secularization, this image is given specific content legible outside of a religious context, for example, it is said that possessing the capacity to reason is the way that humans image God. In this view, the pre-modern account of dignity was misaligned with Christianity (and it developed independent of Christian reflections on the image of God); the transvaluation of dignity that took place with the start of modernity brought dignity into alignment with Christianity, culminating in near coincidence of Catholic accounts of dignity and accounts of dignity in the nascent international legal regime during the mid-twentieth century.[33] The story is certainly more complicated, with the pre-modern view having its own political theology, with the king's dignity guaranteed by his association with the divine, whereas the modern concept of dignity corresponds to a more incarnational theology. But is there any way of understanding black dignity that suggests a relationship to Christian theology?

Many of the black political leaders who have used the language of dignity also participated in or were formed in Christian communities.[34] If dignity means performances that challenge domination, and the end of domination can only be envisioned eschatologically, dignity would have a significant theological resonance. Further, if domination means idolatry, means the machinations of the wealthy and powerful that obscure our perception and ultimately separate us from each other and from the divine, then challenging domination means refusing the ways of the world, refusing to let the world fully define who one is. What remains, marked by that refusal, indicating something wholly other, is what Christians express as the image of God. Note the consequences of this distinctive political-theological configuration. The modern, European account of dignity would have us attend to the dignity of an orphan or leper or impoverished woman, noticing the image of God in her and responding with personal charity or by advocating for social structures that offer assistance. From the perspective of black dignity, the individual in need should not grab and hold our attention. Domination in all its varieties so pervades the world and distorts our perception that any instinct to respond to a particular suffering individual is likely to do more harm than good. Encountering a particular suffering individual is an occasion to notice systems of domination and, as our awareness of domination sharpens, to challenge them more effectively—ideally together with that suffering individual who prompted our reflection. Struggling together against domination, we both perform dignity.

Complications

The historical narrative about dignity's democratization in modernity has come under scrutiny recently by historian Samuel Moyn.[35] He claims that dignity simply was not a relevant concept in the practice of politics until the mid-twentieth century. At that point, the leadership of the Catholic Church began talking about dignity—for example, in Pope Pius XII's 1942 Christmas message that extolled dignity throughout and listed "Dignity of the Human Person" as the first aspect of a well-ordered society—and the concept began making its way into Western European constitutions. The Universal Declaration of Human Rights, adopted in 1948, begins, "Whereas recognition of the inherent dignity and of the equal and inalienable rights of all members of the human family is the foundation of freedom, justice, and peace in the world," and goes on to begin Article 1, "All human beings are born free and equal in dignity and rights." On Moyn's account, such language would have been unthinkable two decades earlier, and even in the two decades following the Declaration's adoption the language of human rights and dignity was slow to spread. There was a very specific set of factors that led to dignity's prominence in the 1940s having to deal with European Catholics' political influence through Christian democratic political parties. In the 1930s, the Church had been speaking of the dignity of workers and of sacraments, rarely of individuals, but moderate French Catholics developed a language of human dignity to navigate between the Scylla of secular liberalism and the Charybdis of totalitarian-friendly Catholic corporatists. After the war, these moderate Catholics captured elite political discourse. In Moyn's view, talk of human dignity today originates in this 1930s French Catholic context.[36]

If Moyn's account is correct, it would call into question dignity's status as a common denominator of black political movements, from Frederick Douglass to Black Lives Matter. At the very least, it would introduce a discontinuity between black dignity before European influence, in the mid-twentieth century, and black dignity after. To explore this possibility, a research assistant and I searched an electronic database of African American newspapers that covered most of the twentieth century for articles that used the word "dignity."[37] We found that the term was used in African American contexts both before and after the shift that Moyn identifies, but the connotations of the term do, indeed, change. A 1906 item in the *Afro-American* refers to "clerical dignity," associating it with solemnity. In 1908, the *Afro-American* reprinted a two-paragraph item from the white-oriented *Ladies' Home Journal* entitled "Rival Dignities." It wittily contrasts English dignity, associated with descent from an ancestor ennobled by a king, and American dignity, associated with descent from an ancestor killed by an Indian. Here, dignity associated with the honors of nobility is mocked; in a sense, dignity is democratized in the American context. Although the figure of the Indian limits this democratization to white Americans, black readers must certainly have appreciated that the thrust of the item was to mock any restriction of dignity to a special class of people. A feisty unsigned column in the *Chicago Defender*, published in 1911 under the title "There Is Dignity in All Labor," complains that a certain local minister described "washing and ironing" as beneath his wife. The *Cleveland Call and Post* reports that an African American social club exists in that city known as "Dignities" that held a high-class dance, suggesting that the name implies nobility or high rank. In 1948, just as the United Nations was enshrining dignity in international law, the *Afro-American* praised City College of New York for "upholding human dignity" by removing an employee who insisted on segregated dormitories, following student protests. By the mid-1950s and following, dignity was widely used in commentaries on racial justice struggles.

If we look even earlier, to the writings of Frederick Douglass, we find many instances of dignity associated with high rank or aristocracy. In *The Life and Times of Frederick Douglass*, his third and longest autobiography, published in 1881, we find the author describing the "great dignity and grandeur" of the Colonel's home, "a dignity and grandeur about the Chief Justice," and a Commodore who "departed himself with much dignity towards us all," for example.[38] There are also several uses of dignity in relation to women, suggesting that women hold a certain nobility-like position—a usage also found in the newspaper archive, including the image of well-dressed women representing the "Dignitaries" dance. But most intriguing are the instances when Douglass uses dignity in a way that pushes against the limits of rank or aristocracy. Douglass notes that Americans "affect contempt for the castes and aristocracies of the old world and laugh at their assumptions," yet "the worth and dignity of manhood" is not consistently respected in the United States—because of the treatment of blacks.[39] Further, retelling the story of his definitive fight with the slave-breaker Covey, Douglass first notes, rather apologetically, that the battle and his narration was "undignified." Yet the struggle was essential to recount, Douglass tells us, because it marks the "turning point" in his life, allowing him to dream anew of freedom. It "revived a sense of my own manhood." Before, Douglass suffered from "crushed self-respect." Now, he was confident and determined, all because of the physical struggle. Douglass concludes, "A man without force is without the essential dignity of humanity."[40]

In short, in African American writing, we find the language of dignity used the way it is used in the ambient culture, to denote high rank or, in the second half of the twentieth century, inherent worth. But we also find a third concept of dignity, black dignity, not accounted for by Moyn, not traceable to 1930s France. Black dignity both admires and mocks the pretenses of American dignity to universality, affirming instead dignity identified with "force"—with struggle against domination, embodied in a slave-breaker or manifested in a system of white supremacy.

Another worry about black dignity comes from a quite different direction. One component of the sophisticated political project advanced by young black activists today is an attack on "respectability politics." By this, they mean black politicians and activists who would offer a certain sort of performance to white audiences in order to be perceived as respectable and so worthy of white attention. Sometimes, the dynamics of respectability are internalized in the black community itself, with black leaders receiving support from the black community because the leader appears respectable, for example, in the way she dresses or speaks or acts. Activists worry that not only are such performances unseemly, they also compromise the content and style of black political demands for an uncertain, and often negligible, pay-off. Put another way, playing respectability politics appears to activists to solicit the respect of whites (or of the white gaze) at the cost of black self-respect, or black dignity.

On the other hand, respectability and dignity seem troublingly close to each other. Are not the words "respectable" and "dignified" used almost synonymously? Are not some of the performances of dignity discussed above, for example, in the "Dignities" dance hall, really attempts to garner respect from whites, either directly or through an internalized white gaze? This worry becomes particularly acute where the language of dignity is applied to women, sometimes by women. Anna Julia Cooper, the Washington, D.C.-based community organizer, adult educator, and foremother of intersectionality writes of the "mission" black women have to represent the race as a whole because "when and where I enter, in the quiet, undisputed dignity of my womanhood, without violence and without suing or special patronage, then and there the whole *Negro race enters with me*."[41] Womanhood is effectively an aristocratic rank, giving black women an opportunity that black men do not have. If they lean on their aristocratic womanhood, black women will be given the honors appropriate to all women and allowed into workplaces—opening the doors for black men to follow. Activists would point out that Cooper's view seems to be acceding to domination rather than challenging it—on two counts, the domination of white supremacy and the domination of patriarchy.

The historian and feminist critic Brittney Cooper has recently argued that Anna Julia Cooper and other early black feminists advance positions "beyond respectability," toward dignity. "The call for dignity and the call for respectability are not the same, though they are frequently conflated. Demands for dignity are demands for a fundamental recognition of one's inherent humanity. Demands for respectability assume that unassailable social propriety will prove one's dignity. Dignity, unlike respectability, is not socially contingent."[42] Here, Cooper the critic leans on the modern, European definition of dignity, indicating inherent worth. If we appeal to the black concept of dignity, in contrast, dignity is understood as a performance located within a social context. Does that dissolve the difference between dignity and respectability? Just the opposite. The performance of respectability aims at creating the appearance of inherent worth. The performance of black dignity aims at challenging domination, which in effect means challenging (rather than replicating) the appearance of inherent worth ascribed to white men.

As we have seen, such challenges can take a variety of forms. Can they include the "quiet, undisputed dignity of my womanhood"? As with all performances of dignity, the audience is called to judge. There may be good reasons on both sides, given the complexities of the cultural setting. If we recall how that line was received, our judgment may be swayed: *When and Where I Enter* became the title of a history of black American women; "In the Quiet, Undisputed Dignity of My Womanhood" became the title of another. Elsewhere, Anna Julia Cooper writes of education for blacks in the post-Emancipation South. She writes elegantly about the sacrifices black women took upon themselves in order to afford to send their children to school. "The work of these schools," Cooper writes, "has been like the little leaven hid in the measure of meal ... diffusing a contagious longing for higher living and purer thinking, inspiring woman herself with a new sense of her dignity in the eternal purposes of nature."[43] For Cooper, dignity does not come about through violent, physical struggle as it does for Douglass, but it comes about through struggle nonetheless. If we understand struggle as a challenge to white supremacy, then the practice of education that Cooper describes here, the "longing for higher living and purer thinking" that is cultivated by schools, most certainly runs against the machinery of domination that would quash all such desires. And here, Cooper returns us to the political theology of dignity. The forces of domination would keep black women and their children tethered to the world, but refusing the ways of the world, refusing white supremacy, and desiring something more elevates us to participate in the eternal.

Notes
1. https://policy.m4bl.org/platform/; "The Gospel Is Not a Neutral Term: An Interview With Rev. Sekou," Theology of Ferguson, https://medium.com/theology-of-ferguson/the-gospel-is-not-a-neutral-term-an-interview-with-rev-sekou-ae7990e66fe2.
2. Honneth, Axel, 1992, "Integrity and Disrespect: Principles of a Conception of Morality Based on the Theory of Recognition," *Political Theory* 20(2), pp. 187-201; applied to the black American case by Bromell, Nick, 2013, "Democratic Indignation: Black American Thought and the Politics of Dignity," *Political Theory* 41(2), pp. 285-311.
3. Such as Boxill, Bernard, "Sympathy and Dignity in Early Africana Philosophy" in *Dignity: A History*, ed. Remy Debes (Oxford, UK: Oxford University Press, 2017), pp. 333-60.
4. By black political thought I do not mean merely an intellectual realm. Thought is, of course, implicit in practice, where practice is understood in the broadest sense, including aesthetics.
5. http://www.thefeministwire.com/2014/10/blacklivesmatter-2/.
6. http://religiondispatches.org/the-role-of-spirit-in-the-blacklivesmatter-movement-a-conversation-with-activist-and-artist-patrisse-cullors/.
7. Khan-Cullors, Patrisse and Asha Bandele, *When They Call You a Terrorist: A Black Lives Matter Memoir* (New York, NY: St. Martin's Press, 2018).
8. http://opaltometi.com/meet-opal-tometi/.
9. http://opaltometi.com/black-lives-matter-co-founder-the-immigration-challenge-no-one-is-talking-about/.
10. http://opaltometi.com/spirituality/.
11. https://policy.m4bl.org/platform/.
12. Hughes, Langston, *The Collected Poems of Langston Hughes* (New York, NY: Alfred A. Knopf), p. 205.
13. Ibid., 339.
14. King, Martin Luther, Jr., *A Testament of Hope* (New York, NY: HarperSanFrancisco, 1991); Idem, *Stride Toward Freedom* (Boston, MA: Beacon, 2010).
15. King, *Stride Toward Freedom*, 15, 29.
16. King, Martin Luther, Jr., *The Papers of Martin Luther King, Jr.* (Berkeley, CA: University of California Press, 1997), vol. 3, p. 432.
17. *The Marcus Garvey and Universal Negro Improvement Association Papers* (Berkeley, CA: University of California Press, 1990), vol. 7, p. 806, 807.
18. Malcolm X, *Malcolm X Speaks* (New York, NY: Pathfinder, 2016), p. 51, 76, 84, 188; 155. See also Sadri Khiari, *Malcolm X: stratège de la dignité noire* (Paris: Amsterdam, 2013).
19. Carmichael, Stokely, *Stokely Speaks: From Black Power to Pan-Africanism* (Chicago, IL: Chicago Review Press, 2014), p. 120. He continues, "Poor white people are not fighting for their

humanity, they're fighting for more money." One way of reading this passage is that white people, because they are implicated in the system of domination that is white supremacy, are unable to have dignity.

20. hooks, bell, *Ain't I a Woman: Black Women and Feminism* (New York, NY: Routledge, 2015), p. 77.
21. Ibid., 7.
22. https://www.theguardian.com/us-news/2016/oct/14/michelle-obama-speech-transcript-donald-trump.
23. Waldron, Jeremy, *Dignity, Rank, and Rights* (New York, NY: Oxford University Press, 2012), p. 32.
24. Because of the brevity of this article, I am not fully demonstrating how this position follows from the sources. The sources in the previous section are intended to suffice merely to make plausible this theory.
25. I have found Linda Zerilli's reflections on political judgment particularly useful, in *A Democratic Theory of Judgment* (Chicago, IL: University of Chicago Press, 2016).
26. The imagery of holding a head high is meant to be evocative, but it also precisely reflects the phenomenology of domination described by recent political theorists such as Pettit, Phillip, *Republicanism: A Theory of Freedom and Government* (Oxford, UK: Oxford University Press, 1999).
27. See especially Badiou, Alain, *Ethics: An Essay on the Understanding of Evil* (London, UK: Verso, 2001); Hal Draper, *Two Souls of Socialism* (Berkeley, CA: Independent Sociality Committee, 1966), https://www.marxists.org/archive/draper/1966/twosouls/The%20Two%20Souls%20of%20Socialism.pdf.
28. For another approach to black dignity in performance, see Jane Cervenak, Sarah, *Wandering: Philosophical Performances of Racial and Sexual Freedom* (Durham, NC: Duke University Press, 2014), p. 153, where she argues in dialogue with performance art that resistance to enslavement involved "exercises in will" that "occasioned illegal movements outside the principles of equivalence and replicability," concluding, "Such resistances forged dignity."
29. On the distinction between performatives and constatives, see Austin, J. L., *How to Do Things with Words* (Oxford, UK: Clarendon Press, 1975); Butler, Judith, *Excitable Speech: A Politics of the Performative* (New York, NY: Routledge, 1996).
30. Mills, Charles W., 2005, "'Ideal Theory' as Ideology," *Hypatia* 20(3), pp. 165-84; Geuss, Raymond, *Philosophy and Real Politics* (Princeton, NJ: Princeton University Press, 2008).
31. Pettit, *Republicanism*; Shklar, Judith, *The Faces of Injustice* (New Haven, CT: Yale University Press, 1990); Lloyd, Vincent, Forthcoming, "What Love is Not: Lessons from Martin Luther King, Jr.," *Modern Theology*.
32. I do not reject moral absolutes, I just reject building them on claims to dignity.
33. Moyn, Samuel, *Christian Human Rights* (Philadelphia, PA: University of Pennsylvania Press, 2015).
34. Even ostensibly secular black nationalists were often formed in Christian communities. Huey Newton's father was a preacher; George Jackson went through a Catholic phase.
35. Moyn, *Christian Human Rights*.
36. See also Chappel, James, *Catholic Modern: The Challenge of Totalitarianism and the Remaking of the Church* (Cambridge, MA: Harvard University Press, 2018).

37. Thanks to Rahma Goran for her excellent assistance. All newspaper clippings on file with the author.
38. Douglass, Frederick, *The Life and Times of Frederick Douglass* (Boston, MA: De Wolfe, Fiske & Co, 1892), p. 44, 439, 500.
39. Ibid, 648. He notes that in Europe, despite their aristocratic conception of dignity or perhaps because of it, "color does not decide the civil and social position of a man."
40. Ibid, 177.
41. Cooper, Anna Julia, *The Voice of Anna Julia Cooper* (Lanham, MD: Rowman & Littlefield, 1998), p. 63.
42. Cooper, Brittney C., *Beyond Respectability: The Intellectual Thought of Race Women* (Urbana, IL: University of Illinois Press, 2017), p. 5.
43. Cooper, Anna Julia, *Voice of Anna Julia Cooper*, 203.

CROSSCURRENTS

A WORLD ON FIRE AND WHITENESS AT THE CORE

Jennifer Harvey

I have extended family in Mississippi. My grandmother took me to visit them once when I was little. But I've never known this part of the family well. Once I made the connection as a child between the civil rights movement and the fact that Mississippi was *in the South*, however, I became fascinated with them.

I asked questions in my immediate family. "Did my aunt make her maid ride in the back seat when she drove her home after her work at my relatives' house?" "Where was my uncle (who held a dean position at the University of Mississippi) and what was he doing when those terrifying fires burned as James Meredith tried to integrate 'Ole Miss'?"

Despite these relationships having always been distant, they generated powerful feelings that have stayed with me. I remember the fear I felt when I made the connection with a fellow seminary student—someone I respected deeply—that we had family in the same town in Mississippi. Instead of the happy recognition that often follows such a discovery, I was immediately unnerved. What if we took the "six degrees of separation" inquiry too far? What if we discovered our family members did know each other? What if my white ones were identifiably and explicitly complicit in subjugation of his Black ones?

I was never satisfied with the answers I got to my family questions. Even as a youngster, they struck me as vague and left me unsettled. "Well, it would have been uncomfortable for everyone at that time (including the maid) for a Black and white woman to sit together in the front of a car. That doesn't mean your aunt liked the way things were."

"Well, he didn't believe segregation was right and did believe everyone should have a good education. He didn't like the way things were."

Then, in summer of 2017—six months into Trump's term—my mom and I were sitting talking about the national racial climate. I was raging about white people's endorsement of a white supremacist president. I was devastated by the passivity of those of us who didn't endorse him, but had allowed conditions to emerge that made way for his election. I was bemoaning a lack of full throttle dissent among whites now that he was in office and predicting that the dissent that was manifesting wouldn't be long lasting; that we'd soon be seduced back to our regularly scheduled lives.

I was trying to find words for the deeper betrayals the spiritual and emotional (let alone political) whiplash of an Obama presidency giving way to a Trump one represented: betrayals long and repeatedly committed by white communities of the most sacred values of humanity and dignity; betrayals of our own humanity as whites, which has been bartered in each generation by the generation that came before it; and betrayals of all people as every white generation has gone on to barter (or explicitly attack or destroy) the humanity of those who are Black, Latino/a, and Native American.

As I tried to find words for this violence we have done to all of our relationships, I found myself, instead, telling my mom about that encounter with my seminary friend. I was desperately trying to convey how flesh-and-blood personal white violence is and how devastating is white apathy. Such a mundane, every day kind of new friend encounter, that moment had contained the sheer immensity and long-term ripple-effects of white tolerance for supremacy.

And next thing I knew my mom and I were talking about that part of my extended family again.

It had never occurred to me to ask about church in all my questioning. So, I was surprised when my mom responded to my story by sharing a piece of family history that was new. She told me that during the civil rights movement, one of the beloved patriarchs in this family wing was on the Board of Deacons at his church. At some point, he introduced a motion to the Board calling on his congregation to de-segregate.

It's relevant to know that I come from a longline of deeply committed Baptists—both American Baptist (U.S.A.) and Conservative Baptist, but conservative and evangelical whichever branch you pick. This type of action, as morally tiny as it appears from today's vantage point, would have been a big deal. My experience of church never approximated anything close to an impulse like the one my mom described. My uncle's move would have been bold in its own way.

At once the fascination I'd had as a child returned, with questions tumbling on its heels: "Why had I never heard this before?" "How did he do it?" "What was his strategy?" "He was so respected, did a moral reckoning and a shift in church practice result?" "Did he lose friends?" "Then what happened?"

The answers that came back felt as vague as those I got in my youngster years. "Nothing happened." "I don't know." "The motion failed." "People in the church weren't ready."

So, then what?

Well, then nothing. My family stayed.

It's the staying that leaves me most unsettled. Following a fleeting impulse toward humanity, my family stayed there in a church that had explicitly said white supremacy was consistent with the gospel. They raised their children and many of their grandchildren there. They prayed and took communion there. They continued to break bread with other whites there. Week in and week out, they listened to Protestant-length sermons there—sermons ostensibly interpreting and then proclaiming the word of God, the good news.

And it's the staying that has become my starting point for wrestling with what happened in the transition from the presidency of Barak Obama to the election of one of the most violently, self-avowedly and explicitly white supremacist men this nation has elected to the highest office since Andrew Jackson—a man whose portrait, non-coincidentally, hangs boldly on Trump's walls and in so many of his photo ops.

I've thought about this part of my white family so much since the election. This isn't because they're uniquely responsible for its outcome or the white supremacist Christian nationalist regime that, as a result, is coalescing in our political landscape. Frankly, I have no idea how they voted. It's not because anecdotes about white peoples' relationships to oppression are the best way to talk about racism or justice. It's most certainly not to enact a kind of public white confession on behalf of my family (a tendency in some white writing about race I find troubling). Finally, and most importantly, I'm not writing to call out this part of my family—folks I still don't know very well. I'm not pointing at them as if they were different. They weren't and they aren't.

My family's response was typical of white Christians then. It remains typical today. In truth, regardless of how any of us voted in the most recent presidential election or responded to the presidency of Barack Obama before it, my family and its history is vividly illustrative of whiteness, of its power, and of the banality of how it functions everyday even now in this era where the reality of white supremacy and battles against it are garnering more widespread public contention than I have ever seen in my nearly fifty years on this planet.

Thinking about my family helps me to wrestle with truths I must internalize as I try to make sense out of what my people—white people—have done. Not only what we've done to this nation, but to a world that seems now on fire with the repercussions. What we've done to other human beings who some of us, sometimes, claim to know, or care about or perhaps even love—the latter being language we're especially likely to be audacious enough to use in white church. Thinking about family and relationships reveals dimensions of soul, heart, purpose, and consciousness that, in white communities, expose so much about how we all ended up here. And thinking honestly about my family helps me see and name the countless losses.

I remember my mom's voice eventually trailing off that night. As I plied her with questions, she could tell I wasn't satisfied with the answers. The exchange was painful. And, I will admit, as my frustration increased my questions became more an outlet for my rage than they were authentic inquiry. She finally went on to say, "Yes, your cousin [the son of the patriarch who introduced the church resolution], was always mad about all of this too. The older he got the more they all fought about it. He told his parents they hadn't done enough. He accused them of having gone along with things too much. But they could have actually done? Should they have moved? Left Mississippi? He ended up estranged from the family and his parents grieved this estrangement for the rest of their lives..."

I offer here less a coherent set of analytical arguments and more my ongoing attempt to wrangle into words these deeper betrayals that evade words, and live in our flesh. This essay is more a pleading—drawing on Emilie M. Townes' articulation of the formative nature of lament, I lament in search of a way into experience and feeling in the hopes that truth-telling lament-filled rage can enable movement as Townes sense of it insists that it can.[1] I write here especially about white women and white church.

And I am enraged. For, as William Stringfellow put it in 1964, "my people is the enemy."[2] Whiteness touches everything. And the loss and carnage seems to be endless.

White women
How we transitioned from the first Black president to one who spews racial vitriol, targeting Black people, Muslims, immigrants (especially Latino/a ones) has been, of course, the subject of much post-election analysis. We've endlessly sliced and diced the data. A strong narrative emerged early that an angry and forgotten "working class" rose up against either (1) liberal elites, or (2) neoliberal economic policies that have forgotten the "working class" and, thus, won the day for Trump. A healthy cacophony of counter-response has also insisted on complicating that narrative into question as well.

The most telling factor, however, was in stark view immediately following the election: race. I will remain forever unwilling to be convinced that, fundamentally, anything other than race was most salient in the election of 2016. Simply put, an overwhelming majority of white people voted for Trump. In fact, as Ta-Nehisi Coates pointed out several months later, if white people alone had voted Trump would have won almost the entire electoral college (389 to 81, to be exact).[3]

Within this data, the number 53 devastates me the most. Fifty-three percent of white women voted for Trump. A majority of we, white women, voted for a man who induced frenzies at his rallies that looked so much like what the frenzies preceding southern lynch mobs seventy years ago must have looked like. Black and brown people, especially, were physically assaulted at his rallies even as he spoke of what "we" would have done to protestors back in the "good old days."[4] A majority of white women voted for a man heard on tape bragging about grabbing women by their genitals. This man stands accused of a sexual assault, at the time of this writing, by no less than nineteen women.[5]

In social media spaces in the weeks after the election, I heard countless Clinton voters, bemoaning the internalized sexism that caused women to not support Hilary Clinton. Even women, so the argument went, couldn't see another woman as president. Even women were influenced by the sexist attacks against Clinton. We women are so aligned with patriarchy we voted against our own self-interest.

Race has now been given a great deal of attention, a year out. So, it may seem a tired repetition to reassert that analysis suggesting internalized sexism as a primary reason women didn't vote for Clinton is perilous and false. It falls as short as does analysis that concludes the "working-class" voted against elites and for Trump. Obviously, in this analysis we're really only talking about *white* women and the *white* working class.

Meanwhile, if this claim were true, how would we possibly explain that Black or Latina women—who overwhelmingly voted for Clinton—were immune to internalized sexism in a way white women aren't and thus knew better than to vote for Trump? Magic? (Non-college-educated and college-educated Black women voted for Clintons at rates of 95 and 91 percent, respectively.[6]) This is just like a claim that ignores the reality that, percentage wise for respective populations, there are far more working class and working-poor people in communities of color than there are in white ones. Working class and poor people of color were not fooled by Trump's "anti-elite" posture but whites were? If this is the case, does that mean they, unlike the white working class, haven't been left behind by neoliberal economic policies? That's a ridiculous proposition.

Race was the difference

It's the only demographic factor that remains constant. To say so is not to say the same explanation for voting behavior can be given for each of the various demographics (white college-educated women may have voted for Trump for reasons different than non-college-educated working class white men). But, it does mean that no explanation that doesn't center race—specifically center whiteness—is coherent. It's worth reasserting this because there's little collective evidence that white people have come to terms with this analysis.

A quick side journey is appropriate here. There's a tendency to experience what happened in 2016 as a strange and quick turn about in white behavior. But the fact of the matter is that white people, in the majority, didn't actually vote for Obama either. In the appropriate elation over the election of the first Black president, this fact didn't get much attention at the time.

It's important we remember this because it keeps our focus unapologetically honed in on race. If the analytical starting point is to explain how "we" who elected a Black president could turn around to elect *the anti-Black* president—a man whose name gets used as a chant of racial harassment at high school sporting events—the strength of white supremacy as explanatory factor recedes. We cannot allow that to happen. In the main, "we" in this county didn't elect the first Black president; people of color in this county did. The analytical turn must presume this more complex recognition. White people first voted against Obama before we overwhelmingly voted for Trump. White women did too. The majority of us voted against Obama—twice (2008 and 2012).[7] 2016 was not outlier.

More than twenty years ago, psychologist Aída Hurtado wrote about the differential relationship to privilege among differently raced women. She analyzed these differentials as fault lines that rendered women of color unable and disinterested in uniting politically with white feminist movements. Among other things, Hurtado argued, the practices of white women's movements were "at odds with the way women of color have been treated by the power structure and therefore feel alien to them."[8] While women of color have been subjugated through rejection by white men, white women, because we are part of familial networks and in other intimate relationships with such men (and desired as child bearers) are "seduced into compliance."[9]

The seduction takes places through psychological and material rewards. Allegiances with white men are made to be "palatable, attractive, and rewarding" to white women They have to be, she claims, otherwise, "... rebellion would ensue."[10]

This analysis means everything in the wake of white women electing Donald Trump. Against a one-dimensional "internalized sexism" assessment, one is forced to conclude that, in fact, white women also voted precisely *with* our interests. We voted with the white men we have relationships with through our racialized social networks. We did so because we have access to racialized rewards. The psychological and material rewards enabled by white supremacy *are* of interest to white women. Given the severity of socioeconomic peril and the pillage of the poor by the powerful, which the election outcome is enabling, it's worth naming here explicitly that the psychological rewards are real even when they exist apart from actual material ones, which many white people really do not get (though we certainly get more of these *per capita* relative to communities of color). This logic goes back to W. E. B. Du Bois' "wages of whiteness" argument.[11]

White women don't need to consciously recognize any of these seductions in order for them to function in our lives nonetheless. We don't even have to have voted with Trump to be implicated in this larger truth as it pertains to the election. Because how this works at a collective level is engendered by stories like my family's. Over and over again, white women have demonstrated our loyalty to white community. Just like my family sticking it out at church, we've tolerated white supremacy with far greater ease than we've been willing to tolerate breaking relationships with other white people. And we've both enabled white supremacy to reign and been ourselves shaped and formed in the process. It's a deadly combination.

Intersectionality, of course, is still relevant. Excavating deeper issues of white loyalty should not be read as downplaying the severity of gender violence, which white women do experience. But if Hurtado is correct—and I believe she is—our (white) racialized desires, access, and insulation is a better point to start to understand collective white women's behavior than is an explanation of internalized sexism. In fact, white women's racial access, as it impacts our willingness to break ranks despite gender subjugation, is a precise illustration of intersectionality. Namely identities and social locations are experienced simultaneously and their intersectional effects, as these identities interact with larger systems, shape our experiences in utterly unique—and not additive—ways.

But let's call it what it is: racial interest. Too often common sense white feminist understandings of intersectionality—in misappropriated use of the concept Black feminists originated—is one-dimensional and flatly pointing in one direction. It starts with gender and goes on to race (maybe). It implies that the fact of gender makes white racial identity less significant for white women in some fundamental way. White women are women aren't quite fully white.

I hear this all the time when I talk to young white women in my classrooms, "Sure, white women experience white privilege. But, we're also women. Because of intersectionality we don't experience privilege as much of it as white men do." (Translation: we're not as guilty.) That's an incorrect use of intersectionality. We're just a guilty. White women have *as much access* to white privilege, racial bonding, and the rewards of white supremacy as do white men. It's just our access is uniquely articulated because of our gender (and sexual orientations, physical abilities, and on and on).

Gendered subjugation remains part of this election mix but race and racial access prevails as the form of seduction. The dangers of downplaying this truth are even more real, right now, as white women are generating public power and complaint against the Trump administration by centering gender. If we white women do not come to terms with the fundamental centrality of whiteness in our collective lives, our capacity to create a different future than the racialized, gendered, anti-queer nightmare we are living now, as movements arise in the form of the Women's March and #metoo, will never come to fruition.

This brings me back to the 53 percent. The pervasiveness of whiteness and its meaning for the election have little to do with whether or not any individual white woman actually voted for Trump. We in the 47 percent don't get to stand back and point at those 53. If we do, we fall prey to an individualistic ideology and simplified interpretation of human experience. Collective white behaviors, consciousness, and culture—continually built through our normal day-to-day relationships and ways of moving through the world—are reflected in the every dimension of the conditions that enabled Trump's election. Virtually all of us, however we voted, remain participants generating the character of this white collective through overarching loyalty to white community and our tolerance for supremacy outweighing our tolerance for breaches in white relationships.

At this point, my family story returns again as relevant. We've stayed. White women who weren't part of the 53 percent have stayed. In some cases, this means we've stayed in familial networks where white supremacist practices and beliefs are present, if not normative. We've failed to challenge and vocalize opposition. In some cases, this manifests in organizations and their priorities. In some cases, this means we've stayed in relationships with other white women for whom powerful and public antiracist commitments are not perceived as important (one end of the continuum) or for whom open acquiescence to racist practices and beliefs are explicit (the other end of the same continuum). However it looks, collectively we've remained part of the white collective.

I'm not throwing accusations here. I am talking about my own white life as much as anyone else's. And it seems so much like what I see when I look back at the behavior of my family's patriarch. We may make, on occasion, impulses toward humanity—but we mostly don't persist in these long enough that they gain traction in our social worlds (family, work, friendships, church). We may hold different beliefs about race than those with whom we are in a variety of relationships and thus conclude this is somehow doing our part. Like I heard when I asked about my aunt, "She didn't like the way things were."

"Not liking it" presumably set my family apart and rendered them less morally culpable or spiritually impacted by the devastating violence of whiteness. But not liking the way things are in our social worlds is an empty way of being sorry because it's always an option to break ranks instead. By breaking ranks, I'm not necessarily talking about ending relationships with other white people—whether in families or workplaces or anywhere else. In fact, people of color both before and since the election have been clear. Many have said those of us bemoaning the racial dimensions of the election must stay in relationships with other white people who are explicitly racist or whose tolerance for white supremacy is high enough they chose to hold their nose and vote for Trump. We who would seek an antiracist way of being—despite being ourselves white—and a future where white supremacy dies or is destroyed have much work to do in these relationships. And not necessarily by physically separating ourselves and definitely not by morally separating ourselves.

But, the questions must constantly be live. What have we been doing in those relationships? What are we doing now while we're in them? The persistence and growth of a white collective characterized by tolerance for white violence is the large-scale effect of white people staying loyal to white communities. Breaking ranks to counter this must mean irrepressible, insistent, vocal, and constant drum beats against white supremacy, against racism, for justice in all of our contexts. In some cases, such insistence may get us kicked out—the separation might end up being physical. But in some cases, it may not. Our insistence must create some ugliness in our nice white family networks, workplaces, churches, and other contexts. But the destabilizing interruption such ugliness represents, if we continue to refuse to comply, creates a fracture in the ethos of a collective white tolerance for the destruction of humanity that is essential. What might come after that?

Consider how different the current moment might be if the 47 percent of us had already long been publicly, insistently repeatedly breaking ranks racially. Wouldn't that have rendered it impossible for whiteness to function the way it has to this point? What if we did this now? That 47 percent represents a lot of people. White culture, consciousness, or the nature of it's collective soul would not remain unchanged in the wake of such dis-allegiance.

I just can't see how a full throttle dissent and revolt among the 47 percent couldn't but mean a defeat of white supremacy. If we broke ranks well enough, for long enough, and adequately enough such that women of color might be convinced to take us back—by which I mean only in the form of a modicum of willingness to engage in strategic and liminal political allegiances (I am under no illusions about what it would have taken for women of color to see white women as "sisters" in the first place, let alone what would be required for them to do so now after this election) we would win. We would absolutely win this soul battle that is raging through the political veins of this nation.

Unfortunately, the extent to which the question that is likely to come tumbling on the heels of this description is "but, what would breaking ranks look like?" is the same extent to which we white women—individually and collectively—have not broken racial ranks. My sense is we're far from the breaking point.

But I want to be clear as we stake our ground in terms of what comes next. White women's failure to do anything racially radical *before* was a pre-condition for the outcomes of the election significant enough that our staying—our loyalty to white community—must be seen as just as central in the election's outcome as were the votes of those among us who actually pulled the lever for Trump. Like my family who continued, week in and out, to break bread with other whites, while mentally conceiving of themselves then and remembered now in our historicized family re-telling to this day, as "the good ones" we have not enfleshed a humanizing, antiracist avowed "no" to the carnage. Transformation depends on reckoning with this.

The meaningful spiritual, moral, and ultimately political question to my mind, then, is not whether or not white women might be prepared to do so now. We're not. The meaningful question is whether we're prepared to now see that choosing to try to figure out how to get prepared is urgent in a world that is on fire; indeed, it's the question of whether we will decide to see that our collective lives depend on our doing so.

It's important to restate here that white women's relationships with women of color—which have never been robust, even among the most liberal white women—have been obliterated by this election: collectively, politically, and interpersonally. I don't know to what extent white women in the 47 percent understand this. But to some extent, it may not matter. Making our case to women of color isn't the work white women should be doing right now. Why should they believe us?

Any hope for a post-white supremacist nation has to see us tenaciously focusing on our work—that of actively seeking to pull the support of other white people away from white supremacy. We must do this through public, insistent reckoning with and a breaking of ranks from whiteness in every venue of our lives and in the most radical, concrete, measureable, and visible ways possible. And we must bring as many others along with us as we go as we can.

There's not space, nor is it this essay's purpose, to give a "to do" list of what the concrete actions here might look like. Happily, a quick Internet search reveals all kinds of excellent and politically wise articles about effective and necessary anti-racism practices for white people. There is list upon list about how to get concrete about this. The question isn't one of resources. The question is whether or not we will re-position our loyalties and decide to search and follow. On that question, the verdict is out. And, on precisely that point, these urgent, rageful explorations now turn to another relevant collective—to the white church.

White churches
In December 2017, the nation waited with bated breath for the outcome of a special election in the South. Doug Jones, a Democrat, was running against Roy Moore, a Republican, for the Alabama Senate seat left vacant after Jeffrey Sessions was appointed to be Attorney General by the Trump administration. Before and after the vote, demographics were again sliced and diced. Much to the shock of many, the Democrat won. Jones barely

won, but he won. This was the first time in twenty-five years, the state of Alabama elected a Democrat to the Senate.

The election's outcome was beautiful from the perspective of those of us (of many races) continuing to rage against the election of Trump and the racial climate he has nurtured. It was a needed victory in the hopescape of those of us who continue to work for a different future than the one that will come to be if white Christian nationalism successfully tightens its grip.

Despite the victory, however, in terms of the longer-term struggle, the racial demographics of the voting were once again ugly. White people overwhelmingly voted for a man who not only made references to slavery as the last time that families were really happy in this nation, but against whom there were multiple, credible public allegations of sexual assault, abuse, and relations with women who were, at the time of the alleged perpetration, as young as fourteen. Yet again white women overall voted with their racial interests: for Moore at 63 percent.

But, an important statistic emerged post-election that merits attention. Moore is an avowed Christian. And white evangelicals voted for him at higher rates than other whites. Among evangelical white women, for example, Moore won at an rate of 76 to 22 percent. But notably, among white non-evangelical women, Jones won and did so handily: 71 percent to Moore's 21 percent.[12] This slice of the demographic pie brings into scrutiny in an explicit way questions about the white church and white Christianity in the United States as it pertains to our national racial crisis.

Racist violence against communities of color and religious minorities has intensified since Trump took office. Self-avowed white supremacists and neo-Nazi's marched and terrorized Charlottesville, Virginia, in August 2017. They viciously beat protestors—even killing one. Every day the president and his administration terrorize Latino/a communities. This terror has included pardoning former Sherriff Joe Arpaio who once bragged about holding racially profiled Latino/as in concentration camp-like conditions. (Arpaio was found guilty of criminal contempt of court for refusing to comply with a 2011 court order to cease detaining people based on suspicion of their immigration status.[13]) The terror has continued with increased ICE activity across the nation. The decision to formally end DACA, the Obama-era program designed to protect young people brought to the United States illegally as children and enable them to legally work and attend school, is the most recent terrorist iteration.[14]

There will be more of all of this and in all of our local communities. But many months before the 45th president of the United States repeatedly insisted "we" are finally going to put "Merry Christmas" back into public discourse (sounding like he's bludgeoning someone every time he says it), before the Moore/Jones vote, and even before Trump declared there were "good people on both sides" in Charlottesville, it was clear that a form of noxious white Christianity is the fuel in this supremacist machinery. We're only a year into this presidency, and the Muslim Ban announcement feels like it was ages ago. That it does is evidence of the extent to which white supremacist Christian nationalism is taking up more and more bandwidth in the public square. With each passing week, we're becoming saturated.

So with each passing week, open questions sit squarely in the center of the sanctuary in predominantly white congregations—evangelical or otherwise. The questions are as wide and searching as those I asked my family members as a child. "Will my pastor speak explicitly about white supremacist hatred this week?" "Will my congregation formally denounce white nationalism with clarity and visibility?" "If we do speak about it, will it be merely in carefully worded prayers about love right before our weekly ritual of passing the peace?" "Or, will there be mostly be silence?"

The mere fact of such questions existence, a year into this administration, speaks volumes. What does it mean that clear and easy denunciation of white supremacist Christian nationalism has not yet manifested as an organized and robust response to the current political moment? I'm frightened to ask it again: What are we willing to live with in order to stay?

In the unsettling call and response that took place between myself and the adults to whom I asked my childhood questions what was implied was that, of course, my relatives were *actually* opposed to white supremacy. They just couldn't do that much about it.

Probably, no family story belies the truth more obviously than the one about church. That story makes it plain. They may not have liked it, but they weren't so opposed to white supremacy that they wouldn't live with it in order to remain part of their community.

Meanwhile, it's easy to look back today on what white Christians did in the 1950s and 1960s and see those days as full of clarion clear crossroads. Surely, if I had lived then, my thinking might go, my church's failure to clear such a low moral hurdle—rejecting segregated church—would have been a crossroads. Surely, I would have made a scene like Jesus in the Temple and left. It's so easy to look back on Nazi Germany today and on German Christians allowing the Naziification of the churches and think, "Not us! We would have stood with the Confessing Church, no doubt."

But, if we're tempted by these responses, we must ask ourselves these explicit questions that have identifiable and factual answers. What happened in our churches the Sunday after Charlottesville? What happened the week after DACA was rescinded? What did we say at church, collectively, during the Alabama race when Moore said families were happy during slavery? Was the gospel spoken? Or was there silence?

Maybe there was prophetic speech in some of our churches. My prayer is that this is the case and, perhaps, a movement is brewing. And there have been visible fits and starts. The Boston Declaration is one. Signed by hundreds of Christian clergy and theologians it begins with the words, "As followers of Jesus, the Jewish prophet for justice whose life reminds us..."[15] and goes on to take a bold stance against the current administration. The Declaration names with specificity the racist, misogynist, anti-trans, and lgbt, violence of this administration. Just over a month after the election, Auburn Seminary convened a group of writers and began an initiative entitled "Dear White Christians: An Invitation to Take on Five Commitments for Racial Justice."[16] This is an attempt as well to publicly break ranks and to energize collective anti-white supremacist movement.

But, I suspect that most predominantly white churches are struggling to find their footing and public declarations are more exception than rule. It may be that some congregations and pastors are silent, or talk about Charlottesville and DACA or "happy families during slavery," only in carefully worded prayers because of an ill-conceived notion that somehow these are political or partisan matters. Such matters are always difficult to navigate in church. But none of this is about politics or partisanship. It's more likely that many of our pastors and congregations are worried about rankling the collective.

But at the end of the day, we are in, in this very moment, in a fierce battle over whose lives matter and whose lives do not in this country. We are embroiled in a soul struggle over who is part of our civic community and who is considered disposable. The last many months and the many yet to come are about whether we actually believe in human rights and dignity in the face of civic hatred, hostility, and violence against Black people and Latino/a people, Muslims and Jews, lgbt people, and women of many different races, religions, and orientations, or whether we really don't.

And what is urgent now are movements in which all of us are engaged in all hands-on deck public struggle. We are a struggle for our lives and for our future as a nation in a world that is on fire. If white Christians aren't *there*, where are we?

Rev. Anna Blaedel has named where we are. Last fall in Creston, Iowa (less than 100 miles from where I live) five high school students posed in hoods, beside a burning cross and a Confederate Flag (one holding a weapon). In response fellow Iowa clergyperson, Blaedel wrote, "hey Iowans: if your church talks about the Iowa / Iowa State [football= game tomorrow but doesn't talk about what happened in Creston, your church is siding with masculinist white supremacy." She was spot on. What's being said or not in our churches this week (and next) is the precise moral measure of what we are actually preaching in our churches.

It's also the case that where we spend our time, how we hold our bodies, what we pray—aloud and in silence, week in and week out, shapes us in the deepest of ways. It shapes our children. It shapes what we're morally and spiritually able to do next and forms how the white collective hurdles through political time and space. It writes on the wall the damage or healing it's going to do.

So, again, the real question, the deepest question is this: Are white Christians going to stay? Will we remain in congregations where the strongest fortitude a pastor or folks in the pews can muster shows up merely as a cautious prayer? Will church remain *white*?

We are at a critical turning point. The world is on fire and it's past time for white church action. Those of us who went to church after Charlottesville, DACA, or the latest racial violence in our community, and were disappointed because our pastors didn't speak, must act. Like white women everywhere must also we too must break ranks. Sitting and not liking what's going on matters as much now as it did to stay in a segregated church while feeling disdain for segregation back then.

Acting must include organizing. We must find others in our congregations who are also disappointed. We must go to our pastors and other leaders in the church and insist they he/she begin to speak justice—gospel—from the pulpit. Those of us who are clergy we must find those in our congregations and denominations who will stand with us as we do the same.

But we must not equivocate. If action is unsuccessful, if silence and cautious prayers remain the norm, it's time to leave. It's time to be kicked out.

It's time for white people to begin leaving our church—that is, if they remain *white* churches. A church that is silent today and in the coming weeks and months is a church beholden to white supremacy. A church silent today is a church tolerating the grip of a white Christian nationalism that is, indeed, taking up more and more bandwidth in our bodies, souls, and minds.

Silence is speech. Silence is the taking of a side. And silence in a so-called sacred space in these times is the opposite of holy.

We are at a crossroads *now*. And it is time to go.

Conclusion

No neat conclusion comes as I try to tie up what is more lament, plea, exploration of betrayal, and articulation of rage. The tendency in writing for the public and in writing for academic space is to tie things up. I'm always tempted to leave with a word of hope. But, I don't feel hope—and I feel warned against it for reasons in regard to which I have found Miguel de la Torre to be persuasive.[17] Hope is (white theological) promise that all things are well and in God's hands. It dissuades us from the urgency and rightness of action, regardless.

But I am also indebted (always) to the work of Marcia Y. Riggs, whose mediated ethic insists that we must leave the experience of tension and unresolved.[18] We must not remove ourselves from conflict and tension-filled realities for the realm of abstract and neat solutions. Instead, she writes, we must mediate the complex, the embodied, the unresolved. We must mediate through these hard embodied realities in the conviction that something we could not possibly see from this vantage point *may* emerge as we do so. Abstract hope, in the midst of a world on fire, is further betrayal. For there is no certainty about anything right now. Suggesting there is can only cause retreat.

But whiteness touches everything. And the loss and carnage seems, right now, to be endless.

Still this I know. Breaking ranks is always an option, and rejecting loyalty to whiteness offers the only possibility for truly living. And so I will continue to rage on.

Notes
1. Townes, Emilie M., "Breaking the Fine Rain of Death: African American Health Issues and a Womanist Ethic of Care" (Wipf & Stock, 2006).
2. Stringfellow, William, *My People is the Enemy* (Garden City: Anchor Books, 1964).
3. Coates, Ta-Nehisi, "The First White President," *The Atlantic*, October 2017, https://www.theatlantic.com/magazine/archive/2017/10/the-first-white-president-ta-nehisi-coates/537909/ (accessed 15 November 2017).
4. Nguyen, Tina, "Donald Trump's Rallies are Becoming Increasingly Violent," *Vanity Fair*, March 11, 2016, https://www.vanityfair.com/news/2016/03/donald-trump-protesters-rally-violence (accessed 15 November 2017).
5. Ford, Matt, "The 19 Women Who Accused President Trump of Sexual Misconduct," *The Atlantic*, December 7, 2017, https://www.theatlantic.com/politics/archive/2017/12/what-about-the-19-women-who-accused-trump/547724/ (accessed 15 November 2017).
6. Mohdin, Aamna, "American Women Voted Overwhelmingly for Clinton, Except the White Ones," November 9, 2016 https://qz.com/833003/election-2016-all-women-voted-overwhelmingly-for-clinton-except-the-white-ones/ (accessed 15 November 2017).
7. Cassidy, John, "What's Up With White Women? They Voted for Romney Too," *The New Yorker*, November 8, 2012, https://www.newyorker.com/news/john-cassidy/whats-up-with-white-women-they-voted-for-romney-too (accessed 10 December 2017).
8. Hurtado, Aída, *The Color of Privilege: Three Blasphemies on Race and Feminism* (University of Michigan, 1996), p. vii.
9. Hurtado, p. vii.
10. Hurtado, p. viii.
11. Du Bois, W.E.B., *Black Reconstruction in America, 1860-1880* (New York: Free Press, 1962).
12. Dowe, Matthew J., https://twitter.com/matthewjdowd/status/941005488560459776 (accessed 8 December 2017).
13. Davis, Julie Hirschfeld and Maggie Haberman, "Trump Pardons Joe Arpaio, Who Became Face of Crackdown on Illegal Immigration," *New York Times*, August 25, 2017 https://www.nytimes.com/2017/08/25/us/politics/joe-arpaio-trump-pardon-sheriff-arizona.html?mcubz=3&_r=1 (accessed 10 December 2017).
14. Contrera, Jessica, "Ending DACA Will Change Thousands of Lives: Here's How it Already Upended One," *The Washington Post* September 9, 2017, https://www.washingtonpost.com/lifestyle/style/ending-daca-will-change-thousands-of-lives-heres-how-it-already-upended-one/2017/

09/08/e8f53cd2-93e0-11e7-89fa-bb822a46da5b_story.html?utm_term=.3898a4bb330a (accessed 10 December 2017).

15. "The Boston Declaration: A Prophetic Appeal to Christians of the United States," November 20, 2017, https://thebostondeclaration.com/blog/2017/11/18/the-boston-declaration (accessed 10 December 2017).

16. "Dear White Christians," http://auburnseminary.org/dear-white-christians/ (accessed December 12 2017).

17. de la Torre, Miguel, "Toward a Theology of Hopelessness," March 14, 2015, https://ourlucha.wordpress.com (accessed 10 December 2017).

18. Riggs, Marcia Y., *Awake, Arise and Act: A Womanist Call for Black Liberation* (Pilgrim Press, 1994).

DO BLACK LIVES MATTER TO WHITE CHRISTIANS?
A Theological Reflection in Three Movements

Rubén Rosario Rodríguez

Introduction

In the spring of 2009, shortly after Barack Obama assumed the Office of President of the United States, I was invited to lecture at the Perkins School of Theology at Southern Methodist University in Dallas, Texas, on the topic of whether or not the election of the nation's first African American president signaled a new post-racial era in American politics. Back then I wrote, "The election of our nation's first African-American president is a giant step forward on the journey toward Martin Luther King Jr.'s 'beloved community,' but we cannot presume that one single step can end what has been a very long, and very painful journey. Yet, as ridiculous as it sounds, some pundits have proclaimed that President Barack Obama's election has brought about a new "post-racial" era in which race no longer matters and racism and discrimination no longer keep people of color from full participation in American society." Then, as now such naiveté about America's racist history does not inspire confidence in political punditry.

From the outset, however, President Obama remained a political realist on issues of race: "At the inauguration, I think there was justifiable pride on the part of the country that we had taken a step to move beyond some of the searing legacies of racial discrimination in this country...But that lasted about a day."[1] Thankfully, the President was under no illusions that a single political victory could erase the stain of hundreds of years of slavery, degradation, discrimination, and racism that marks our nation's history. Instead, Obama viewed his election as an opportunity to "continue the long march of those who came before us, a march for a more just, more equal, more free, more caring and more prosperous America."[2] While Obama's political realism was undoubtedly tempered by a lifetime of growing up black in a white supremacist culture, it was more immediately occasioned by the first of many trials he would face on the race relations front as President: two Constitutional challenges, one to the Congress's extension of the Voting Rights Act and a second targeting a controversial affirmative action program in New Haven, Connecticut.

The first Supreme Court case, *Northwest Austin Utility District v. Holder*, challenged Congress's reauthorization of the Voting Rights Act in 2006 on the basis that this particular district had no history or claims of racial discrimination in any of its elections therefore ought to be exempt from §5 of the Voting Rights Act requiring certain (Southern) states to receive pre-clearance from the Federal government before enacting changes in their electoral law. Ultimately, the Supreme Court ruled unanimously (9-0) that the Austin district was exempt from the §5 requirement because of technical wording in §4(a) and §14(c)(2) about what constitutes a "political subdivision," thus preserving the Federal government's oversight of election law changes while avoiding a ruling on the Constitutionality of §5 by a vote of 8-1, with Justice Clarence Thomas dissenting, arguing that §5 is no longer Constitutional.[3] The second case before the Supreme Court, *Ricci v. DeStefano*, was brought forward by nineteen white (and one Hispanic) firefighters who claimed discrimination under Title VII of the Civil Rights Act of 1964 after they had passed the test for promotion to management positions yet the city declined to promote them. The city of New Haven, Connecticut, invalidated the test results because none of the black applicants who took the same test scored high enough on the test to warrant promotion to a management position. The Supreme Court ruled 5–4 that the city's decision to ignore the test results violated Title VII and also "criticized New Haven for using "raw, racial statistics" to invalidate a promotional examination, but stopped short of ordering broad changes to race-and-hiring laws sought by the firefighters and their supporters around the country."[4] While this case did not overthrow the affirmative action provisions of the Civil Rights Act of 1964, it did set the stage for how accusations of "reverse discrimination" and white backlash would come to characterize race relations in the United States during the eight years of the Obama presidency.

In 2008, white liberal optimism viewed the Obama presidency as an opportunity for racial reconciliation, but political realism soon demonstrated its opposite, a rise in white backlash as a direct result of electing the nation's first black President: "according to the Southern Poverty Law Center, the election of the first black president had triggered more than 200 hate-related incidents…a sobering reminder of the work that remains ahead."[5] This white backlash reached its nadir with the emergence and popularity throughout his presidency of the "birther" movement, a far-right conspiracy theory that claimed Barack Obama was born in Kenya and therefore Constitutionally prohibited from holding the office of President. These allegations first surfaced during the Democratic primaries in 2007, and while not directly linked to Hillary Rodham Clinton, there is evidence that these rumors were forwarded via e-mail by a Clinton campaign volunteer (subsequently fired), and more damning, that the idea of attacking candidate Obama for his "lack of American roots" was first proposed by Clinton campaign strategist Mark Penn.[6] Not surprisingly, these allegations resurfaced during the 2016 Presidential campaign, when GOP candidate Donald Trump, for years one of the more high-profile proponents of the "birther" movement (in 2011 he told NBC news, "I would like to have him show his birth certificate, and can I be honest with you, I hope he can"), reversed his position while blaming Democrat candidate Hillary Clinton "of starting the birther movement during her 2008 Democratic primary campaign against Obama."[7] Sadly, instead of leading the nation in a new conversation on racial reconciliation, the Obama presidency came to be characterized as timid on race relations for the sake of advancing other political agendas like the Affordable Healthcare Act. Even though Obama, who campaigned on a platform promising change entered office in 2008 riding a wave of optimism, in 2017 he left office with a mixed record on race, as evidenced by the simple fact that Black Lives Matter, a youth-led movement responding to acts of police brutality targeting black communities, was born during his presidency.

People of faith, most especially the nation's progressive white Christians, have to deal more frankly and openly with the realities of racism in post-Obama America after the election of Donald Trump, a candidate whose path to the White House was made possible by the empowerment of fringe white nationalist groups collectively labeled the Alt-Right movement.[8] This became evident in Charlottesville, Virginia, the weekend of August 11–12, 2017, as several hundred white nationalists from all over the nation descended on the small college town nestled in the idyllic Blue Ridge Mountains for a "Unite the Right" rally. Ostensibly a protest against the removal of a Confederate monument to Robert E. Lee, the rally was also a calculated move to draw national media attention to the various factions comprising the Alt-Right in an effort to move from the internet fringes of U.S. politics into the Trump-era mainstream. Protesters included white supremacists, white nationalists, neo-Confederates, Klansmen, neo-Nazis, and various, heavily armed, militia groups. Amidst the chants of "white lives matter," "Jews will not replace us," "Whose streets? Our streets!" (co-opting a Black Lives Matter slogan used during the Ferguson protests), and the Nazi slogan, "Blood and soil," marchers carried signs with anti-Semitic slurs, brandished Nazi swastikas and waved Confederate flags, while also carrying "Trump/Pence" signs. Yet, instead of immediately repudiating the heinous acts of white nationalism that led to the death of Heather Heyer, a peaceful counter-protester, and the beating of DeAndre Harris, President Trump vacillated, claiming there were "very fine people on both sides," and that the mob chanting hateful racist propaganda included, "a lot of people in that group that were there to innocently protest and very legally protest."[9]

Throughout its history, far right white supremacy movements have tended to identify with Protestant Christianity and have co-opted Christian language and imagery—for example, the use of burning crosses as an instrument of terror by the Ku Klux Klan. Indeed, as James Cone's *The Cross and the Lynching Tree* reminds us, "between 1880 to 1940, white Christians lynched nearly five thousand black men and women in a manner with obvious echoes of the Roman crucifixion of Jesus. Yet these 'Christians' did not see the irony or contradiction in their actions."[10] This raises the question: How many "Christians" were there among those clean-cut, well-dressed, college-age white protesters chanting hateful Nazi slogans at progressive Christians gathered in peaceful prayer at St. Paul's

Memorial Episcopal Church on Friday night, August 11? How many professed "Christians" were there among those who harassed and goaded clergy and other faith leaders on their peaceful walk to Emancipation Park on Saturday, August 12, and then gathered for worship in a "Christian" church on Sunday, August 13?

A spiritual Turing test

Watching the documentary news footage from the Unite the Right rally in Charlottesville, I remember seeing the hatred in the faces of the (mostly) young, white males wearing the preppy "business casual" look that allows them to blend seamlessly into corporate America carrying torches and chanting Nazi slogans, and asking myself, "Are they even human?" Such anger, such hatred…What events unfolded in their lives that would cause them to spew such hateful and dehumanizing bile about their fellow human beings? But that is the crux of the matter: The ideology that leads to such actions is grounded in denying all who oppose them—be they black, brown, yellow, Catholic, Jew, Muslim, gay, lesbian, or transgender—human status. When you can objectify the other and reduce them to an obstacle in your way rather than acknowledge them as fully living breathing human beings, it becomes easier to trample them beneath your boots or under the wheels of your car.[11] It was at that moment that I had the following thought: What if we could develop a "spiritual" Turing test that would allow us to determine whether or not the hateful bigots fighting for white supremacy still possess some spark of humanity? Are they capable of dialogue? Is conversion from their hateful ways possible? Or are they so far gone down the path of racial hatred that we ought not waste our breath?

Alan Turing, an English philosopher and mathematician who contributed to Great Britain's code-breaking efforts that ultimately enabled the Allies to defeat the Nazis during World War Two, was a pioneer in computer science and artificial intelligence. In 1950, he developed the Turing test, an experiment designed to evaluate whether or not a machine is able to emulate intelligent behavior equivalent to or indistinguishable from human intelligence.[12] In this landmark paper, Turing considers the question, "Can machines think?" Acknowledging that "think" is a philosophically difficult and highly contested concept, Turing suggests replacing his initial question with a similar, but less ambiguous question: "Are there imaginable digital computers which would do well in the *imitation game*?"[13] Turing describes a simple party game in which Player A is male, Player B is female, and Player C (either male or female), who is unable to see or hear either Player A or B, attempts to determine which player is male and which female. Unknown to Player C, Player A's role is to attempt to trick Player C into making the wrong choice while Player B's task is to help Player C make the correct choice. To maintain the anonymity of both Player A and B, the players communicate with one another by means of written notes. Turing adapts this parlor came into an experiment evaluating "machine intelligence" by modifying a digital computer "to have an adequate storage, suitably increasing its speed of action, and providing it with an appropriate programme," so that the computer could replace Player A in the game, then unbeknown to Player C, both the computer and Player B are trying to deceive Player C into making the wrong choice.[14] This time, however, the challenge to Player C is to determine which player is a computer and which player is human. Turing argues that if human Player C is unable to distinguish between the computer-generated statements and the statements typed into the terminal by human Player B, then the computer wins the game and takes an important step toward creating an artificial intelligence capable of emulating human cognitive capacities. Turing's stated goal in developing the Turing test is not to determine whether the digital computers of his day and age were capable of artificial intelligence, but given future advances in technology, "whether there are imaginable computers" that could do well enough to win the game.[15]

Most philosophers and scientists agree that the Turing test does not determine whether or not a machine *is* intelligent; rather, it is designed to evaluate whether or not a computer can be programmed to *imitate* a human being well enough to fool a human interrogator. Not surprisingly, many Artificial Intelligence (AI) researchers argue that trying to pass the Turing test actually distracts from more important advances in AI, and point out that very few academic or commercial researchers are actually interested in implementing the Turing test.[16] Nevertheless, Alan Turing's thought experiment has captured the popular imagination, appearing in movies and fiction in one form or another, and resurfacing in 1996 when Deep Blue, a chess-playing computer developed by IBM, defeated reigning world champion Garry Kasparov in game one of a six-game match. Today, chess-playing software has become increasingly complex and much faster than Deep Blue, so that in 2006 a chess program called Deep Fritz defeated world champion Vladimir Kramnik 4 games to 2, taking advantage of its computational speed of eight million positions per second to successfully emulate human reasoning well enough to defeat a world champion.[17]

So as I watched the cold, empty, hateful glares of the white racists protesting in Charlottesville, Virginia, my mind immediately thought: "Are they human? Or are they soulless automatons? Could these carbon copy, golf-shirt wearing clones be the creation of some evil genius intent on turning back the clock of human progress by returning us to the 1950s pre-Civil Rights South?" Which is when it hit me that a "spiritual" Turing test could help us determine whether these protesters are in fact twenty-first century humans, or some facsimile designed to imitate human behavior just well enough to fool us into treating them with proper respect and civility. I then began to formulate a possible experiment, like Turing's "imitation game," consisting of a battery of yes-or-no questions (Are all human beings equally image of God? Did slavery come into existence because of the Curse of Ham? Can you affirm faith in a black Christ?), designed to help us identify the genuine Christian from the racist ideologue. Yet, this kind of thinking, however tempting, is a shibboleth that very quickly leads down the slippery slope toward demonizing the other and treating them as objects to be controlled, manipulated, or eliminated. The term shibboleth has come to mean any distinguishing word or phrase used to distinguish members of a group from outsiders, and in many societies such linguistic (or cultural) differentiations are used to justify segregation as a way of maintaining group purity. Its origins date to the book of Judges in the Hebrew Bible:

> Then the Gileadites took the fords of the Jordan against the Ephraimites. Whenever one of the fugitives of Ephraim said, 'Let me go over,' the men of Gilead would say to him, 'Are you an Ephraimite?' When he said, 'No,' they said to him, 'Then say Shibboleth,' and he said, 'Sibboleth,' for he could not pronounce it right. Then they seized him and killed him at the fords of the Jordan. Forty-two thousand of the Ephraimites fell at that time. (Jgs 12:5-6, NRSV)

The purpose of a shibboleth is exclusionary, as evidenced by the biblical tale in which persons whose way of speaking reveals their status as an outsider are viewed as threats to the community, and then are executed by the dominant group. Therefore, while it is tempting to have some quick and simple test to determine whether the hateful bigot in front of me is capable of conversion and therefore worth engaging in dialogue, or is beyond redemption and therefore incapable of conversation (let alone conversion), the act of developing and implementing a "spiritual" Turing test can easily become a form of theological totalitarianism as reprehensible as the neo-Nazis and white nationalists spouting hatred in Charlottesville.

Consequently, a Christian engagement of white racism—especially in its most virulent form, white nationalism—is better served by a dialogic approach. Admittedly, some interlocutors are not interested in conversation, but this ought not to deter one from making the effort. Furthermore, within the confines of U.S. politics, these interlocutors are not the neo-Nazi extremists themselves, but rather their mainstream allies and facilitators within the GOP and other social and political institutions who have tolerated—even encouraged—such right-wing extremism for the sake of gaining a few percentage points at the polls. In the aftermath of the Michael Brown shooting in Ferguson, Missouri in 2014, I began a conversation on racism and Catholic social teaching with one of my graduate students, a white male police officer in the Ferguson police department, which has blossomed into friendship. As a liberation theologian who leans left-of-center on most issues, there is much we disagree on, yet despite our differences, we are able to discuss sensitive issues and, more importantly, disagree while managing to treat each other civilly. It is not an overstatement to say we actually enjoy each other's company. Not surprisingly, many of his colleagues on the force are baffled by our relationship and seem worried that I will "infect" him with some sort of liberal contagion. Nevertheless, we have had some deep and meaningful conversations analyzing the situation in St. Louis and have reached some areas of agreement: (1) St. Louis is a radically segregated city, part of the Jim Crow era legacy, so the high crime rates and social unrest currently plaguing the city need to be understood within the context of this racist history[18] ; (2) increased incidents of police violence against potentially armed suspects are in part the result of cuts to *community policing* that eliminated the practice of two-officer patrol cars[19] ; and (3) long-term strategies to diversify police departments cannot be divorced from public education reform efforts since only 59 percent of African American males graduate high school (despite a national all-time high graduation rate of 81 percent in 2012–13), given that applicants to the police academy need to have a high school diploma or its equivalent (not to mention no felony convictions or "unfavorable" police record).[20]

Over time, our conversations have broadened beyond the crisis in Ferguson to consider the impact of racism and economic injustice on a whole host of issues impacting the nation, yet my student's insights are always grounded in his experiences as a police officer in Ferguson. He admits that police are now "even further alienated from their communities," and attributes some of the increased police violence to the day-to-day fears patrol officers live with: "Now guns are everywhere and officers know it. They also know that there is nothing they can do about it. Frankly, if an officer isn't afraid today he's a psychopath and shouldn't be out there. Part of the problem is they feel like sitting ducks." Unfortunately, this problem is exacerbated by the fact that police departments and police unions do not have the political capital or courage to stand up to the NRA and the gun lobby,[21] which is why he prefers that I protect his anonymity. In a conversation following the mass shooting in Las Vegas on October 1, 2017, he confided: "Stuff I can't say in the public arena...referencing Las Vegas. As I mentioned, the current gun laws are a disaster for policing. The much stricter gun laws of the 1980's were never considered unconstitutional. I brought in a gun a night and did so following the rules. There was no perceived threat to the Constitution on either side of the fence. I would like to think that I had some impact. If young black males were dying of anything *other* than puncture wounds as the result of an incoming round, NIH would declare an epidemic. It is a frustrating feeling of helplessness. Sad." In a later conversation, he added: "The further we walk down this gun road we are on, the more paranoid (justifiably I would argue) the police become. We are human and the chance for mistakes increases with every gun on the street. As you said, we are banging our heads on the wall expecting different results." Finally, in assessing the Federal study done in the aftermath of the Michael Brown shooting, this officer expressed the opinion that this was a "missed opportunity" by the Department of Justice because its use of consent decrees in Ferguson and Baltimore have actually increased mistrust of law enforcement while simultaneously "destroying any trust that officers had in the process that was established to take bad officers off the street. I don't see officers coming forward about bad officers."

Ultimately, any way forward on these issues begins and ends with trust. The idea behind the very concept of neighborhood or community policing is to increase trust between police officers and the communities they patrol, because the "need to close the gap between cops and the community has become increasingly apparent in recent years."[22] In St. Louis County, the strategy implemented guarantees that "officers patrol the same beat, within the same neighborhood and are provided with a yearly computer schedule that is designed to allow the beat officer an opportunity to get to know the residents, businesses and schools where our children attend and grow."[23] Churches, vital resources in every community, ought to take the lead on these issues, speaking *prophetically* against abuse and brutality by law enforcement, while *simultaneously* supporting community and trust-building efforts by local governments and police departments. Some police departments are encouraging more transparency during investigations of police-shooting incidents by sharing information with local African American clergy and NAACP representatives, while developing outreach efforts in African American communities with the hope of moving "the police force closer to some of its most disenfranchised and suspicious stakeholders."[24] As, for example, in Tulsa, Oklahoma after a recent officer-involved shooting, when potential hostilities were stilled by the community's trust in Mayor Dewey Bartlett. According to the Reverend Warren Blakney, church pastor and president of the local branch of the NAACP, Mayor Bartlett "has worked hard to establish ties with the black community in north Tulsa, attending Sunday services at African-American churches most weekends."[25] More and more, as "racial tensions continue to simmer in the wake of the deaths of unarmed black men at the hands of white officers in Ferguson, Mo., New York City and elsewhere, churches have offered themselves up as trusted go-betweens for the police and angry residents, particularly in black communities."[26] While community policing is still viewed with suspicion by many African American activists, some local chapters of Black Lives Matter have taken steps toward building the kind of trust necessary to not only change the culture of police departments, but also transform how police are perceived in predominately African American communities.²⁷

How to silence 200 nineteen-year-olds in St. Louis, Missouri

For years, Dr. Martin Luther King's "Letter from a Birmingham City Jail" (1963) has been required reading in my introductory Theological Foundations course at Saint Louis University (SLU). Most semesters we read this text in the latter half of the semester after a solid grounding in the biblical foundations of the Christian faith and exposure to such perennial theological favorites as Augustine's *On Christian Doctrine*, Anselm's *Why God Became Man*, and Bonhoeffer's *The Cost of Discipleship*. This school year, however, I made the decision to begin with Dr. King's letter given the events that took place in Charlottesville mere days before the start of the semester. In hindsight, I made the correct decision insofar as a few weeks later the city of St. Louis was once again rocked by violent protests after the acquittal of a white police officer, Jason Stockley, charged with murder for the 2011 shooting death of a black driver, Anthony Lamar Smith.²⁸ In a matter of hours, these protests moved from downtown to midtown, from midtown to the suburbs, and even onto the campus of Saint Louis University where, I am proud to say, I saw many of my students marching and partaking in nonviolent direct action in the tradition of Dr. King.

The Monday after the first wave of protests, I was lecturing to my class of 200 first-year undergraduate students, making a point about Christian just-war theory in an effort to explain why the Bush doctrine—a strategy of "preemptive strikes" as a defense against an immediate or perceived future threat to the security of the United States²⁹—violates Christian moral reasoning. To illustrate my point, I asked a (white) male student to stand up and said to him: "Imagine we are walking toward each other on the street. Unknown to you I have had a very bad day so I am in a foul mood. As I approach you I happen to give you a mean look. Applying the Bush doctrine to this situation you interpret my look—keeping in mind that I am brown and weigh 250 pounds—as a potential threat to your life, and this being Missouri (a concealed carry state), you pull out your 9 mm GLOCK pistol and shoot me dead. I ask you, is this a legitimate case of self-defense?" The class was somewhat shocked by my example, and most just sat there in silence, but a few voices could be heard saying, "No!" At that moment, when I was certain I had their attention, I said loudly and clearly, "Unless, of course, you are a white police officer in the United States." Time stopped. The room was deathly still, and I let the silence linger for a moment longer before returning to the lecture at hand, my point made. I then related the Christian tradition of just-war reasoning to the issue of racially targeted police brutality by drawing concrete parallels to the Stockley acquittal, in which the accused white officer planted a gun on the victim yet only Stockley's DNA could be found on it. Ultimately, the judge ruled that the state failed to prove "beyond a reasonable doubt that Stockley 'did not act in self-defense,'" despite the fact that Stockley admitted to carrying unauthorized weapons with extra rounds while on duty.[30] Undoubtedly, my actions and statements made an impact on students (which I am sure will reflect both negatively and positively on my student course evaluations), as evidenced by the comments students made on their way to their next class. The young man whom I had drafted to take part in my lecture illustration actually said, "That was funny. I appreciate how you used sarcasm to make your point." One African American student, who had been among the protesters the night before, came up to me and said, "Thank you for that." Regardless, I had learned from personal experience how to silence an auditorium full of usually loud and talkative nineteen-year-olds in St. Louis, Missouri.

My decision to begin our semester by reading Dr. King's "Letter from a Birmingham City Jail" in order to locate Black Lives Matter (BLM) within our nation's historical struggles for civil rights was motivated by the fact that this movement has had a major impact in St. Louis since Michael Brown's 2014 shooting death yet there is much misinformation in the local media about the movement, its goals, and its tactics. The Black Lives Matter movement came to national prominence in the aftermath of the murder of African American youth Michael Brown by a white police officer in Ferguson, Missouri on August 9, 2014. However, it was actually founded in 2013 by three radical organizers—Alicia Garza, Patrisse Cullors, and Opal Tometi—in response to the acquittal of George Zimmerman, a neighborhood watch coordinator for a gated community in Sanford, Florida, who had murdered African American teenager Trayvon Martin (a guest at a town home in the gated community) with a 9-mm semi-automatic pistol. According to the movement's mission statement,

BLM is "an ideological and political intervention in a world where Black lives are systematically and intentionally targeted for demise," committed to affirming "the lives of Black queer and trans folks, disabled folks, undocumented folks, folks with records, women, and all Black lives along the gender spectrum. Our network centers those who have been marginalized within Black liberation movements."[31] When Michael Brown was murdered in 2014, BLM worked with local organizers in Ferguson, Missouri, to coordinate a series of nonviolent protests (that led to civil unrest) designed to draw international attention to the systemic pattern of brutalization of African Americans by law enforcement. While the movement has since become an international network with over thirty local chapters, their involvement in Ferguson highlights the founders' desires to work as a decentralized network without a formal hierarchy. It is worth noting that despite the growth of the movement and subsequent incidents of police fatal violence targeting African Americans in places like Baltimore and Minneapolis-St. Paul, the BLM website still credits local organizers and activists in Missouri for their ongoing frontline work: "the folks in St. Louis and Ferguson who put their bodies on the line day in and day out, and who continue to show up for Black lives."[32] As theological ethicist Jermaine M. McDonald has noted, much of the backlash from within the African American civil rights establishment directed at Black Lives Matter stems from the fact that BLM is "primarily composed of younger activists, it conflicts with elders in the black community over tactics and strategies, and it is not committed to any particular religious worldview."[33]

Though not explicitly theological—and definitely not linked to any single confessional tradition—Black Lives Matter has often invoked Martin Luther King, Jr. to differentiate, situate, and defend itself from external criticism. Specifically, the movement's founders have responded to criticisms that their involvement in the rioting in Ferguson betrayed the nonviolent legacy of Dr. King, arguing instead that they are "recovering the radicalism of King's methods and message for the twenty-first century"[34] by retrieving and reclaiming King's "Letter from a Birmingham City Jail" (1963) and his infamous address at Riverside Church in New York City, "A Time to Break Silence" (1967), in order to drive home the urgency of the current situation in which black lives continue to be brutalized and murdered by agents of the state. Therefore, BLM stands on the same principled call to "direct action" that brought Dr. King to

Birmingham in 1963, because there "comes a time when the cup of endurance runs over, and men [sic] are no longer willing to be plunged into an abyss of injustice where they experience the blackness of corroding despair."[35] With Dr. King, they have learned from "painful experience that freedom is never voluntarily given by the oppressor; it must be demanded by the oppressed"[36]; like Dr. King, they do not shy away from controversy by affirming their unapologetic "blackness" in a white supremacist culture in much the same way Dr. King refused to back down when he was criticized for using his fame to address issues beyond civil rights in order to condemn the U.S. war in Vietnam: "A nation that continues year after year to spend more money on military defense than on programs of social uplift is approaching spiritual death."[37]

A movement like Black Lives Matter eschews traditional religion and focuses primarily on advocating for those who have been marginalized within established black liberation movements while presenting itself as an emancipatory spirituality for *all* black lives. Recognizing that their revolutionary goals necessitate tactics that might not meet with the approval of the older, more ecclesiocentric Civil Rights Movement, the founders of BLM have struggled to differentiate their movement and its goals while nonetheless locating themselves within the rich history of African American struggles for liberation. In an interview for *Teen Vogue* magazine, Patrisse Cullors, one of the three founders of Black Lives Matter, expressed the resistance she and her two comrades experienced: "The first challenge was making sure that people knew who *actually* were the creators of Black Lives Matter—pushing back against our own erasure. I have never felt the grips of patriarchy and its need to erase black women and our labor...so strongly until the creation of Black Lives Matter."[38] However, the greatest resistance has come from the white mainstream, which has labeled Black Lives Matter a terrorist group.[39] Thus, even supposed white allies come under the critical lens of BLM and its consistent message that racism is alive and well in post-Obama America: "We forced folks to look at the Democratic party as a party that has historically said it's on the side of black people but instead it hasn't been, and the policies have shown that."[40] George Wayne Smith, the tenth Anglican Bishop of Missouri, focuses the vague spiritual urge underlying the activism of groups like BLM within an explicitly theological framework with the suggestion that the site of Michael Brown's murder on Canfield Avenue in Ferguson has become a shrine:

> People go to that place and weep, or they rage, or they sing, or they stand in slack-jawed silence. The place allows people to express deep emotion, and it lets them hope. Some even pray. The pavement is still visibly marked by Michael Brown's blood. Protestors sometimes paraphrase Genesis 4 in saying that his blood cries out for justice. But the place is also saturated by the anger, the hopes, and the prayers of thousands. It is an important place. Dare I call it holy?[41]

This spiritual urging that gives voice to an entire people's history of suffering and dehumanization occupies the liminal space where the love of God coexists with innocent human suffering but in place of *theodicy*—a rational explanation for the existence of evil—the Spirit offers *mystery*, turning the tragedy of Michael Brown into a sacramental encounter with God in the midst of our broken human history.

Concluding unscientific postscript

In the words of the apostle Paul, the Christian church is called to be a community in which "There is no longer Jew or Greek, there is no longer slave or free, there is no longer male or female; for all of you are one in Christ Jesus" (Gal 3:27–28, NRSV). It was foolish to expect the election and presidency of Barack Obama to erase the problem of racism in the United States; yet, many are surprised by just how strong the white male resentment has become now that Obama has left office. The truth is, this resentment was seething just below the surface all along. Cory Booker, then mayor of Newark, New Jersey, and now the junior Senator from New Jersey (a much-talked-about potential presidential candidate for 2020), described the promise and challenge of racial reconciliation following the election of the first African American President:

> We are a nation that celebrates racial diversity. We're not Norway; we're not South Korea; we are the United States of America. The story of America is one of bringing such differences together to manifest a united set of ideals—not a united culture, not a united language, not a united religion, but a united set of ideals. That was what made America dramatic when it was founded, the first

country of its kind in humanity. So I reject [the idea of a post-racial America]. I want to celebrate all of America: its richness, its diversity, its deliciousness... God forbid if we ever get to a point where we "transcend our race."[42]

This tension identified by Cory Booker is a topic I addressed in my first book, *Racism and God-Talk* (2008)[43] —the desire to affirm racial and ethnic particularity while embodying the apostle Paul's inclusive vision of the church as a community where we are no longer Jew or Greek, slave or free, male or female but *one* in Christ Jesus. The "Silent Majority" that elected Donald Trump in 2016 has become an emboldened white supremacist reactionary political movement with deep pockets and nationwide organizational support led by former Trump staffer Steve Bannon (who was fired by Trump less than a week after the Unite the Right rally in Virginia).[44] This shift in U.S. politics, which elevates and celebrates "whiteness" as if white people were a repressed minority suffering under generations of oppression finally being delivered from captivity, ought to prompt bold and thoughtful theological responses from the church as it resists white identity politics without erasing the racial and ethnic diversity that constitutes our nation in order to build a "more perfect union."

Do black lives matter to white Christians? The empirical evidence is lacking, and centuries of enslavement, abuse, rape, and murder of black lives by the dominant white culture of the United States suggest not. Instead of demonstrating how black lives matter, far too many white Christians offer up a supposedly Gospel-tinged counternarrative that says, "*all* lives matter." Still, James Cone's *The Cross and the Lynching Tree* (2011) documents the extent to which black lives have not mattered in this country—even to a progressive white Christian icon like Reinhold Niebuhr, whose "lack of a strong empathy with black suffering prevented him from speaking out passionately for justice on behalf of black people."[45] Niebuhr, while opposed to racism, "showed little or no interest in engaging in dialogue with blacks about racial justice, even though he lived in Detroit during the great migration of blacks from the South and in New York near Harlem, the largest concentration of blacks in America."[46] For Cone, this tone-deafness on matters of racial justice is best illustrated by Niebuhr's reserved reaction to the lynching of two black teenaged boys, in which he described a lynching as "a general fete to which men, women, and children are invited," yet refused to name the town in Mississippi where he witnessed this "public gallows."[47] The current historical moment, in which white Christians have allowed white bigots to hijack the language and symbols of the Christian religion for their hateful ideology, then employed the language of love, forgiveness, and tolerance to undermine the radical urgency of Black Lives Matter by proclaiming "all lives matter," exposes the cultural and political impotence of liberal mainstream Christianity.

As a Latino/a theologian, I have written about and critiqued the black/white dichotomy that dominates the nation's racial conversation, and I do not want to minimize the very real threat to brown lives in the era of Trump's exclusionary policies targeting immigrants from Latin America and the Middle East.[48] However, at this moment in U.S. history, the outcry and organized response to white supremacy originates within the African American community, and Black Lives Matter deserves the support of brown, yellow, red, white, straight, gay, trans, poor, rich, working class, and all other lives. To quibble about who suffers most under the culture of white supremacy undermines what is perhaps the most effective effort at dismantling our nation's racist infrastructure since the Civil Rights Movement of the 1950s and 1960s, and allows the political manipulators to divide and conquer: "As long as communities of color fail to build the necessary coalitions to combat the prevailing reality that all nonwhite and nonstraight lives live in peril, the social structures protecting white privilege will remain intact."[49] Miguel De La Torre correctly concludes, neither "black lives nor brown lives will succeed in the crucial work of dismantling the racist and ethnic discriminative institutionalized structures undergirding law enforcement until brown folk stand in solidarity at Ferguson, and black folk stand in solidarity on the border."[50] In the meantime, working toward mutual solidarity need not prevent brown lives from standing united with Black Lives Matter here and now. Nor, for that matter, white lives.

Undergirding a black theology of liberation is this central question: Is Christianity the religion of the slave owners, or the religion of the slaves? In *Black Theology and Black Power* (1969), James H. Cone argued that, "If the Gospel of Christ...frees a man [sic] to be for those who labor and are heavily laden, the humiliated and abused, then it would seem that for twentieth-century America the message of Black Power is the message of

Christ himself."[51] Cone, influenced by both Dr. King's nonviolent direct action and Malcolm X's philosophy of Black Power, elevated political self-determination, racial pride ("Black is beautiful"), and resisting white supremacist violence as the concrete goals of a black theology of liberation. In *A Black Theology of Liberation* (1970), Cone concludes that the message of the Gospel *is* liberation, so in order for theology to be genuinely "Christian" it must side and identify with the oppressed in a struggle to change their condition. Accordingly, so long as black lives continue to be exploited, brutalized, and destroyed with impunity, God is most clearly revealed in the suffering of black men and women. If as Christians we believe in the Incarnation—that in becoming human God has made the suffering of the oppressed God's own—then we must be able to affirm that Christ is black. Consequently, for white Christians who want to live in solidarity with black lives, Cone's Christological assertion that Christ is black is one obvious point of departure. Granted, James Cone is not making a historical assertion about the Jesus who walked this earth in the first century of the Common Era. Rather, he is making a theological assertion about the Risen Christ's blackness today: "I begin by asserting once more that Jesus was a Jew. It is on the basis of the soteriological meaning of the particularity of his Jewishness that theology must affirm the christological significance of Jesus' present blackness. He is black because he was a Jew."[52] Therefore, all Christians—not just black Christians—ought to resist white supremacy in an America where black lives still don't seem to matter, because the Savior who revealed God's self to the world as a Jew in Roman-occupied Palestine now chooses to become incarnate in the suffering of black lives. In this context, the cross becomes the lynching tree, inverting "the world's value system with the news that hope comes by way of defeat, that suffering and death do not have the last word, that the last shall be first and the first last."[53]

Earlier, with tongue in cheek, I suggested our society needs a "spiritual" Turing test for distinguishing white nationalists from the rest of society. Upon further reflection, I have come to realize that what is needed—at least within the Christian churches—is a "spiritual" Turing test for identifying those Christians who pay lip service to tolerance and inclusion but in the end blandly proclaim, "all lives matter," and genuine Christians who stand with Black Lives Matter *because* Christ is black. Proclaiming a black Christ is possible for all people, regardless of skin color, so long as they opt to follow Christ in his suffering, because the God revealed in the Gospels is one who chooses to identify with the oppressed of the world in order to overturn their oppression: "Hate and white supremacy lead to violence and alienation, while love and the cross lead to nonviolence and reconciliation."[54] Granted, "Loving whites who hated and killed them was not easy for African Americans. Only God could empower black Christians to love hateful whites, and even God could not guarantee that they would return love for hate, nonviolence for violence."[55] Perhaps there is no way to convince the majority of white Christians that black lives matter, but a black theology of liberation continues to struggle in hope, convinced that in offering resistance, blacks "not only liberate themselves from oppression, they also liberate the oppressors from an enslavement to their illusions."[56] Ironically, black lives are the ones most concerned about the well-being of *all* lives, despite the rhetoric of many well-meaning white Christians. Come, Lord Jesus!

Notes

1. Quoted in Justin Ewers, "Obama and Race Relations: Civil Rights Leaders Aren't Satisfied," in *U.S. News & World Report*, posted April 30, 2009 (accessed on November 25, 2017). https://www.usnews.com/news/obama/articles/2009/04/30/obama-and-race-relations-civil-rightsleaders-arent-satisfied

2. Obama, Barack, "A More Perfect Union," published as "Barack Obama's Speech on Race," in *The New York Times*, posted March 18, 2008 (accessed on November 25, 2017). http://www.nytimes.com/2008/03/18/us/politics/18text-obama.html

3. Liptak, Adam, "Justices Retain Oversight by U.S. on Voting Rights," in *The New York Times* (June 22, 2009), A1.

4. Mahony, Edmund H., "New Haven Firefighters To Get $2 Million In Discrimination Lawsuit: City Also Agrees To Pay Enhanced Pension Benefits," in *Hartford Courant*, posted July 28, 2011 (accessed on November 25, 2017). http://articles.courant.com/2011-07-28/news/hc-newhaven-firefighters-0729-20110728_1_white-firefighters-new-haven-frank-ricci

5. Early, Gerald, Susan M. Glisson, Curtiss Paul De Young, Melvin Bray, and Chris Rice, 2008, "What's changed? Obama and race in America," in *The Christian Century* **125** (26), December 30, p. 21.

6. Green, Joshua, "Penn Strategy Memo, March 19, 2007," in *The Atlantic*, posted August 11, 2008 (accessed on November 25, 2017). https://www.theatlantic.com/politics/archive/2008/08/penn-strategy-memo-march-19-2008/37952/

7. Figueroa, Laura, "Donald Trump on birther issue: Barack Obama born in U.S.," in *Newsday*, posted September 16, 2016 (accessed on November 25, 2017). https://www.newsday.com/news/nation/donald-trump-admits-barack-obama-was-born-in-the-united-states-1.12326105

8. The Southern Poverty Law Center (SPLC) website defines the Alternative Right, known in the media as the Alt-Right, as "a set of far-right ideologies, groups and individuals whose

core belief is that "white identity" is under attack by multicultural forces using "political correctness" and "social justice" to undermine white people and "their" civilization. Characterized by heavy use of social media and online memes, Alt-Righters eschew "establishment" conservatism, skew young, and embrace white ethno-nationalism as a fundamental value." For example, after the *National Review*, a traditional bastion of U.S. conservatism, vehemently opposed the candidacy of Donald Trump, members of the Alt-Right used social media to attack the publication and promote Trump's presidential bid (accessed on November 25, 2017). https://www.splcenter.org/fighting-hate/extremist-files/ideology/alt-right

9. Thrush, Glenn and Maggie Haberman, "Giving White Nationalists An Unequivocal Boost," in *The New York Times* (August 16, 2017), A1.

10. Cone, James H., *The Cross and the Lynching Tree*, paperback edition (Maryknoll, NY: Orbis Books, 2013), p. 31.

11. See Caron, Christina, "Friends Recall "a Strong Woman" Who Stood Up Against Discrimination," in *The New York Times* (August 14, 2017), A14.

12. Turing, Alan, "Computing Machinery and Intelligence," in *Mind*, Vol. LIX:236 (October 1950), pp. 433–60.

13. Ibid., p. 442.

14. Ibid., p. 434.

15. Ibid., p. 436.

16. See Shieber, Stuart M., 1994, "Lessons from a Restricted Turing Test," *Communications of the ACM*, **37**(6), pp. 70–8; and Russell, Stuart J. and Peter Norvig, *Artificial Intelligence: A Modern Approach*, 3rd edition (Upper Saddle River, NJ: Prentice Hall, 2010).

17. "Chess champion looses to computer," in *BBC News*, posted December 5, 2006 (accessed on November 26, 2017). http://news.bbc.co.uk/2/hi/europe/6212076.stm

18. See *Papers of the NAACP Part 5. The Campaign against Residential Segregation, 1914–1955* (Frederick, MD: University Publications of America, 1986); St. Louis passed a residential segregation ordinance stated that if 75 percent of the residents of a neighborhood were of a certain race, no one from a different race was allowed to move into the neighborhood. The NAACP challenged the ordinance in court, and in 1948, Shelley v. Kraemer ruled these "racial covenants in St. Louis were unconstitutional, but not before the city had become racially segregated in what is now known as the "Delmar Divide," in which the neighborhoods north of Delmar are overwhelmingly black and economically deprived. This legacy contributed to the incidents and unrest in Ferguson and is reinforced by the recent study that named St. Louis the tenth most segregated city in the United States. See Michael B. Sauter, Evan Comen, and Samuel Stebbins, "16 Most Segregated Cities in America, "posted in *24/7 Wall St.*, July 21, 2017 (accessed on November 25, 2017). http://247wallst.com/special-report/2017/07/21/16-most-segregated-cities-in-america/2/

19. See del Carmen, Alejandro, and Lori Guevara, 2003, "Police Officers on Two-officer Units: A Study of Attitudinal Responses Towards a Patrol Experiment," *Policing: An International Journal of Police Strategies & Management*, **26**(1), pp. 144–61; Griffith, David, "Two-Officer Cars: The Buddy System," in *Police: The Law Enforcement Magazine*, October 16, 2015 (accessed on November 26, 2017). http://www.policemag.com/channel/patrol/articles/2015/10/the-buddy-system.aspx

20. See Bidwell, Allie, "Racial Gaps in High School Graduation Rates Are Closing," in U.S. News & World Report, posted March 16, 2015 (accessed on November 26, 2017). https://www.usnews.com/news/blogs/data-mine/2015/03/16/federal-data-show-racial-gap-in-high-school-graduation-rates-is-closing; Brown, Emma, "Report on Black Males' Graduation Rates Shows that Data are Muddy," in The Washington Post, posted February 11, 2015 (accessed on November 26, 2017). https://www.washingtonpost.com/local/education/report-on-black-males-graduation-rates-shows-that-data-are-muddy/2015/02/10/368bac0c-b16b-11e4-886b-c22184f27c35_story.html?utm_term=.2026f0738e5c

21. See Lott, John R. Jr., "Gun Control Is Not the Answer to Shootings that Kill Police Officers," in *National Review*, posted July 26, 2016 (accessed on November 26, 2017). http://www.nationalreview.com/article/438327/gun-control-police-officers-overwhelmingly-support-second-amendment-rights; for a contrasting view, see Robertson, Campbell and Timothy Williams, "States Widening Gun Rights Lose Longtime Ally: Police," in *The New York Times* (May 4, 2016), A10; Kaste, Martin, "Gun Debate Divides Nation's Police Officers, Too," in *National Public Radio*, posted October 9, 2015 (accessed on November 26, 2017). https://www.npr.org/2015/10/09/446866939/gun-debate-divides-nations-police-officers-too

22. (accessed on November 26, 2017) https://www1.nyc.gov/site/nypd/bureaus/patrol/neighborhood-coordination-officers.page.

23. (accessed on November 26, 2017) http://www.stlouisco.com/LawandPublicSafety/PoliceDepartment/Services/NeighborhoodPolicing

24. Calhoun, Jack, "How Law Enforcement and the Faith Community Can Work Together for Cities," in CitiesSpeak: National League of Cities, posted April 27, 2017 (accessed on November 26, 2017). https://citiesspeak.org/2017/04/27/how-law-enforcement-and-the-faith-community-can-work-together-for-cities/

25. Ibid.

26. Banks, Adelle M., "Police Chief To Black Churches: 'We Can't Do This Without You Guys'," in *Huffington Post*, posted January 11, 2015 (accessed on November 26, 2017). https://www.huffingtonpost.com/2015/01/11/police-black-churches_n_6443664.html

27. Chappell, Bill, "Police And Black Lives Matter Hold A Cookout, And Praise Rolls In," in *National Public Radio*, posted on July 19, 2016 (accessed on November 26, 2017). https://www.npr.org/sections/thetwo-way/2016/07/19/486581466/police-and-black-lives-matter-hold-a-cookout-and-praise-rolls-in

28. Berman, Mark, Wesley Lowery, and Andrew deGrandpre, "Police and protesters clash in St. Louis after former officer who shot black driver acquitted on murder charges," *The Washington* Post, posted September 16, 2017 (accessed on December 1, 2017). https://www.washingtonpost.com/news/post-nation/wp/2017/09/15/st-louis-tenses-for-verdict-in-murder-trial-of-former-police-officer/?utm_term=.14872d492acb

29. See Dolan, Chris J., *In War We Trust: The Bush Doctrine and the Pursuit of Just War* (Burlington, VT: Ashgate Publishing, 2005), pp. 47–64.

30. Berman, Lowery, and deGrandpre, "Police and protesters clash in St. Louis," (September 16, 2017).

31. See https://blacklivesmatter.com/about/, and https://blacklivesmatter.com/about/herstory/, for an introduction to and defense of the movement (accessed on October 13, 2017).

32. Ibid.

33. McDonald, Jermaine M., 2016, "Ferguson and Baltimore according to Dr. King: How Competing Interpretations of King's Legacy Frame the Public Discourse on Black Lives Matter," *Journal of the Society of Christian Ethics* **36**(2), Fall/Winter, p. 149.
34. Ibid., pp. 150–1.
35. King, Jr., Martin Luther, "Letter from a Birmingham City Jail," in *A Testament of Hope: The Essential Writings of Martin Luther King, Jr.*, ed. James Melvin Washington, (San Francisco: HarperSanFrancisco, 1991), p. 293.
36. Ibid., p. 292.
37. King, Jr. Martin Luther, "A Time to Break Silence," in *A Testament of Hope: The Essential Writings of Martin Luther King, Jr.*, ed. James Melvin Washington (San Francisco: HarperSanFrancisco, 1991), p. 241.
38. Anthony Blades, Lincoln, "Patrisse Cullors of Black Lives Matters Discusses the Movement," in *Teen Vogue* (August 24, 2017), https://www.teenvogue.com/story/patrisse-cullors-of-black-lives-matter-discusses-the-movement (accessed on October 13, 2017).
39. Currently, there is a popular movement petitioning the White House to declare BLM a terrorist group on par with ISIS and Al-Qaeda; the White House responded saying, "The White House plays no role in designating domestic terror organizations," nor does the U.S. government "generate a list of domestic terror organizations." See https://petitions.whitehouse.gov/petition/ formally-recognize-black-lives-matter-terrorist-organization; and Erroll Barnett, "White House responds to petition to label Black Lives Matter a "terror" group," CBS News (July 17, 2016), https://www.cbsnews.com/news/white-house-responds-to-petition-to-label-black-lives-matter-a-terror-group/ (accessed on October 16, 2017).
40. Ibid.
41. Smith, George Wayne, 2015, "Blood Cries Out from the Ground: Reflections on Ferguson," *Anglican Theological Review* **97** (2) Spring, p. 261.
42. See http://www.christiancentury.org/article.lasso?id=6040 (accessed on December 13, 2017).
43. Rodríguez, Rubén Rosario, *Racism and God-Talk: A Latino/a Perspective* (New York: New York University Press, 2008).
44. See Blake, Aaron, "Why Steve Bannon's threat to primary almost every GOP senator should frighten Republicans," in *The Washington Post*, posted October 10, 2017 (accessed on November 25, 2017). https://www.washingtonpost.com/news/the-fix/wp/2017/10/10/why-steve-bannons-targeting-of-incumbent-senators-is-a-serious-threat-to-the-gop/?utm_term=.1262a36b9135; also see, Desiderio, Andrew, "Bannon's Revenge: Bannon Defeats Trump as Roy Moore Cruises to Victory in Alabama," posted on *The Daily Beast*, September 26, 2017 (accessed on November 25, 2017). https://www.thedailybeast.com/bannon-defeats-trump-as-roy-moore-cruises-to-victory-in-alabama
45. Cone, *The Cross and the Lynching Tree*, p. 43.
46. Ibid., p. 42.
47. Ibid., p. 46.
48. See Miguel A. De La Torre, "Being Brown While Black Lives Matter," in *Our Lucha*, posted August 29, 2015 (last accessed December 13, 2017). https://ourlucha.wordpress.com/2015/08/29/being-brown-while-black-lives-matter/
49. Ibid.

50. Ibid.
51. Cone, James H., *Black Theology and Black Power*, 1989 edition (Maryknoll, NY: Orbis Books, 1997), p. 37.
52. James H. Cone, *God of the Oppressed* (Maryknoll, NY: Orbis Books, 1977), p. 123.
53. Cone, *The Cross and the Lynching Tree*, p. 2.
54. Ibid., p. 71.
55. Ibid., p. 79.
56. Cone, James H., *A Black Theology of Liberation*, 40th anniversary edition (Maryknoll, NY: Orbis Books, 2010), pp. 185–6.

CAN THESE BLACK BONES LIVE?
Addressing the Necrotic in US Theo-Politics

Antonia Michelle Daymond

> He said to me, 'Mortal, can these bones live?'
>
> Ezekiel 37:3

The inquiry, "Can these bones live?" appearing in the biblical canon posed by Yahweh to the prophet Ezekiel can be hermeneutically analyzed in two ways. On one hand, it calls into question whether desiccated and de-fleshed bones of the Israelite people can be resurrected to become alive again. These bones, residing in a valley of blood-soaked slaughter from Babylonian persecution, are the end result of benumbed bodies excavated from life rendering their remains illegible and "truly dead that they no longer made skeletons."[1] Massive murder, alienation, exile, and abandonment were exacted on Israel, which led to a mammoth of dead bones seemingly "void of sanctuary and redemption",[2] prompting Yahweh's rhetorical question of whether death can be reversed and ultimately asking whether death has the final word.

On the other hand, as Robert Jenson proposes, there is another interfaced layer to Yahweh's query undoubtedly significant for modern society: Despite the Christian proclamation that death does not win due to the resurrection of Jesus Christ, is Christian theology nevertheless a pile of dried up bones incapable of addressing the issues of the modern human.[3] Jenson situates his theological investigation to empathize the challenges modernity poses to the church such as nihilism, methods of textual/historical interpretation, and so on. However, in what follows, my emphasis differs. I am interested in grounding the twin nature of Yahweh's inquiry within the United States' twenty-first century sociopolitical climate, a fragile climate perpetually vexed by sundry afflictions against black life through the nation's sociocultural processes that bear an open valley of raced black bodies through its institutional infrastructures, namely its courtrooms, cells, classrooms, and even church pews.

Hence, I'm rephrasing our guiding question—"Can these bones live?"—with a formal distinction to examine "Can these *black* bones live?" Perhaps this inquiry defies an abrupt, affirmative answer given that black life in America has been historically cast on the edges of the outside consistently wedded to death as a result of the state's negligence to shield black bodies from violence and ensure justice to black communities via the distribution of necessary life resources and equal rights. What's required, then, is to consider, as João Vargas and Joy James critically ponder: "What will happen … if instead of demanding justice we recognize (or at least consider) that the very notion of justice—indeed the gamut of political and cognitive elements that constitute formal, multiracial democratic practices and institutions—produces or requires black exclusion and death as normative?"[4]

With Vargas and James' question in mind, I consider grounding structural violence and death as constituent elements of blackness as a reward that sidesteps relying on surfaced theological prescriptions and attend to those unsettling conundrums that seemingly appear theologically irresolvable. In other words, our engagement here is worth the expense of proposing inadequate liberatory options and grounds precisely the paradox undergirding this essay: How can we put forward theological prescriptions that liberate the conditions of black being despite the plaguing doubt that racism will ever end given the ways that the state and its corresponding mechanisms of power imbue the nation's everyday culture, a culture that complies with and commands participation in the ceaseless creation of Black Death?

Because Christianity and its concomitant myths and logics are politically flexed within the United States since the nation's inception, particularly as it is collapsed within cultural logics and pathologies about race and gender, the charge of this essay considers the extent to which Christian myths/logics embolden (or even constitute) stiffening structures of Black Death helping to pulsate a necroideological fantasy that structures the United States' neoliberal democratic pathologies, making Christian claims implausibly dormant to those who face the raw confinements of state-sanctioned terror, racialization, and dehumanization. In doing so, I consider the ontological sensibilities offered by black critical studies, especially black feminist thought, regarding the singular positioning of blackness, which situates the racialized black subject as not only exposed to deathly social processes ascribed to the impactful horrors of slavery and the reorganized domination in slavery's afterlife, but considers that the very residence of blackness positioned on the outside of civil society is what holds together and informs other non-black categories that are positioned on the inside. Next, I conceptualize the tripartite relation to race and religion and the American nation through theodicean grammar to consider the ways that current racist deities (portrayed in divine garb) in the United States' social and political architecture rationalize violence and black subjection through use of the Christian social imaginary, revealing the ease with which black suffering and death are often romanticized, normalized, neutralized, disregarded, or even relegated to sacrificial terms. Finally, I conclude by proposing an idea of the cross as that which calls us to have a theological temperament of refusal, which involves a process of "wake work" that necessarily acknowledges the presence of black suffering and death and necessarily disallows its normalization through a politics of refusal and defiance.

On black life and the necrotic
Achille Mbembe's seminal essay "Necropolitics," the titular and conceptual formulation I'm somewhat purloining here, traces the necrotic condition, that is "the subjugation of life to the power of death" historically occurring in (post)-colonial territories, through the imposition of war and conquest. With a keen focus on the African continent, Mbembe foregrounds the place of race within modern political discourses dominated by violence and human subjection to account for not only the sovereign's lone ability to will overt death among its inhabitants but also its "creation of death worlds" which are "new and unique forms of social existence in which vast populations are subjected to conditions of life conferring upon the status of *living dead*."[5] In interrogating colonial sovereignty's formations, which possess the power to dictate who may live and who may die tout court, Mbembe's "Necropolitics" succinctly describes

the modern nation-state's capacity to merit certain bodies as possessing the right to life, whereas other bodies are seen, to use Derrida's term, as always already in peril and materially antagonized by the fate of the necrotic, inconsequentially not mattering at all. To be clear, the saturnine positioning of these bodies operates in tandem to strengthen and solidify sovereign power.

To be sure, Mbembe's essay offers a lexis of theoretical reflection on the more contemporary production of ordinary and extraordinary "death worlds" that encompass the ever-evolving obscenities of violence and death foisted on black bodies by state power and racist ideology. In contemporary America, we can consider the ways that the nation organizes lifespans by inscribing raced bodies as disposable through zones of death such as, for example, the impoverished zone of Flint, Michigan, by which the state allowed poor blacks to consume and be baptized in toxic water rejecting these inhabitants with fundamental resources for human survival. This profane death world is among many that serve as the state's necrotic apparatuses that freely relate racial blackness to anesthetized spaces of the living dead.

And yet, although I find much value in Mbembe's conceptual acuities, I follow Jared Sexton's contention that we cannot fully integrate Mbembe's analytical frame to substantially elaborate the inimitable ways that necropolitical processes assemble and position black subjectivity in America. For Sexton, Mbembe's quick slippage of universalizing the colony's "peculiar terror formation" with US chattel slavery makes necropolitics's analogical inferences too conveniently clean.[6] To be clear, Sexton acknowledges that Mbembe presents American chattel slavery in exemplary fashion, describing it as "one of the first instances of biological extermination," and indexes its race logics and technologies of power as a protuberant source of death production in global "states of exception"; however, Sexton deems that Mbembe's "meditation on the peculiar institution ... loses track of the fact ... that the crucial aspects of 'the peculiar terror formation' that Mbembe attributes to the emergence of colonial rule are already institutionalized, perhaps more fundamentally, in and as the political- juridical structure of slavery."[7]

Further, for Sexton, the conceptualization of race within the death worlds that Mbembe presents not only lacks novelty but also devalues the integral practice of gendered subordination underlying state polities of terror and violence. To stress this point, Sexton refers to Saidiya Hartman's vital text (which he also says Mbembe mismanages), *Scenes of Subjection*, which examines the ways that the very status of the captive female within the system of American racial slavery serves as the originary structure of catastrophic violence licensing other paradigmatic structures for modern regimes of power. In this regard, Hartman examines the constitutive role that the manifold processes of violence, racialization, and domination that were enacted on captive female bodies informed the gendered category of "woman" creating ontological difference between black and white female subjectivity.

In doing so, Hartman obfuscates the very dominant conceptualization of woman as based on who qualifies within the normative conditions of white womanhood, which is traditionally characterized as universal or already known, and is, by extension, inaccessible to the enslaved female. As such, Hartman brings the captive enslaved woman to the fore and reckons with the contingent and diverse production of gender, "in the context of very different economies of power, property, kinship, race, and sexuality."[8] The sexual exploitation, subordination, and kinship negation levied upon the captive black female and the ways that racial and gender hierarchies relied on acts of sexual violence and injury toward the captive black female body—offenses not legally recognized or reproved by law because of the sanctioning of captive bodies as property—divergently produce the category "woman." The female slave as subsumed to the dominion of mere accumulation and fungible property cannot be ontologically aligned with a white woman who may be in a subordinate position such as an indentured laborer or a house servant, since white women are nonetheless still viewed as human;[9] hence, Hartman's point that a white woman's children can be legally described as "illegitimate" while the female enslaved is marked as "not legitimate." Therefore, Hartman (and Sexton) reposition gender and class as not intersecting with but directly produced through the social formation of racial slavery as the matrix of violently sorting humans from "anti-humans" and property from persons.

In a similar manner, Hortense Spillers' "Mama's Baby, Papa's Maybe" also critically examines race and the violence thrust upon captive bodies, raising the question of whether gender and sexuality can be applicable to the condition of the captive community since chattel slavery instigated an unvarnished and figurative *"theft of the body*—a willful and violent ...

severing of the captive body from its motive will, its active desire." Spillers continues, "under these conditions we lose at least gender difference in the outcome, and the female body and the male body become a territory of cultural and political maneuver, not at all gender-related, gender specific."[10] Thus, Spillers distinguishes the body and the flesh in the service of metaphorically differentiating captive and liberated subjects. On one hand, the body represents those subjects who are beneficiaries of dominant gender and kinship roles through which ascriptive designations are made intelligible. Yet, when captive bodies are subsumed as property, the body is violently disunited and reduced to "ungendered" flesh, which, as Alexander Weheliye notes "while representing both a temporal and conceptual antecedent to the body, is not a biological occurrence seeing that its creation requires an elaborate apparatus"[11] such as Spillers' perspicuous examples of "eyes beaten out, arms, backs, skulls branded, a left jaw, a right ankle, punctured; teeth missing, as the calculated work of iron, whips, chains, knives, the canine patrol, the bullet."[9] These carnages dispense "a kind of hieroglyphics of the flesh,"[10] relegating black existence to an indecipherable outlaw status to which the symbolic order, what she calls the "American grammar," depends on to inform its episteme and structure itself.[12]

Often categorized as "pessimistic," the deft analyses offered by Hartman and Spillers demonstrate the violent antagonism persistently shadowing and structuring blackness. Here, black bodies remain exposed to violence and death even as black people have acquired rights and liberties to their own bodies. Thus, in positioning persons racialized as black in the United States as being primarily constituted through the violence of slavery, blackness, then, is ontologically banned from the category of human being, rendering them socially dead in relation to all other racial positions in the modern West. Put slightly differently, the structural condition of blackness is indelibly marked by the provenance of slavery and its afterlife to which gratuitous violent offenses against black flesh remain omnipresent and immutable.

To be sure, these viewpoints advanced by Hartman, Spillers, Sexton, and others have been understood as constraining, negligently fueling stagnant ideologies concerning black pathology and suffering, which reduce black subjectivity to a life of totalizing death. This applies especially to critical meditations within the broad project of black studies that suggest we cannot elide the agency of the slave who dared to overcome its spatiotemporal, sociopolitical circumstances and "redeem the religion the master had profaned in his midst."[13] To do so, would be to disavow the peculiar history of black American life, a life that not only carries the historical weight of suffering and the perils of white anxiety and rage, but in addition, one in which black folk are not barricaded by these realities but exist as a progressive humanity—detached from the racial imaginary of the white psyche—that re-creates the world and not alienated from it. After all, as Weheliye tells us, there must be "the existence of alternative modes of life alongside the violence, subjection, and racialization that define the modern human."[11] In other words, black people have found transformative ways to live their best life and have personified the highest capacity for self-making and self-expression.

This territory is very familiar within the discourse of black theological circles to account for current real-world black identities that supersede blackness as being primarily defined through its relation to ontological death.[14] Specifically, it is *de rigueur* to be preoccupied with difference as black theological paradigms have (rightly) gone beyond liberation motifs in the service of not reducing black life/experience to forms of racial oppression/suffering but to consider the cultural differences and fluidity in contemporary black life, the contested and complex black subjectivities therein, as well as the necessity to foreground black bodies (and the multiple levels of power intersecting on them) in African American theological analysis. There is no space here to rehearse these developments nor is my purpose to offer critical perspectives on them in this work. However, I do make one necessary qualification, which animates what I'm pursuing here: In order to offer a sustained treatment of black life/death, I associate the notion of God with a meaningful engagement of blackness, whose space, time, and being remain undercut by structural violence inaugurated by racial slavery. This is to say that the lived experiences of black folk remain imperiled and devalued "by a racial calculus and a political arithmetic" as Hartman terms it, evidenced in the "death worlds" propagated from the nation's racial gestations, which perpetually dictate who may/should live and die; hence, life is yet carte blanche for black folk.[15] To provide a brief example, the contemporary phenomenon of ghetto and mass incarceration by which black existence continues to be excluded, quartered, and stockpiled as objects within a spatial boundary mirrors or is at least contiguous with slavery's commodified scene of buying and trading captive bodies transgressed as fungible property resorted to a statistical quantity interminably compliant for use and exchange.[16] Put simply, the nonsensical stockpiling of black bodies continues to reify the quandary for black folk successively abjecting blackness to liminal space established from kidnapping to the Middle Passage to enslavement to Jim/Jane Crow and to the tripartite eras of Reaganomics, "Crime" Bill Clinton Centrism, and the Bush War Years and so on. That is, despite the multifarious identities/differences in black life as well the intermittent social progress made in modernity, there still remains a unitary essence in black humanity, which entails dismantling a violent past wrought with black subjugation, which is inextricably interwoven into the present and will continue to suture and structure our postmodern world well into the future.

Hence, my belaboring here is intentional as it helps us to grapple with not so much the various ways black people perform their identities or the expressive capacities of black agency but in how black being is situated in the antagonistic structure of US power relations.[17] As a matter of fact, focusing on a theological account of race and racialization must be complex and capacious enough to mien the position of the subjected, which although is arguably understood as residing at the "bottom" or negatively cast as outside of civil society as socially dead; nevertheless, this erasure, exclusion, and violation fund a politics of being and relating, sounding, and imagining, that enact other non-black subjectivities in/and a parallel present. It is the Duboisian peculiarity that persistently foregrounds blackness—namely that of being necessary to whiteness and its statehood but not of it. At this juncture, then, my aim here is not to reconcile theological notions of hope with the pessimistic tendencies advanced by these critical perspectives but to consider its modality of analyses as a horizon to check, monitor, and ground the racialized black subject along the lines of slavery as an essential way of defining the production of racialization and its interface with state violence, death, and dehumanization. Ultimately, placing this process of racialization as shot through the binary of life and death provides insight into America's theopolitical dogmatics by which "black living" has not been its ultimate concern.

The impingement of racist deities: the shadow of theodicy

The issue laid bare has theodicean implications, for, as Sylvia Wynter suggests, race, amid its wide-ranging imports, is a bodicy. Reminiscent to Mbembe's proposition referenced earlier, Lewis Gordon clarifies Wynter's statement, suggesting that "the theodicean grammar of the world in which race was constituted is also, we should understand, one about the negotiation of life and death. Among its many consequences, race is about in one sense who lives and who dies. In another sense, its normative significance leads to a rephrasing of who is *supposed* to live and who to die."[18]

Gordon goes on to investigate the etymological manifestations of race through the lens of theodicy, especially at the level of nature and history, which concerns itself on what is permissible in the world contra to what is not. Such theodicean deliberations raise the question on why the world and history, affirmed as teologically good, becomes a slaughterhouse to those deemed impermissible. Hence, at the outset, Gordon primarily focuses on the foundational elements of theological naturalism, which were based on what was considered as natural and unnatural and served as a primary source to legitimate the supremacy of white modern Europe. "Natural" and "theological" were coterminous concepts and/or realities, which eventually created a raced classification system that designated a natural order of things to which white norms/traits constituted its base. Those groups marked epidermally by blackness were viewed as a deviation from this normativity—which was never quite severed from its deific stature—and were rationalized as unnatural, which consequently necessitated its extinguishment. According to Gordon, this mode of thinking is so robust that "Even secular societies may have a theodicean mode of rationalization, where the society itself or some system of treasured knowledge or values occupies the deific role. In theology this is called idolatry.... Idolatry offers a theodicean grammar or form. Its rationalization depends on rendering its contradictions *external*, which means, from a systemic point of view, systematically "dead."[19]

To reckon with the state violence inflicted on black communities, evidenced in the frequent exonerated police killings of black women and men in the United States, Stephen Finley and Biko Mandela Gray draw upon Gordon's reflections to address what they view as an immanent concern by which the state occupies a deific role, who as god, is the absolute judge of innocence or guilt and is legally and divinely authorized to terrorize black people.[20] They insist: "Black life, thus, has come to matter *negatively* within the context of our sociopolitical life, emerging as always already guilty in the eyes of a state that sanctions Black Death as necessary to the maintenance of social order—in other words, as a theodicy or defense of the goodness and sanctity of the state: the state-as-god *is* a white racist."[21]

Extending Jones' reflections to address a more immanent concern, Finley and Gray's conceptualization of the state *as a deity*, identifying it as a divine racist whose routinized violence toward black citizenry is often sanctioned through theodicean reasoning is useful in considering how black suffering/death becomes justified as the very presence of blackness negates from or threatens the "law and order" established by the all-powerful idolized state sanctioned to brazenly murder black life. Despite historic gains and setbacks, the ordination of this type of racist ideology against blackness catalyzed through the savage infringements of power and violence facilitated by the state has remained consistent since the debasement of chattel slavery. From obscene sexual intrusion—to the lash—to the rope—to the bullet, black bodies have been a whipping board in America's archive.

I am conceptualizing these fixated death-ridden or "necrotic" effects on black life, by drawing on Frantz Fanon's larger framing of the modern west's historical racial schema as "affective ankylosis." Ankylosis, a medical term for the stiffening, calcification, and rigidity of the joints resulting from the melding of bones, for Fanon describes the stagnant existence of white racism.[22] More specifically, if we consider US racial history that normatively segregates "Man"[23] and "Woman,"—primarily defined as white, supremacist, propertied, and heteropatriarchal—from its "others," an obstinate continuity in the nation's racial assembly persists subjecting blackness to wanton violence and literal, social and figurative death. To be clear, in his lecture on "Racism and Culture" Fanon would later go on to clarify that although the presence of racism remains static and immobile, its cultural manifestations are polyvalent often morphing into unidentifiable forms persistently haunting and vitiating American culture.[24] Thus, culturally, the nature of racism is a crude, ubiquitous, and self-organizing element, which evolves in mutable forms.

Accordingly, Fanon absolutely contests the notion that racism has vanquished as a consequence of human and societal progress evinced through so-called non-/post-racial mechanisms and practices to which race and racism are phantastically suppressed. For instance, the mere fact that American society advanced from the explicit scene of black bodies or "strange fruit" hanging decadently on poplar trees to the dramatic optic of inaugurating a black man into the highest political position on the very land to which those trees still sit, is not enough, for Fanon, to suggest that racism has been defeated. Rather, Fanon would implore us to examine the grand dynamism of racism within new cultural moments that subvert everyday life observing that: "[Racism] has had to renew itself, to adapt itself, to change its appearance. It has had to undergo the fate of the cultural whole that informed it.... For a time it looked as though racism had disappeared. This soul-soothing, unreal impression was simply the consequence of the evolution of forms of exploitation."[25]

Granting that the revivifying proliferations of racist discourses and formations in the United States' violent instated race/gender regimes are fluidly fertile and constantly emerging in a state of renewal, there exist other interconnected, racist deities to state violence that unconsciously/consciously rationalize and reinforce the stunning character of black suffering and death through what I shall call malignant and benign discourses. I'm defining the malignant as those cancerous constellations that are explicitly exposed through its exclusionary discourses composed of flagrant rhetoric, rallies, and rituals of retrieval that seek to reclaim the nation's more visible and pervasive white dominance. These malignant endeavors have no veil and are seen in plain sight and strive to, for example, "Make America Great Again." Although malignant manifestations are apparent throughout the course of American history, I am also interested in the benign, which are those ambiguous yet audacious discourses in which the structures of blackness and anti-blackness continue to entrench every speck of American democracy producing a regular death toll in black life despite loud claims of universal racial progression and racist regression.[26] My sights here are set on the Obama moment and the benign continuances in its wake, which evidently triggered, generated, and further exasperated nostalgic fantasy about race to which the predicate "post" became the grounding modifier for identities of difference, paradoxically impeding differentiation in the service of a politics of universalism. However, while a black presidency gave rise to a somewhat more diversified and inclusive democracy, it could not be severed from a racialized/racist script lucidly evident in the persistent production of racial and gendered hierarchies; the visual piling of dead black bodies at the hands of the state; and the election of a president whose exclusionary ethics are proudly touted evidenced in his proclamation that, "The only important thing is the unification of the people — because the other people don't mean anything."[27] These benign discourses, then, cannot escape the nation's time-honored fantasy and fear around race to which the constant production of Black Death and subjection resume business as usual.

Thus, I have chosen to look elsewhere to consider what I contend is a particular reoccurring deity that remains potent and dangerous to black being in our current sociopolitical atmosphere for its idolatry rationalizes Black Death through its benign nature and theodicean inferences: This is the deity of "exceptional universality." I'm defining exceptional universality as the teleological appeal to America's divine goodness and blessed exceptionality by which the nation's democratic ideals are cast as resources available to *all* despite its flagrant violations to the rule of moral concern. Often circulated and proclaimed in sociopolitical realms and daily mundane life, these teological appeals to America's universal goodness disregard the ways that violent racial and gender hierarchies are deeply embedded into the democratic project, a project whose governance consistently enacts material and physical death to black flesh, flesh seen as residing outside the borders of white heteronormativity. To push this problem even further, in conditions of emergency where petitions to America's moral ideals are fervently proclaimed amid political chaos and debates (say the polarizing election of Trump) or even in progressive movement discourses (say white liberal feminist or queer movements) blackness is only made visible (or allegorized and neutralized) within these discourses and narratives, which have had the pleasure of being bestowed a positioning *within* civil society due to not being racialized as black. At times, in the midst of such emphatic identification, black suffering and death are rationalized or suppressed altogether.

My concern is the ways that the logic of exceptionalist universalism often employs bourgeois Christianity and its contemporaneous myths/logics to rationalize the US nation's death grip of racial treason. The totalizing project of universality is the foundation of nascent Western modernity made possible by its intimate relation to a very political Christian religion. The epistemological and ontological privilege birthed by this relationship, to which whiteness or "Man" was reasoned to look like the universal, the one, the transcendent Christ, resulted in what Charles Long has defined as a process by which whites are assumed as a "colorless color" to which epistemological categories remained transparent, rendering a political status revelation that must be empirically, historically verified through the white lens. Such romantic universalism did not coalesce with a particular subjectivity, namely, blackness, which is always regarded as "colored" disjoined from conceptual personhood and rational cognizance. Christianity, securing universal dominion in time and space, solidified Christ's status as head of what was rationalized as the authentic human race (i.e., white humanity) followed by Christian claims to universal empire.[28]

These theological filters came to define and influence American "democracy," which was originally about an accomplishment of the chosen Teutonic race (white Anglo European North American), claiming that white men could only advance a democratic state because of their inherent sapient ability. The attainment of this democracy, and other so-called advanced civil societies, specifically required homogeneity so that citizenship was delineated to whites, their property, and privilege.[29] In order to legitimate such homogenous, economic, and sociopolitical aims (which were coded as universal), racial and gender hierarchies emerged and became deeply embedded into the democratic project through the violation of captive slave bodies, which in turn undergirded the nation's sociopolitical processes.[30] Thus, if we grant that there are necropolitical tendencies within U.S. democracy, then, perhaps, this concept can also be characterized as "necrotheological" in the nation's marriage to assign and cosign power and life to its version of "all" (read: whiteness) to the point that titanic death, in slow and premature forms, becomes reasoned and acceptable by which disposability is normatively sentenced (exacted) to black populations.

The problem, then, is that the claim of "universality" and the defense of its goodness therein which is frequently projected in sociopolitical realms dissimulate the underlying supremacist history of American democracy, neutralize the singular experience and position of blackness, abolish distinctions by transcending racial and gender boundaries and flout the specificity of anti-blackness in the service of galvanizing an imperfect American union and its dream. Russ Castranovo, in his work on the nineteenth-century archive, defines this modal process as "necro ideology," a reasoning that deadens and disembodies the material histories of slavery, exclusion, and violence in US democracy in order to establish the liberal concepts of freedom and citizenship as concrete and universally accessible.[31]

In light of this, though it is well established that the violent imposition of slavery and its afterlife shadow black life, the historical project of universalism has been at the crux of the American democratic project continually seeking to thrive and reinvent itself. This project of universality, which credits itself with the capacity to achieve democratic ideals of freedom, justice, and equality, has nevertheless burdened black people, with its declarations that progress, freedom, and individuality have been realized or are attainable because of so-called high moments in history relegating and numbing the capricious sociopolitical status of black life. Again, Hartman's work is helpful. Hartman unsettles the full-blown liberatory tenor of the emancipation by framing it as a non-event since slavery served as an undulating menace that continued to shadow black life after the emancipation. Recognizing that black life is not unscathed by slavery's impact, Hartman stresses the precise teleological inference of blackness insofar as the candid aphorism suggests "white folks present is always black folks future." Her insistence on "the double bind of freedom" describes black freedom as being: "freed from slavery and free of resources, emancipated and subordinated, self-possessed and indebted, equal and inferior, liberated and encumbered, sovereign and dominated, citizen and subject."[32] Hartman's explanation of the deeply paradoxical and encumbered nature of black life is not only evinced post-emancipation but has consistently undergirded black folk's claims of freedom from the first reconstruction through to the afterlife of a black president.

It is worth mentioning that Obama himself chose to, by virtue of managing America's empire, exercise and sustain America's exceptional universalism. As Cathy Cohen points out, the state did not transform its traits after Obama's successful election; rather, its guise was merely racialized with a black body leading and facilitating its system of white power structures.[33] Obama, who Melayne T. Price identifies as the "race whisperer" attributed to his unique ability to simultaneously conjure narratives of blackness, whiteness, and migration, was able to frame his own personal narrative as universal (and thus race-less). According to Price, "The success of [Obama's] campaign pivoted on Obama's ability to play up universal messages that promote cross-racial appeal. He relied on race-neutral themes or themes related to aspects of African American history that have become apart of America's universal understanding of itself....that so-called postracial rhetoric is decidedly not race neutral and instead reinforces the existing racial order."[34]

This would be easy for Obama as the black faith tradition has, like the larger project of American theo-politics, drawn upon biblical tropes for faith and self-understanding and social political purposes. For example, while American exceptionalism has, for the most part, relied on the narrative's theme of "chosenness" and "conquest," black people drew upon the narrative's bondage—liberation paradigm to not only understand their condition and plight but also built a democratic vision around the narrative by taking up the American nation's ideas of race, gender, and citizenship, which informed expressions of black culture that continued long after emancipation. The vocabularies of "chosenness," "liberation," "wilderness," "Promised Land," "mountaintop," "equality," the "beloved community," and "the dream realized" are contextualized by the specific political realities of Jim/Jane Crow, the Ballot, and a host of other democratic ideals.

Undeniably, the advent of Obama's arrival marked new significant meanings for African American biblical hermeneutics, particularly its shift from the "Moses" generation leading its people out of bondage to the "Joshua" generation, which sees themselves entering into the Promised Land. For instance, on the night of the 2008 presidential election, Christine King Farris, the sister of Martin Luther King Jr. spoke to a massive audience at the Ebenezer Baptist Church proclaiming, "As he [King] predicted the night before he left us, 'I may not be with you, but as a people we will reach the Promised Land,' that Promised Land was realized Tuesday. Yes, it is our Promised Land."[35] If we consider the meaning of Farris' declaration, namely: "That Promised Land was realized," especially her moving the narrative from anticipation to realization, it is palpable to say that even though the symbol of Obama's election signaled black progress, it wasn't enough to transform anti-black racist ideas and the devaluation of black bodies. Even more importantly because Obama led, maintained, and facilitated America's system of white power structures, black folks have had to reckon with the reality that the American presidential election of a man with black skin doesn't ensure black freedom/flourishing or access to the American "Promised Land." Rather, the gaze on these categories of black suffering becomes in a sense so mundane (faddish adages if you will) that they ironically become performed, commoditized, romanticized, and popularized in American culture in a way that doesn't evoke any radical social change; on the contrary, they valorize and reinforce the language and grammar of black subjection and captivity.

What's at stake is the degree to which Christian tropes and themes continue to serve as instruments in the sociopolitical arena to propagate the underlying structures of universality, which consequently tend to *rationalize* black suffering and death in concrete and affective ways. It is here that pastoral Christian logics become pervasive forcing us to think critically about the ways they play a part in rationalizing Black Death in sociopolitical realms.

A case in point: black execution at mother Emmanuel
On June 17, 2015, Susie Jackson, Ethel Lance, Sharonda Coleman-Singleton, Cynthia Hurd, Myra Thompson, Clementa Pinckney, Tywanza Sanders, Depayne Middleton-Doctor, and Daniel Simmons Jr. were executed at the hands of a white racist and domestic terrorist during a bible study at the historic Emmanuel AME Church in Charleston, SC. On the day of his bond hearing, the unapologetic white killer, who admitted that it was nothing wrong with him psychologically, sat in the courtroom room to hear the pained relatives of the victims express their insurmountable grief, anger, and shock on the premature death of their beloved ones. During this courtroom spectacle, the presiding judge made an outlandish plea to the public stating: "We have victims, nine of them. But we also have victims on the other side. There are victims on this young man's side of the family. No one would have ever thrown them into the whirlwind of events that they have been thrown into." Of course, the public attention toward the killer's family is in no way parallel to the victims' families grappling with the grotesque and senseless murder of their loved ones attributable to black hatred. Nevertheless, the judge attempted to bring a sense of neutrality to court, leveling black pain with the shame and embarrassment of the killer's family.

The public was in deep awe of the victims families' expressions of forgiveness toward the killer—to the point of disbelief—, especially the daughter of Ethel Lance, Nadine Collier, who boldly professed as a woman of (Christian) faith, "I forgive you" on a worldwide stage. The circumstances in that moment reflect the historical relationship between blackness, forgiveness, and death, which as Letoya Eaves contends is undergirded by a necessity for survival: "Given the structural and social ills that form the North American landscape, a choice to forgive becomes one of the only options for black people. Forgiveness is a tool for survivability for black people and communities to function in a regular state of pain."[36]

The following week, Obama delivered the eulogy (also a political exhibition) for Rev. Clementa Pinckney, Emmanuel's slain pastor. The president, in this moment of unbearable black tragedy and black suffering, was able to "wield racial appeals as instruments of mobilization to bring together diverse and divergent groups" in his rehearsed manner.[37] Flanked by black clergy whose visible demeanor expressed pride and delight with Obama's presence, the president centered himself in the pulpit and delivered words of benevolent comfort, consensus, and correctives. Describing the black church as the nation's "beating heart," Obama reflected on the remarkable contribution of the black faith's tradition to the nation's problematic racial history, specifically pointing out its racial bias and division as well as its difficulty in discussing issues related to race, thereby declaring that the country must move forward to embrace each other's histories and experiences. In so doing, Obama praised the nation for rallying together with "big-hearted generosity and, more importantly, with a thoughtful introspection and self-examination that we so rarely see in public life."

Obama would then foreground his eulogy in the Christian notion of "grace" and "forgiveness" stating that the killer:

> didn't know *he was being used by God*. Blinded by hatred, the alleged killer *could*
>
> *not see* the grace surrounding Reverend Pinckney and that Bible study group...
>
> The alleged killer could have never anticipated the way the families of the fallen would respond when they saw him in court – in the midst of unspeakable grief, with words of forgiveness.... As a

> nation, out of this terrible tragedy, God has visited grace upon us, *for he has allowed us to see where we've been blind. He has given us the chance, where we've been lost, to find our best selves.*[38]

Obama's quick slippage of invoking divine providence via grace alongside Black Death and suffering in order for the inherently good nation to "see" its unjust racist culture has problematic theodicean inferences, that is, too often it takes explicit forms of Black Death—in tragic and terrible appearances—instead of the everyday concrete and amorphous ones, to awaken America of its attachment to white supremacy and anti-black racism. To renew and restore America's moral consciousness, which is divinely exemplified to be in the end "good," dead black bodies need not be rationalized or romanticized as the sacrificial impetus for the nation's altar call to redemption. Such thinking has untoward effects in cosmic proportions, as slain black bodies were never divinely appointed to provide clarity to a diseased societal endemic that has been tangibly diagnosed and is transparently seen. Although forgiveness was utilized to uplift the legacy of the slain; the quick shift to blindness endangers blackness as it is used to redeem the legacy of America in the service of sanitizing whiteness over and against Black Death in its expediency of proclaiming universal grace.

Moreover, the emphasis on blindness as teamed up with the notion of forgiveness in Obama's political remarks, as well as his media lauded rendition of "Amazing Grace" specifically the lyrics, "I once was lost but now I'm found. Was blind but now I see" have biblical origins, especially in Christ's plea to his father to "forgive them for they know not what they do" during the dramatic scene of his execution at Golgotha. Indicating a sense of ignorance among Christ's so-called inculpable offenders, the narrative chronicles that the divine extends to humanity salvation, grace, and forgiveness through the murder of his only son. To be sure, there is an incredible fidelity to relate the terms of black suffering with the paradoxical symbol of the cross as this symbol represents a martyred Jesus conquering death in the end. As James Cone puts it in his compelling work, *The Cross and the Lynching Tree*: "A symbol of death and defeat, God turned it into a sign of liberation and new life. The cross is the most empowering symbol of God's loving solidarity with the 'least of these,' the unwanted in society who suffer daily from great injustices."[39] At this point, it is not my aim to discuss whether there is redemptive power in Christ's sacrificial act, which has been vividly discussed in theological projects, especially in Womanist and Feminist discourses.[40] However, I will contend that in order to confront America's sin of anti-black racism and white supremacy and illuminate the opacity of these transgressions in the service of authentic reconciliation and just healing, we must exercise a theology of refusal that resists the suggestion that America is "blind." To not do so is to succumb to the necroideological tendency to express "the need for the *innocent* black subject to be victimized by a racist state in order to *see* the racism of the racist state...."[41] More specifically, the nation must not use the expediency of blindness as a prophylaxis against accountability but express repentance not based on grammars of ignorance or loss of sight but in its sheer culpability on its wages of terror inflicted onto black flesh.

Thus, if we relate the terms of the cross to the crucified realities of black social life, a theological praxis of refusal can be enacted to read the cross beyond mere identity and performance and position it as an imposturous yet concrete event that requires a disposition of defiance at its material existence. This means that we refuse the absurd assertion that God must utilize black suffering to forge redemptive, salvific change among America's so-called universal good. This involves refashioning a Christology and Soteriology of praxis that defies the notion that the death of Jesus had to happen to bring about new life recognizing that the original structuring of the world before the engulfing and hijacking of white political and theological fantasy was that the Christ came so that we can have life and to live life abundantly (John 10:10). This is to say that at the moment when God became flesh, a salvific, primordial consciousness of an intervening, freeing, loving God was disclosed via the "essence" of the Incarnate Christ yielding an absolute dependence on God within black subjectivity, which, means that black people are compelled to live, have lived, and have always been predestined to live despite the realities of suffering and death. In so doing, black people have the ingenious ability to defy recurring and new manifestations of racial subjugation and the multiple levels of power imposing on black life seeking to shape our sense of self and constrain what we can be.

In this regard, our current sociopolitical climate requires a defiance at the conditions of participation in the violent archive of America's carceral logics recognizing that just as we live in the afterlife of the cross which illumines the opacity of sin, we also live in and through what Christina Sharpe describes "the afterlife of property," whereby the gratuitous violence of slavery and its antagonisms still tug at black life. Consequently, Sharpe suggests that black folk must undergo a process of "wake work" or "staying in the wake" understanding "that we are Black peoples in the wake with no state or nation to protect us, with no citizenship bound to be respected, and to position us in the modalities of Black life lived in, as, under, despite Black Death: to think and be and act from there."[42] Thus, Sharpe insists that we attend to the spatial, legal, psychic, and material realities of the grave that resist peeling away at the horrific evidence of black subjection, violence and death. As David Marriot describes, it is the "need to affirm affirmation through negation... not as a moral imperative... but as a psychopolitical necessity."[43] Thus, this wake work finds that this process of negation is a redemptive component to liberation insofar as acknowledging the absurdity of the grave's existence and its graveyard politics making no room for appeals to blindness, ignorance, or romanticized redemption concerning black suffering.

Such wake work is exemplified in Harriet Jacob's *Incidents in the life of a Slave Girl*, which portrays Linda, a fugitive slave returning to the graveyard where her mother and father are buried and describes the necrotic conditions surrounding her:

> The graveyard was in the woods, and twilight was coming on. Nothing broke the death-like stillness except the occasional twitter of a bird. My spirit was overawed by the solemnity of the scene. For more than ten years I had frequented this spot, but never had it seemed to me so sacred as now. A black stump, at the head of my mother's grave, was all that remained of a tree my father had planted. His grave was marked by a small wooden board, bearing his name, the letters of which were nearly obliterated. I knelt down and kissed them, and poured forth a prayer to God for guidance and support in the perilous step I was about to take. As I passed the wreck of the old meeting house, where, before Nat Turner's time, the slaves had been allowed to meet for worship, I seemed to hear my father's voice come from it, bidding me not to tarry till I reached freedom or the grave. I rushed on with renovated hopes. My trust in God had been strengthened by that prayer among the graves.[44]

Linda's spiritual meditation on the irrational scene of death surrounding her as well as the stirring depth of her father's voice prompt a resolute disavowal to not let death have the final word. Among the graves that housed her mother and father's black bones, she conjures an inward divine consciousness that ignites a forceful tenacity that she is predestined to live freely and to persist until freedom is fulfilled or death greets her.

Notes
1. Jenson, Robert, *A Theology in Outline: Can These Bones Live* (New York: Oxford University Press, 2016), p. 11.
2. Wilderson III, Frank B., Samira Spatzek, and Paula von Gleich, 2016, "'The Inside-Outside of Civil Society': An Interview with Frank B. Wilderson, III," *Black Studies Papers* 2(1), p. 7.
3. Jenson, Robert, "A Theology in Outline," p. 11.
4. Vargas, João Costa and Joy James, "Refusing Blackness-as-Victimization: Trayvon Martin and the Black Cyborgs," in *Pursuing Trayvon Martin: Historical Contexts and Contemporary Manifestations of Racial Dynamics*, ed. George Yancy and Janine Jones (Lanham: Lexington Books, 2013), pp. 193-204.
5. Mbembe, Achille, 2003, "Necropoilitics," trans. Libby Meintjes, *Public Culture* 15(1), p. 40. Italics in the original.
6. Vincent Lloyd has suggested that Mbembe's theoretical offerings including his telling of the historical triumvirate relation between racialization, colonization, and Christianity are valuable to the discourse of black theology. See Lloyd, 2016, "Achille Mbembe as Black Theologian" in *Modern Believing* 57(3), pp. 241-251. For Lloyd, Mbembe and the discourse of black theology (especially James Cone) share similar impulses especially understanding the Judeo-Christian tradition in unique relationship with sites of black suffering. For Mbembe, the post-colonial, African and black experience as sites of suffering (which are not reducible to this status), all provide "the strongest possibility of encountering and fully appreciating the death of God (of God-in-the-human.)..." (249). Further, these sites inspire hope that resurrection can occur bringing about new life to resist the Western symbolic order of things as humanity realizes new life through "reason, emotion, imagination, and practical wisdom." Lloyd sees value in a particular dynamism within Mbembe's work that is able to foreground "the death and resurrection of God as human—that takes different forms at different places and times, just as oppression takes different forms at different places and times. Africa may now be the privileged site for theological reflection, but this has not always been the case and it will not always be the case; similarly, the particular way that reflection comes into language will change." (250). However, because of the incontestable role of gender violence in chattel slavery, especially the inhumane violence toward the captive female body which informed other categorical identities with the US racial framework still prevalent to this day, I do consider the black American experience as not only singular, but will remain a (not the only) privileged site of suffering incapable of being fully universalized due to its positioning within the regime of US power relations. In this way, if we consider the absurd violence dispersed onto the captive black female, this then may implicate how we view the scandal of Christ's death and resurrection differently from Mbembe's theological resolve. I briefly discuss this point on Christ's crucifixion in this

essay and will expand more fully in future work. Further, this concern on atonement theories concerning black women has been brought forth in Womanist theological discourse. See for example Williams, Delores, *Sisters in the Wilderness: The Challenge of Womanist God-Talk* (Maryknoll, NY: Orbis Books, 1993).

7. Sexton, Jared, 2010, "People of Colorblindness on the Afterlives of Slavery," *Social Text* 28 (2), pp. 32-3.

8. Hartman, Saidiya, *Scenes of Subjection: Terror, Slavery and Self-Making in America* (New York: Oxford University Press, 1997), p. 60.

9. Although the phrasing is changed here slightly, this point explicitly comes from Frank Wilderson in his interview with Hartman, Saidiya, 2003, "The Position of the Unthought," *Qui Parle* 13(2), p. 186.

10. Spillers, Hortense J., 1987, "Mama's Baby, Papa's Maybe: An American Grammar Book," *Diacritics* 17(2), p. 67.

11. Weheliye, Alexander, G., *Habeas Viscus: Racializing Assemblages, Biopolitics, and Black Feminist Theories of the Human* (Durham: Duke University Press, 2014), p. 39.

12. Ibid., 68.

13. Thurman, Howard, *Deep River and the Negro Spiritual Speaks of Life and Death* (Mills College: Eucalyptus, 1945), p. 34. For alternative proposals to pessimistic thought, see Robinson Cedric, *Black Marxism, The Making of the Black Radical Tradition*, 2nd ed. (Chapel Hill: University of North Carolina Press, 2000). See Moten, Fred, 2013, "The Subprime and the Beautiful," *African Identities* 11(2), p. 242. See also Moten, Fred, and Stefano Harvey, *The Undercommons: Fugitive Planning and Black Study* (New York: Minor Compositions, 2013) Also see, Carter, J. Kameron and Sarah Jane Cervenak, 2016, "Black Ether," *The New Centennial Review* 16(2), pp. 203-24. See also Carter and Cervenak, 2017, "Untitled and Outdoors: Thinking with Saidiya Hartman," *Women & Performance: A Journal of Feminist Theory*, (27), pp. 45-55.

14. A prime example is Anderson, Victor, *Beyond Ontological Blackness: An Essay on African American Religious and Cultural Criticism* (New York: Continuum Publishing, 1995).

15. Hartman, *Lose Your Mother: A Journey Along the Atlantic Slave Route* (New York: Farrar, Straus, Giroux, 2006), p. 6.

16. R.L. "Wanderings of the Slave: Black Life and Social Death," in *Mute*, June 5, 2013, http://www.metamute.org/editorial/articles/wanderings-slave-black-life-and-social-death

17. Again, on this point, I am heavily indebted to the theoretical lens of Afro-pessimism and especially appreciative of Frank Wilderson's meticulous analysis on the "structure of U.S. antagonisms" in his work *Red, Black and White: Cinema and the Structure of U.S. Antagonisms* (Durham: Duke University Press, 2010).

18. Gordon, Lewis, 2013, "Race, Theodicy, and the Normative Emancipatory Challenges of Blackness," *The South Atlantic Quarterly* 112(4), p. 725.

19. Gordon, Lewis, "Race, Theodicy and the Normative Emancipatory Challenges of Blackness," 727.

20. Finley, Stephen C. and Gray, Biko Mandela, 2015, "God Is a White Racist: Immanent Atheism as a Religious Response to Black Lives Matter and State-Sanctioned Anti-Black Violence," *Journal of Africana Religions* 3(4), pp. 443-53.

21. Finley and Gray, "God *Is* a White Racist," p. 447.

22. Fanon, Frantz, *Black Skin and White Masks*, trans. Charles Lamm Markmann (London: Pluto Press, 2008), p. 92.
23. See Wynter, Sylvia, 1993, "Unsettling the Coloniality of Being/Power/Truth/Freedom: Towards the Human, After Man, Its Overrepresentation—An Argument," *The New Centennial Review* 3(3), pp. 257-337.
24. Fanon, Frantz, "Racism and Culture," in *Toward the African Revolution: Political Essays*, trans. Haakon Chevalier (New York: Grove Press, 1964).
25. Fanon, "Racism and Culture," 32, 37.
26. Here, I am indebted to Kaiama L. Glover's analysis on benign discourses in the "First World's" anxious relationship to the "Third World," which, according to Glover, despite these discourses being presented as deracialized, blackness is always seen as "other." See Glover, Kaiama L., 2017, "Flesh Like One's Own": Benign Denials of Legitimate Complaint," *Public Culture* 29(2), pp. 235-60.
27. Cited in Müller, Jan Werner, "Populism and Constitutionalism" in Cristobal Rovira Kaltwasser, Paul A. Taggart, Paulina Ochoa Espejo, and Pierre Ostiguy, eds., *The Oxford Handbook on Populism* (Oxford: Oxford University Press, 2018), p. 593.
28. See Mbembe, Achille, *On the Post Colony* (Berkeley: University of California Press, 2001), see especially chapter 6; Jennings, Willie James, *The Christian Imagination, Theology and the Origins of Race* (New Haven: Yale University Press, 2010); Carter, J. Kameron, *Race: A Theological Account* (New York University Press, 2008). See also Douglas, Kelly Brown, *Stand Your Ground: Black Bodies and the Justice of God* (Maryknoll, NY: Orbis Books Press, 2015), see especially part 1.
29. Hawkesworth, Mary, *Embodied Power: Demystifying Disembodied Politics* (New York: Routledge, 2016).
30. Ibid.
31. Castronovo, Russ, *Necro Citizenship: Death, Eroticism, and the Public Sphere in the Nineteenth Century United States* (Durham: Duke University Press, 2001).
32. Hartman, *Scenes of Subjection*, p. 117.
33. Cohen, Cathy, "Afterword: When Will Black Lives Matter? Neoliberalism, Democracy, and the Queering of American Activism in the Post Obama Era," in Travis L. Gosa and Erik Nielson, eds., *The Hip Hop and Obama Reader* (New York: Oxford University Press, 2015).
34. Price, Melayne T., *Barack Obama and The Political Uses of Race* (New York: New York University Press, 2016), p. 18.
35. The above vignette was taken from http://www.boston.com/news/nation/articles/2008/11/10/black_congregants_reflect_on_obamas_victory/. (Accessed on November 10, 2008).
36. Eaves, Letoya E., 2016, "We Wear a Mask," *Southern Geographer* 56(1), p. 23.
37. Price, *The Race Whisperer*, p. 19.
38. Obama, Barack, "Remarks by the President in Eulogy for the Honorable Reverend Clementa Pinckney." June 26, 2015. https://obamawhitehouse.archives.gov/the-press-office/2015/06/26/remarks-president-eulogy-honorable-reverend-clementa-pinckney (Accessed on June 30, 2015). Italics Mine.
39. Cone, James H., *The Cross and the Lynching Tree* (Maryknoll, NY: Orbis Books Press, 2011), p. 156.
40. See, for example, Williams, Delores, *Sisters of the Wilderness*; Terrell, JoAnne Marie, *Power in the Blood? The Cross in the African American Experience* (Maryknoll, NY: Orbis Books Press,

1998); Douglas, Kelly Brown, *Stand Your Ground*, chapter 5. See also Ruether, Rosemary Radford, *Introducing Redemption in Christian Feminism*, Introductions in Feminist Theology, no. 1 (Sheffield: Sheffield Academic, 1998), chapter 6.

41. Hartman and Wilderson III, "A Position of the Unthought," p. 189.

42. Sharpe, Christina, *In the Wake: On Blackness and Being* (Durham: Duke University Press, 2016), p. 22.

43. Marriott, David, *Haunted Life: Visual Culture and Black Modernity* (New Brunswick: Rutgers University Press, 2007), p. 273.

44. Jacobs, Harriet Ann, *Incidents in the Life of a Slave Girl* (Cambridge: Harvard University Press, 2000), p. 138.

CROSSCURRENTS

WHEN HOPE APPEARED IN FLESH
From Black Power to Barack Obama and the Spirit of the American Jeremiad

Terrence L. Johnson

When the tall, lanky 24-year-old Stokely Carmichael stood between hundreds of fatigued Black activists and the dozens of white police officers encroaching upon them in Greenwood, Mississippi, his booming voice diverted their locked eyes. "This is the 27th time I have been arrested—I ain't going to jail no more, I ain't going to jail no more," cried out Carmichael, the new head of the Student Nonviolent Coordinating Committee (SNCC), who had been arrested earlier in the day for his role in organizing the march. The marchers perked up, gesturing with waved hands and shouts of support as Carmichael's speech echoed a familiar black preacher's cadence. He then silenced the enthusiastic supporters with four chilling words: "We want black power!" The words were arresting, nearly as suffocating as the fear of being beaten by police officers and bitten by their dogs. Carmichael shouted black power again. Some gasped at the phrase, and others cheerfully clapped their hands and shouted back "Black Power!"[1]

When Dr. Martin Luther King, Jr., received word of Carmichael's unprecedented speech, his heart sank. He felt betrayed by his protégé in what appeared to be an effort to undermine King's and the Southern Christian Leadership's approach toward garnering group political rights. Interestingly enough, King was not so bothered by either the rhetoric or the political and economic message of Black Power; instead, he feared the employment of Black Power as a political tool and strategy would sabotage the Civil Rights Movement's effort to secure meaningful legislation for blacks and further marginalize moderate and progressive whites from the coalition work he believed was necessary for fulfilling social justice.

The disagreement between King and Carmichael was a fight for the direction of Black politics in the United States. They stood at the intersection of a political movement struggling to obtain an identity and social coherence. Once dominated by Christian symbols, puritan relics, a theory of nonviolence, racial uplift ideology, and the politics of respectability, the core philosophical principles of the civil rights agenda faced increasing interrogation from groups like SNCC as the growing anxiety over the Vietnam war and economic exploitation widened. To be sure, this was a debate between two ambitious and astute men, a fight for the right to steer the imagination of the race for the next generation. Underlying this motivation was patriarchal normative commitments; that is, the subtext of economically powerless men dueling for control over the rhetorical and symbolic vestiges of power among a landless people, the bastard children of the nation. King characterized this point aptly: It was a debate over (Black) national consciousness and the (moral) conscience of a nation and people.

Black Power was a direct attack against King's moral egalitarian vision. Framed by a notion that all persons are deserving of respect by virtue of their personhood and rational capacity, King's early political project assumed the acquisition of political rights would cement the political status of Blacks based on equality and respect. In a lengthy *New York Times* essay, which was later published in *Where Do We Go from Here: Chaos or Community*, King challenged the political and moral veracity of Black Power. He fundamentally argued against the viability of a political strategy that alienates allies. For instance, before King left the Meredith march, he overheard among the young participants debates concerning the veracity of nonviolence in a social context like Mississippi, where violence against Blacks was a cultural pastime. Moreover, they wondered aloud why "white liberals" were marching alongside them, "invading" their political movement. King seemed shocked by their remarks.

> I guess I should have not been surprised. I should have known that in an atmosphere where false promises are daily realities, where deferred dreams are nightly facts, where acts of unpunished violence toward Negroes are a way of life, nonviolence would eventually be seriously questioned.[2]

King acknowledged the existential need for Black Power. It emerged from what he called a "cry of disappointment," born from the "wounds of despair."³ But he feared the bitterness would create existential despair and lead to political and moral blindness, a frame of thinking that would foreclose political friendships and solidarity across racial and ethnic lines.

More than half a century later, the debate between Black liberalism (traditional civil rights voting rights strategy) and Black leftist politics (the inheritors of Black Power) haunts Black politics and the legacy of the Barack Obama presidency. After decades of domestic turmoil, U.S.-led wars in the Middle East, and rollercoaster dips and turns in the economy, the United States seemed ripe in 2007 for a new message and messenger. Hope appeared in plain sight without much fanfare. Similar to the infamous spirit eerily emerging from the swamp in Toni Morrison's acclaimed *Beloved*, Barack Obama surfaced in public life without the usual acclaim one might expect for a Harvard-trained Black law professor and U.S. Senator. According to a March 2007 article in the *Guardian*, Black voters even after his enormously praised 2004 DNC speech still supported Senator Hillary Clinton three-to-one. Obama landed "the blessing of Oprah Winfrey and Halle Barry but has yet to get an endorsement from any of the major black political figures."⁴ But Obama's retrieval of the American jeremiad and Black preaching style captured the nation's imagination and reinvigorated national conversation on race and politics.

Establishing a political campaign on a message of hope, Obama borrowed the best of the counter-public tradition of the Black church to recast the existing political narrative of fear and isolationism following the George W. Bush presidency. When Obama announced his presidential campaign at Abraham Lincoln's birthplace in Springfield, Illinois in 2007, the then-Senator centered his talk on the need to build "a more perfect union," invoking the jeremiad narrative as a tool to restore a broken land torn by discord and despair. "In the face of a politics that's shut you out, that's told you to settle, that's divided us for too long, you believe we can be one people, reaching for what's possible, building that more perfect union."⁵ Similar to previous invocations of the jeremiad by presidential candidates, Obama warns the nation of its social and political shortcomings, while pointing to the great promise of prosperity and peace awaiting the nation if it heeds the call to justice. Unlike his predecessors, however, Obama falls short of proclaiming America as the greatest nation on earth. Instead, he recasts hope as a tool to correct previous social harms.

Beginning with his announcement to run for the highest office of the land, we can see a striking theological and political reorientation of the jeremiad: invoking a lamentation to inspire "an unyielding faith" in promoting "change" with and through the hands of individual Americans.

> The genius of our founders is that they designed a system of government that can be changed. And we should take heart, because we've changed this country before. In the face of tyranny, a band of patriots brought an Empire to its knees. In the face of secession, we unified a nation and set the captives free. In the face of Depression, we put people back to work and lifted millions out of poverty. We welcomed immigrants to our shores, we opened railroads to the west, we landed a man on the moon, and we heard a King's call to let justice roll down like water, and righteousness like a mighty stream.[6]

Taken at face value, this is a resounding rebuke of moral complacency, a condemnation of Americans who stand, sit and watch in silence as institutions violate and harm the least off. In other words, Obama chastises *all* Americans for their complicity in oppressing their neighbor, the stranger, and the foreigner. At the symbolic level, the location of Obama's kickoff campaign is remarkable. While President Lincoln is heralded for signing the Emancipation Declaration in 1863, which freed slaves in the Confederacy, Lincoln's first and major emphasis on saving the Union nonetheless symbolizes the nation's ambiguous understanding of slavery and its relationship to the descendants of African slaves. Slavery was a necessary and protected evil until it threatened the long-term political and economic development of the United States. Barry Schwartz writes in *Society*, "Even to say that Lincoln considered emancipation secondary to the Union is to overstate its importance, for he never thought about emancipation independently of reunification."[7] A safer, politically appropriate backdrop of a concert hall, farm, or office suite would have mirrored his predecessors. His departure from the tradition is both noteworthy and symbolic. The same can be said when Obama declined an offer by journalist Tavis Smiley to attend the highly successful and popular Annual State of the Black Union Conference. (His opponent Senator Hillary Clinton attended the conference, where she received thunderous support.) Obama's absence can be taken as a rejection of representational Black leadership and possibly as a sign of his dubious relationship to mainline Black male leadership.

Herein lies the argument I want to explore: Barack Obama's presidency inaugurates a moral imagination that upends and reconfigures the American jeremiad to disrupt the binary dividing liberal and conservative politics. His moral vision of hope indicts both Black representational politics of racial solidarity and cultural conservative ideologies rooted in forms of antiblack racism, xenophobia, bigotry, and sexism. In both instances, appeals to individualism, crude racial ontologies, and American exceptionalism emerge and take precedence at the expense of building sustained conversations on how to transform institutions, religious fundamentalism, nationalism, and ethnocentrism. This moral vision is influenced by American religion, specifically the Black church and Black preaching, shaped by the American jeremiad, and informed by debates between Black liberals (King) and Black leftists (Carmichael).

Obama's moral imagination is an invitation to lean into the boundaries of our familiar terrain, hoping against all odds that our collective and individual political struggles and resistance against oppression will expand, ever so gingerly, the horizons of our social, economic, and cultural possibilities. It is a moral imagination encompassed by a vision of political actors entangled in the messy work of disrupting and destabilizing tyranny and abusive institutions. This is the *radical* hope steering Obama's campaign, a strategy shaped by a theo-political vision of an "unyielding faith" in wo/man's capacity to overshadow evil and transform institutions.

To be sure, President Obama's enduring message of hope, optimism, and lamentation during his two-term presidency faced fierce persecution from among his own party and triggered an insurrection within both the Tea and Republican parties that stalled the president in the congressional legislature and federal judiciary. From questioning his place of birth and challenging his solidarity with Blacks to calling the self-identified Christian a Muslim, the barrage of criticisms from all corners of the American landscape points to a singular but shifting theme in American culture: affected racism, or the decision to choose self-injury and societal deterioration instead of policies and practices that could lead to racial justice. A case in point: Obama's victories would not have happened without multiracial and multiclass coalitions. He never won the majority of white votes and barely made a dent into the (white) evangelical vote. Yet, his successor, Donald Trump, ran a campaign steered by racist, xenophobic, and sexist rants and landed the overwhelming majority of white evangelical voters (80 percent) and the majority of white women (52 percent). Trump's victory is characterized as the symbol of the rise of the white working class and voters seeking political and economic change. And while the rhetoric is emblematic of the political vocabulary subgroups of Americans leaned on to justify their vote for Trump, I believe Trump's victory exemplifies a broader decline in the American jeremiad in national politics and a return of overt racism and discriminatory practices in public life. Lawrence Bobo reminds us that "a core if not the primary factor in Donald Trump's electoral success and much of what so far appears to be his policy agenda rests on deep-rooted racism and white supremacist presumptions in US institutions and culture."[8]

As we reflect on the legacy of the Obama presidency and the normalization of xenophobia, antiblack racism, sexual assault, and bigotry in the public sphere during the campaign and subsequent presidency of Donald Trump, the conversation demands an attention to the competing and overlapping roles religion and race play among white evangelical Christians and moderate Republicans in shaping debates on economic anxiety, immigration, and elitism in government and the media. Both white evangelicals and moderate Republicans often justify their support of an openly racist, xenophobic, and accused sexual predator based on preexisting norms and principles that align with their guiding moral and political beliefs. On the one hand, Trump's commitment to nominating conservative and pro-life jurists to the Supreme Court and federal courts attracted white evangelicals. On the other hand, Trump's call to overhaul taxes for corporations and the middle-class in the name of economic growth won over moderate Republicans. But what's missing from this narrative is the extent to which the majority of white Americans, at least since the election of Ronald Reagan, have never supported a presidential platform based on an explicit rejection of the racist institutions and governmental policies from which many whites have benefitted socially and economically. Nor have the majority of white Americans supported in a presidential election any jeremiad appeals to live up to the justice sketched in the American jeremiad and affirmed through Scripture and the "Founding Fathers" until the Obama campaign. Herein lies the theological and moral crisis facing the nation: The election of Obama to the presidency was a direct *rejection* among white voters of the American jeremiad as a tool to dismantle domestic social and economic injustice *and* the repudiation of any national effort to build and promote a color-blind society. The argument is counterintuitive, it might initially appear. I believe it begs a far a deeper conversation. If we examine the Obama election in the context of his predecessors, let's say beginning with Ronald Reagan, the voting patterns of Americans follow a predictable and familiar pattern: Their votes reflect, on some level, their comprehensive traditions that may or may not align with the policies ascribed to the candidate at hand. In other words, American voters elect presidential candidates based on the familiar: what looks, feels, and sounds like what is reflected when one stands in front of a mirror. Moreover, the election of Trump deepens my point: Evangelicals and college educated white women, the two groups likely to have been the most offended by Trump's outlandish behavior and revelations during the campaign, voted for Trump in numbers that Obama would never have dreamed of securing.

Contesting Black Power: King and Carmichael
In 1966, James Meredith organized the March Against Fear, a 220-mile march from Memphis, Tennessee to Jackson, Mississippi to encourage Black voter registration and to protest white violence against Blacks. The march was a homecoming of sorts for Meredith, who was living in New York and attending Columbia University Law School. But on the second day, the march took an ugly turn. Meredith was shot in the back. The shooting stunned the marchers. Even though they had grown accustomed to violence, no one anticipated it at a march led by one of the patron saints of the Civil Rights Movement. The march continued without its leader, despite increasing concerns. Ten days or so into the march, the movement produced a major shift in Black politics: the birth of Black Power.

These two words, Black Power, changed the fundamental ethos and direction of the Civil Rights movement. Instead of relying on the moral good will of the nation and benevolence of white lawmakers and politicians, Carmichael was attempting to reconfigure the political aims and aspirations Blacks were seeking to acquire. In a rhetorical sense, Black Power was designed both to awaken a lethargic people and shield them from white supremacist beliefs in Black inferiority. The issue at stake here is what I call the moral problem of blackness, cultural beliefs in the moral inadequacy of Blacks and Black bodies. But in a conceptual sense, Black Power was aimed at reimagining individual and group power, and exploring how that power might be executed to confront economic exploitation and dismantle ill-conceived constructions of race, politics, culture, and religion.

The swift emergence of Black Power points to one of the most unnoticed but drastic changes in Black politics and the counter-public of the Black church: the move away from voting rights as the primary method of acquiring equality, political freedom, and economic justice. Appealing to the moral conscience of the nation and relying on the exceptional nature of American democracy as resources for overhauling the country, the major principles of the Civil Rights Movement, appeared obsolete to SNCC members.

Though King applauded the "positive" elements of Black Power to build economic and political power among Blacks, he was not sure those goals could be obtained because of the "problem of power," the "confrontation between the forces demanding change and the forces of power dedicated to preserving the status quo." He seems to imply here that the acquisition of economic and political power without a fundamental *tweaking* of power would reinforce and re-inscribe the very same hegemony Black Power was attempting to transform. The rhetorical move ought to include, King admonished, a discussion of the relationship between power and love, and how the two concepts are linked and dependent on each other within the framework of his Beloved Community. Indeed, King held that

> power without love is reckless and abusive and that love without power is sentimental and anemic. Power at its best is love implementing the demands of justice. Justice at its best is love correcting everything that stands against love.[9]

King believed that the historical interventions of Black political philosophy, which sought to achieve its goals through "love and moral suasion devoid of power," represented the best path to pursue. The focus on power, especially expressed as acquisition and domination, mirrored the abusive use of power King believed remains operative within the current political liberal framework and among racist whites.[10] "It is precisely this collision of immoral power with powerless morality which constitutes the major crisis of our times."[11] Here, King urges the leaders of Black Power to resist the tendency to replicate imperialism as it forged a democratic theory and philosophy of liberation.

Finally, King believed Black Power is a "psychological call to manhood."[12] That is, Black Power is a public pronouncement of the humanism or humanity inscribed within black bodies and a denouncement of slavery's attempt to link political and social "depravity" to biology or the inherent nature of blacks.[13] Indeed, King argued, the origins of Black Power date back to slavery, where moral beliefs in black inferiority created the cultural and political conditions in and through which the nation created the legal codes to justify the inherent criminality and moral deficiency of Blacks.

The legacy of the King-Carmichael struggle fundamentally altered the guiding political models and moral vocabulary informing mid-twentieth-century Black political thought: the Black church and the American jeremiad. To this end, Black Power upends the primary moral resources developed within the Black counter-public, casting a veil over and limiting the uses of the jeremiad. Political freedom and economic justice, then, have been torn away from God's hand and placed in the hands of political agents. This new theo-political terrain leads to seismic changes in and responses to Black politics.

American Jeremiad and Obama

The American jeremiad as a Puritan rhetorical device formed and fashioned within colonial America a national narrative based on a belief in the fledgling nation's sacred history and eschatological future. The fragments from the jeremiad have been widely documented in American literature, politics, and Protestant Christianity. Twentieth-century examinations describe the jeremiad as a primary epistemic resource for establishing competing and overlapping American traditions such as the Social Gospel Movement, African-American Prophecy, and secular Social Criticism. In these prominent examples, the jeremiad is often portrayed as a counter-religious tradition that attempts to lift the veil to gross poverty and injustice in and outside of the United States.

Soon after Black Power and SNCC's collapse, the nation experienced a steady increase in attacks on efforts to address structural racism by expanding opportunities in the private and public sectors, and the reasons for the backlash almost always pointed to culturally destructive and nihilistic "behavior" among Blacks and particularly among Black men as the reason why structural changes were neither needed nor justified. Indeed, the cultural wars, The Bell Curve, and Cornel West's *Race Matters* all reflect and speak to discourse bandied about both to illumine the Black problem and justify why Blacks did not warrant economic, social, and educational aid.

The tension between cultural conservatives and Black public intellectuals deepened and reached an impasse until the election of Bill Clinton. The outsider and moderate Democrat attempted to create a bridge to reconcile these groups through public deliberations and by expanding representational leadership by appealing to American exceptionalism. His cabinet was one of the most diverse ever within the White House and he inaugurated a public conversation on race, a kind of national dinner-table discussion on race and reconciliation.

Reading the American jeremiad in the context of recent presidential elections, we see a major shift in how politicians appeal to the tradition. In the broad sense, contemporary appropriations of the jeremiad have distorted the tradition for partisan purposes. According to M. Cathleen Kaveny, the nation has "retained the Puritan ideal of chosenness without the context which shaped it toward responsibility."[14] The presidency of Bill Clinton, in particular, is a clear example of the shift Kaveny describes. President Clinton deflated the jeremiad of its institutional responsibility to care for the poor and working class while advancing global trade based on the nation's providential role in world leadership. As President Clinton noted in a 1993 speech: "If we walk away from this, we have no right to say to other countries in the world, 'You're not fulfilling your world leadership; you're not being fair with us.' This is our opportunity to provide an impetus to freedom and democracy in Latin America and create new jobs for America as well." At the same time, President Clinton's support of welfare reform and stiffer prison sentences minimized the nation's leadership and responsibility to the poor and working class. President

Clinton's appointment of prominent Blacks to his Cabinet buffered criticisms from Black liberals. This move speaks to a broader concern. According to Claire Jean Kim, "[Clinton] repudiated this orthodoxy, essentializing racial/cultural differences and arguing that the race problem consisted not of White racism but of the threat these differences posed to national unity."[15]

The longtime narrative of the American jeremiad, which united dissident political and religious groups around a collective belief in the sanctity of America and its divine role in shaping both domestic and global politics, was no longer applied to domestic politics and social reform at the local level. Instead, the jeremiad found a new role within Empire as a guiding narrative to justify war and the expansion of American power globally.

According to Philip Klinkner, Bill Clinton's welfare reform undermined the poor when he agreed to a balanced budget with congressional Republicans. "Together, these agreements almost exactly inverted the programmatic legacy of Roosevelt's New Deal by cutting programs for the poor and working class and providing tax cuts for the wealthy."[16]

Critics of Obama and the Jeremiad

The fiercest critics of the Obama presidency have surfaced from the Black left and Black public intellectuals, a group of mostly highly educated Black men from the nation's premier schools and institutions. The Rev. Jesse Jackson, Sr., bemoaned in 2008 that Obama was "talking down to black people." To make matters more interesting, many of these brothers come from the Black church, or at the very least rely on the Black church or the academic study of religion as a source of their income. Why is this demographic so damn mad at Obama? The answer isn't clear. Listen to any sermon by any Black preacher of repute and one will hear, at some point during the calendar year, a sermon chastising *and* encouraging brothers to do better. Minister Louis Farrakhan is a prime example. Black women and men applaud Farrakhan for his bold and unabashed criticisms. Of course, a fair rebuttal acknowledges that one is hard pressed to find a similar speech addressing corruption, fraud, and drug abuse on Wall Street among mostly white men.

According to Cornel West, a towering philosopher whose tireless prophetic witness and prolific writings eroded disciplinary boundaries long before interdisciplinary studies was mainstream, Obama's "neoliberal" economic policies, increased "militarism," and lackluster education policies warranted harsh feedback. "The age of Barack Obama may have been our last chance to break from our neoliberal soulcraft. We are rooted in market-driven brands that shun integrity and profit-driven policies that trump public goods."[17] Joining in the chorus of critics is Ta-Nehisi Coates. Writing in "My President was Black," Coates argues that Obama invoked his racial identity to "lecture black people for continuing to make 'bad choices.'"[18] Far less acerbic than others, Coates paints a refreshingly nuanced view of the struggles facing the first Black president who worked with a legislative body armed to destroy his presidency.

In a *New York Times* opinion piece, Frederick C. Harris lamented near the end Obama's first term in office that "the last four years must be reckoned a disappointment. Whether it ends in 2013 or 2017, the Obama presidency has already marked the decline, rather than the pinnacle, of a political vision centered on challenging racial inequality. The tragedy is that black elites—from intellectuals and civil rights leaders to politicians and clergy members—have acquiesced to this decline, seeing it as the necessary price for the pride and satisfaction of having a black family in the White House."[19] Contrary to an earlier position raised in this essay, Harris blasts Black elites and public leaders for blindly supporting the president simply because he is the nation's first Black president.

The sad truth is that the boisterous attacks on Obama, especially from Black public intellectuals and white cultural conservatives, stem from the ironic decline of two important aspects of liberal American philosophy: the American jeremiad and the Black church. In both instances, religion, race, and politics overlapped in competing and complementary ways to launch moral criticisms of social and economic injustice. The moral outrage and indignation produced rhetorical weapons, a tradition of employing language in varying literary and poetic ways to disrupt, dismantle, and deconstruct public policies as the orator simultaneously encouraged, admonished, and raised Black audiences. Rhetorical weapons of defense were the only tools available among a people without significant economic and political power. The goal: In a fashion mirroring the rhythmic genius of jazz and Black preaching, one repudiates racial subjugation while simultaneously affirming the epistemic resources informing the counter-publics in Black life. Black Power and the Black Lives Matter movements exemplify the best examples of how rhetorical weapons of defense are employed in public and counter-public spheres. To this end, retrieving rhetorical weapons of defense in the public sphere was not only the expected but the normative mode of discourse for any Black (male) leader of note.

The rhetorical weapons of defense emerge from Black religion in general and the Black church in particular. Described by Harvard Professor Evelyn Brooks Higginbotham as a "counter-public," the Black church is a constant but shifting American institution that, as Melissa Harris-Perry notes, serves as a "cultural training ground" and a primary epistemic resource for defining black political discourse and cultural traditions.

President Obama is a son of the Black church and inherited what Michael Eric Dyson calls "black speech."

> To understand what Barack Obama does with language—how syllables sound and words crackle in his mouth, and how his voice elevates or dips, and the sentences simmer, or sometimes sing—one cannot simply turn to theories of rhetoric or listen to other gifted presidential communicators like John F. Kennedy and Bill Clinton.[20]

Obama studied and learned from the best: Dr. Martin Luther King, Jr. and Rev. Jeremiah Wright. Obama's former pastor Rev. Wright is an exemplary model of the tradition: fiery, erudite, and folksy. And yet, Obama learned from the tradition but took a detour when he decided to devote his life to public service. What he accomplished was historic: entering the White House on a message of hope and courage. Maybe this is part of the reason he is despised: He's a Black preacher with the intelligence of an Ida B. Wells-Barnett or W.E.B. Du Bois whose thoughtfulness and integrity subverted, albeit briefly, the white supremacist stronghold on the office of the presidency. Obama's campaign frustrated many Black and white men, especially politicians and civil rights leaders who believed Obama hadn't paid his dues to deserve the presidency so soon after entering national politics. As late as January 2008, nearly one-third of the Congressional Black Caucus supported then-Senator Hillary Rodham Clinton. Many backed Clinton despite growing criticisms from among their constituents. Congressman John Lewis bemoaned that "as an elected official you have to lead...sometimes [your constituents] don't follow, but you still have to lead and not be afraid."[21] A month later he endorsed Obama.

Though Obama is criticized for "talking down" to Black audiences, I believe the contrary is true: Obama speaks to Black audiences as an *insider*, embodying the charisma of Malcolm X and the oratory skills of Martin Luther King, Jr. When he stands in front of Black audiences, he is the *healer-and-priest*, embracing the people with love and lifting them to higher places. This is not the case in any other setting. This begs an important question: Has President Obama ever characterized an audience as *family* or the space as *home* in a "public" speech other than in the confines of Black counter-publics? I am not suggesting Obama holds a preference for Blacks or Black audiences; instead, his presidential speeches in counter-public spheres address the wounds of Black folk, and within the Black church this involves affirmation, chastisement, and pastoral love. President Obama, unlike any other Black male public figure since Dr. King, has occupied the role of healer-in-chief of Blacks for the last eight years or so. For this reason, Black males who have traditionally occupied this space—preachers, professors, and politicians—appear to hold a deep resentment against him. The nature and depth of public rebukes against Obama by Black men is unprecedented. The closest example is the fight between W.E.B. Du Bois and Marcus Garvey, during which Du Bois called Garvey "a little, fat black man," to characterize his frustration with Garvey's political agenda. Unlike Du Bois or Garvey, who legitimated the public spaces they occupied as writers and intellectuals, Obama is transformed when he enters the counter-public sphere. This can only happen when there exists a deep love for and belief in the people. Du Bois and Garvey saw themselves as prophets; Obama sees himself as a healer.

Perhaps Obama as healer-in-chief is filling a new need among Blacks. According to Melisa Harris-Perry, Black religion has experienced significant changes in the last three decades. In particular, two new religious phenomena are challenging the core of Black life in general and Black politics in particular: the "un-churched" and the "mega-churched."[22] These categories, employed by Professor Harris-Perry, characterize both the steady decline in Black church membership within mainline Black churches and the rise of independent Black mega churches.

For Harris-Perry and others, mega churches promote religious doctrines of individualism and prosperity at the expense of liberation theology and the jeremiad tradition. In both instances, Black politics suffer because of the decentralization of the black community and the inability to organize among those with shared political values. This translates for some into the death of the Black church as a kind of political *and* spiritual engine of Black life.

President Obama reinvigorates in public life the Black sermon motif that emphasizes collective responsibility alongside individual transformation through intellectual and economic entrepreneurialism. Three examples demonstrate the point I am attempting to argue: the fatherhood "sermon" at the Chicago apostolic church, the Morehouse commencement speech, and the Charleston eulogy. In each instance, similar motifs emerge through signification: Obama identifies the setting as his *home*, recovers the fragments of Black history to illumine their collective beauty and tragic history, names the courage and shortcoming of a people, and pours his deep love on the people. To this end, Obama transforms the jeremiad tradition he inherits by using lament, admonishment, and love to invigorate a people and remind them of their human destiny. This is the primary role of our healer-in-chief. A case in point: In what was likely his most theological sermon, the Charleston eulogy, Obama explores the Afro-Christian conception of grace to unite the mourners around the gift of God's grace. "This whole week, I've been reflecting on this idea of grace. The grace of the families who lost loved ones. The grace that Reverend Pinckney would preach about in his sermons," said Obama. "According to the Christian tradition, grace is not earned. Grace is not merited. It's not something we deserve. Rather, grace is the free and benevolent favor of God, as manifested in the salvation of sinners and the bestowal of blessings."[23]

In few other settings do we find Obama at once exuberant, sober, and euphoric. It is a position at odds with Obama's role as commander-in-chief, but it is nonetheless where Obama emerges as an exemplar healer-and-priest in a setting among a people whose pride in his accomplishments cultivates itself in a deep love that bursts from the seams in his presence.

Let's explore in more detail the Charleston eulogy of Rev. Clementa Pickney, delivered June 26, 2015. In his remarks, Obama emphasizes three critical points: the strength of the Black church, God's grace in times of social turmoil, and the ongoing racial subordination and subjugation of Blacks. President Obama characterizes the shooting as a logical, though disturbing, extension of racism and the cultural symbols that keep racial subordination alive. "Maybe we now realize the way racial bias can infect us even when we don't realize it, so that we're guarding against not just racial slurs, but we're also guarding against the subtle impulse to call Johnny back for a job interview but not Jamal."[24]

Obama solidifies his home within the service and among Christians watching via Internet or cable television when he sings "Amazing Grace" during his eulogy. If anyone doubted his faith prior to the Charleston eulogy, Obama's sermon and subsequent singing proved beyond a doubt that he possessed a moral and spiritual fiber rarely invoked by politicians. "By the second bar of Obama's hymn, the mourners were on their feet and applauding. By the line 'saved a wretch like me,' the organ had joined him, followed by hundreds of voices."[25]

Other than grace, two additional points stand out in his sermon. First, Obama claims that the tragedy allows the living to find an example for imagining a more profound life. "As a nation, out of this terrible tragedy, God has visited grace upon us, for He has allowed us to see where we've been blind. He has given us the chance, where we've been lost, to find our best selves." Second, Obama acknowledges to the world the complex role of Black churches both in the nation's history and among Blacks. Not only is the Black church a sanctuary of worship, but it has been "rest stops for the weary along the Underground Railroad; bunkers for the foot soldiers of the Civil Rights Movement."

During the Morehouse College commencement address, Obama asserts his allegiance to the mostly Black crowd in plain sight of all Americans without anyone taking notice of the President's expressions of solidarity with one of the most despised and disciplined groups in the country, black men. Representing nearly 34 percent of the prison population, Black males are by all accounts overrepresented in prison and the overall judicial system. With this backdrop in mind, Obama embraces the community of men at Morehouse as a brother, a fellow traveler in a world where Black men face astonishing odds.

> [For] the last 50 years, thanks to the moral force of Dr. King and a Moses generation that overcame their fear and their cynicism and their despair, barriers have come tumbling down, and new doors of opportunity have swung open, and laws and hearts and minds have

been changed to point where someone who looks just like you can somehow come to serve as President of these United States of America.[26]

This past should give them "hope," not in the form of sentimentalism but radical political and moral praxis. He places this charge in the context of admonishing Black men who choose neither to work nor to support their families.

President Obama acknowledges the ongoing need for Morehouse as a place of higher education for Black men, despite the long fought battles to end slavery, segregation, and discrimination. Indeed, "some came in search of community" where one would find other high achieving Black males. For others, the community at Morehouse was an extension of their high school experience. In either case, young men entered Morehouse hoping to fulfill the "unique sense of purpose that this place has always infused—the conviction that this is a training ground not only for individual success, but for leadership that can change the world."[27] He invokes Dr. King, perhaps Morehouse's most distinguished alumnus, to remind the young men of the tall challenge that is within reach: the courage to fight for social justice at all costs. In fact, it is Morehouse's DNA, and it is therefore within the possibility of the young men sitting before him to "look past the world as it [is] and fight for the world as it should be." He reminded them of the double standards they would find in graduate school or corporate America: Blacks must be twice as good as whites in order to succeed. Though many Black public intellectuals lashed out at Obama for preaching a "clean up yourself" mantra, I believe the backlash is unwarranted in light of the counter-public's tradition of addressing "home" audiences. Indeed, Obama's speech is no more conservative or critical than any number of sermons delivered in Black churches by the preachers such as Malcolm X or the Rev. Jesse Jackson, Sr. Self and communal-criticism are welcomed *and* expected in most counter-public settings.

To be sure, Obama's self-representation is significantly modified in different spaces. David Remnick suggests that Obama's Philadelphia race speech characterized the then-Senator as a "racial Everyman."[28] This move was an explicit attempt to situate himself within the grand narratives of American exceptionalism and among the nation's shining leaders of hope and transformation. Eric Sundquist writes that Obama's race speech allowed him to "stand in the mythic shadows of King and Lincoln, and through them the Founders themselves."[29] But within Black counter-public spheres, Obama is different. He's no longer the commander-in-chief. He stands as the healer-in-chief of a subjugated and scorned people in need of healing.

The Trump Presidency unleashed demons the country has tried to avoid: racial hatred and fears of economic and political displacement of whites. Bobo reminds us that in spite of "much positive change and development, the presumption of white privilege and of black and brown inferiority—in a cultural if not more 'essential' way—continue to exert effects in the American body politic."[30] Instead of addressing widespread economic and political changes on *all* Americans as a result of expanding technologies and shifting demographics, many whites shift the conversation to identity politics to justify how their political displacement or economic loss stems from a particular group such as Blacks or immigrants without interrogating the system they feel advantages others over them.

The tragic nature of Obama's presidency is a cautionary tale as to what happens when you push the boundaries of the familiar. Empire, and sometimes your own people, will strike back. Maybe this is the price of claiming Black people as human, normal, and frail. Maybe this is the price of not standing in solidarity with Black men, the primary gatekeepers in our counter-public spheres. The challenge we face is towering but not impossible to embrace, but it demands that we wrap ourselves in hope.

Notes

1. Gene Roberts, "Mississippi Reduces Police Protection for Marchers," *The New York Times*, June 17, 1966, 33.
2. Martin Luther King Jr., *Where Do We Go From Here: Chaos or Community?* (New York, NY: Harper and Row, 1967), p. 26.
3. King, 33.
4. Gary Younge, "Is Obama black enough?" *The Guardian*, March 1, 2007. Retrieved from http://proxy.library.georgetown.edu/login?url=https://search.proquest.com/docview/246630478?accountid=11091.
5. Associated Press, "Illinois Sen. Barack Obama's Announcement Speech," [italics] Washington Post, February 10, 2007, http://www.washingtonpost.com/wp-dyn/content/article/2007/02/10/AR2007021000879.html. (Accessed on February 9, 2018).
6. Ibid.

7. Barry Schwartz, "The Emancipation Proclamation: Lincoln's Many Second Thoughts," *Society* 52, no. 6 (October 2015): 590-603.
8. Lawrence D. Bobo, "Racism in Trump's America: Reflections on Culture, Sociology, and the 2016 Presidential Election," *The British Journal of Sociology* 68, no. S1 (November 2017): S86.
9. King, 36-37.
10. Ibid.
11. Ibid.
12. Ibid., 38.
13. Ibid.
14. M. Cathleen Kaveny, "The Remnants of Theocracy: The Puritans, the Jeremiad and Contemporary Culture Wars," *Law, Culture and the Humanities* 9, no. 1 (January 2013): 67.
15. Claire Jean Kim, "Clinton's Race Initiative: Recasting the American Dilemma," Polity 33, no. 2 (Winter 2000): 175.
16. Philip A. Klinkner, "Bill Clinton and the Politics of the New Liberalism," in *Without Justice for All: The New Liberalism and Our Retreat from Racial Equality*, ed. Adolph Reed, Jr., (Boulder, CO: Westview Press, 1999), 11.
17. Cornel West, "Pity the Sad Legacy of Barack Obama," *The Guardian*, January 9, 2017, https://www.theguardian.com/commentisfree/2017/jan/09/barack-obama-legacy-presidency. (Accessed on November 7, 2017).
18. Ta-Nehisi Coates, "My President was Black: A History of the First African American in the White House—and of what came next," *The Atlantic*, January/February 2017, 51.
19. Frederick C. Harris, "The Price of a Black President," *The New York Times*, October 27, 2012, http://www.nytimes.com/2012/10/28/opinion/Sunday/the-price-of-a-black-president.html. (Accessed on January 2, 2018).
20. Michael Eric Dyson, *The Black Presidency: Barack Obama and the Politics of Race in America* (New York, NY: Houghton Mifflin Harcourt, 2016), 70-71.
21. Joseph Hearn, "Black Caucus divided over Obama," *Politico*, January 17, 2008, https://www.politico.com/story/2008/01/black-caucus-divided-over-obama-007948. (Accessed on February 10, 2018).
22. Melissa Harris-Perry, "Righteous Politics: The Role of the Black Church in Contemporary Politics," *Cross Currents* 57, no. 2 (Summer 2007): 182.
23. Julia Zauzmer and Pulliam Bailey, "How Obama's remarkable Charleston eulogy shows his Deep Roots in the Black Church," *Washington Post*, June 26, 2015, https://www.washingtonpost.com/news/acts-of-faith/wp/2015/06/26/watch-obama-bust-out-his-version-of-amazing-grace-at-eulogizes-after-eulogizing-charleston-pastor/?utm_term=.3c61c6a19644. (Accessed on February 10, 2018).
24. Barack Obama, "Remarks by the President in Eulogy for the Honorable Reverend Clementa Pinckney," Office of the Press Secretary, June 26, 2015, https://obamawhitehouse.archives.gov/the-press-office/2015/06/26/remarks-president-eulogy-honorable-reverend-clementa-pinckney.
25. Zauzmer and Bailey, "How Obama's remarkable Charleston eulogy."
26. Barack Obama, "Remarks by the President at Morehouse College Commencement Ceremony," Office of the Press Secretary, May 19, 2013, https://obamawhitehouse.archives.gov/

the-press-office/2013/05/19/remarks-president-morehouse-college-commencement-ceremony. (Accessed on February 10, 2018).

27. Obama, "Remarks by the President at Morehouse."

28. David Remnick, *The Bridge: The Life and Rise of Barack Obama* (New York, NY: Alfred K. Knopf, 2010), 524.

29. Eric J. Sundquist, "We Dreamed a Dream: Martin L. King, Jr., & Barack Obama, *Daedalus*, 140, no. 1 (Winter 2011): 120.

30. Bobo, "Racism in Trump's America," S99.

CROSSCURRENTS

TO INSTILL LOVE FOR MY PEOPLE
Reassembling the Social in a Time of Mass Criminalization

Laura McTighe, with Reverend Doris J. Green

People are more than the shackles that bind them; this is the truth of Exodus narratives. During the Great Migration, seven million people traded the southern landscape for the northern Promised Land. Today, more than seven million people are imprisoned, on probation, or on parole. The continuities between slavery and imprisonment are undeniable, and segregation laws under Jim Crow nearly parallel the policies formerly imprisoned people navigate today. However, marginalization through the prison system is only part of the story, just as legalized subordination was only part of the story for black people a century ago. Scholars of religion have illuminated the uniquely urban sacred order created by southern transplants to northern meccas, and, in so doing, have shown how migration itself was a salvific event, not just the result of socioeconomic push-pull factors. Our narrative of religion in a time of mass criminalization must take this consciously liberatory turn: to refuse to yoke black life to the stranglehold of punitive punishment and to dwell instead in the complexities of being and being-together inside our prison nation, where currently and formerly imprisoned people and their families are building their own Promised Lands.

Drawing on fieldwork undertaken in partnership with Reverend Doris Green and the Men & Women In Prison Ministries (MWIPM) she began in Chicago more than three decades ago, this article centers the everyday and intimate work of holding communities together across prison walls. From this standpoint, I examine the raced and religious underpinnings of our nation's collective obsession with punishment. I also excavate the religious ideas and practices that offer MWIPM such tremendous possibilities for imagining and generating more just ways of doing justice. Within the communities hardest hit by mass criminalization, I argue that prophetic talk provides a grammar for bearing witness to the mass disappearance and reappearance of residents, and for imagining a world beyond prisons. Thinking with the lives and witness of the MWIPM community not only challenges some of our commonsense ideas about the concept of "religion;" it also forces us to think about *criminalization* differently. Prisons are often treated as total and static institutions. With MWIPM, I argue, however, that mass criminalization is better understood as a system of forced migration.[1] When we move with imprisoned people and their families across lockups, this truth comes into focus. We can also see the radical analysis that undergirds MWIPM's approach to care, service, healing, and restoration. MWIPM is moving in order to hold together the relationships that mass criminalization would sever, to bring *and keep* family members home, and to restore community wholeness. By mobilizing community networks to these ends, they are reassembling the social; they are also attacking mass criminalization at the roots.

Relationships are central to this story; they also continue to make possible the research that drives it. I (Laura McTighe) first met Reverend Doris Green in the spring of 2008. We were part of a group of twenty or so AIDS activists and prison abolitionists brought together in an upstate New York retreat center to envision how to build a national movement that would address the role of mass imprisonment in driving the domestic HIV epidemic. In preparation for the meeting, I had been asked to put together a "think piece" on possible policy goals for this burgeoning coalition. Looking back on the document now, it reads to me as my first articulation of the critical reframing of reentry and recidivism that guides my research partnership with Reverend Green and the MWIPM family. Rather than rehearsing the grim narrative of the two-thirds of formerly imprisoned people who will be rearrested within three years of their release, my think piece centered the lifeworlds and work of the one-third who are not. *Who are they? And who are the people that support them?*

Reverend Green's flight had been delayed, which gave her unexpected time to read the "think pieces" prepared for the meeting. When she finally made it to the retreat center, she was on a mission to find that woman who had been able to capture the pain of families in her writing. On break the next morning, she pulled me aside. "How did you know?" Seeing the confusion on my face, she paused. Reverend Green had spoken at length about her prison work in Chicago in our morning discussion. Almost in passing, she had mentioned that her husband, Mike, was incarcerated. "There's no place for me to talk about that in most of these advocacy discussions. But you made a place. How did you know? You are my child and I've never even met you." Many of the details of that moment are lost to me. But I remember clearly the tears welling up in Reverend Green's eyes, which summoned tears in my own, and the sun beating down on our heads, unexpectedly after a gloomy morning of rain. Somewhere there is a picture someone snapped of us talking, and another of us facing forward squeezing each other tightly. It was settled. From that day forward, I had a mother in Chitown and a father in the Illinois state prison system.

Ending mass criminalization is intimate work. That is the point. Staying in the intimacies of our relationships provides a different lens for understanding the assemblage of *mass criminalization* through the disassemblage of entire communities.[2] It also provides a launch point for reexamining the stories we tell about punishment in the United States. Most work on religion and criminalization starts with the penitentiary model in Pennsylvania, or the labor reform model of New York's Auburn Prison. I argue, however, that these northern models do not help us understand the enduring religious character of American punishment. In the first section of this article, I re-center this narrative in the American South after the Civil War. By zeroing in on the convict lease system (and its critics), I contend that what we see is not religion as *discipline*, but rather religion as *expulsion*. Then, in section two, I work through the words and writings of Ida B. Wells on the occasion of the 1893 Chicago World's Fair to stitch this analysis of expulsion into an enduring black feminist critique of race, religion, and punishment in the United States—a tradition of which Reverend Green is a part. In the third section, I fast-forward one hundred years to the founding of Chicago's MWIPM by Reverend Green in 1982 and its growth into a vibrant statewide organization built through the patient work of women moving across prison walls and in and out of police lockups to reconnect the severed threads of community. Now, more than thirty years later, the team of formerly imprisoned people united through MWIPM works to bring hope and healing to the communities that have been most impacted by mass criminalization. I spend a bit of time on the texture of this work in order to understand why providing support in a time of mass criminalization has the MWIPM team on the move so much. Then, in section four, I ask what MWIPM's work might help to illuminate about our current moment of mass criminalization. Importantly, here I connect the dots from Ida B. Wells' organizing in the nineteenth century to Reverend Green's in the twenty-first century using the theme of expulsion, arguing that mass criminalization is better understood as a system of forced migration through which individuals and entire communities are uprooted and then made-stuck. Finally, in the last section, I turn back to MWIPM to think about the radical *potential* and *critique* in the work to move with the people scattered across prison walls in order to reassemble entire communities. I argue that what appears at first glance to be *pastoral* work (sending letters, caring for families) is actually deeply *prophetic* work to decarcerate American society and realize a world beyond prisons.

The spirit of American punishment
To speak of religion and criminalization in the United States is to conjure a vexed and uncomfortable history. Just a decade after the Declaration of Independence proclaimed the equality of men and their God-given inalienable rights, a group of middle-class religious progressives got together to develop a carceral method befitting this new nation of rights-bearing men. They called it the *penitentiary*. In 1790, sixteen cells in Philadelphia's Walnut Street Jail were converted from holding areas for those awaiting public corporeal punishment to sites of solitary confinement. The imprisoned were left to penitently reflect, repent, and realign themselves with that of God in them. Other states added their own twists on the penitentiary model in the decades to follow, most notably New York's Auburn Prison launched in 1817, which combined silent group work during the day and solitary confinement at night.[3] The underlying rationale, however, was the same. These antebellum institutions were spirited by two principles: *first*, the inalienability of the atomized redeemable soul, and *second*, the power of concrete, seclusion, and forced labor to stimulate personal transformation.[4]

In the postbellum South, we began to see *another* system of punishment emerge. This is the genealogy of "mass incarceration" that we are perhaps more familiar with.[5] After the end of the Civil War, southern whites responded to black people's claims on freedom with the exceptional violence of the lynch law and the quotidian terror of the convict lease system. They redefined crime by creating "Black Codes" and used them to imprison thousands of black men and women—often sentencing them to work on the very plantations they had just been freed from! It was by many accounts "worse than slavery."[6] And scholars have paid considerable attention to *how* it was worse than slavery. In the shift from an agricultural slave society to an industrializing South, the assemblage of the Jim Crow carceral sphere was not merely slavery in new clothes. The economic system had changed, and so, too, had the system of modern state racism undergirding it.[7] Whatever language was used to conceal it, Jim Crow justice had nothing to do with crime, punishment, and redemption. It was a key infrastructure for producing and reinforcing the impossibility of black freedom.[8]

Today we are living through an era of criminalization that is without international parallel or historical precedent.[9] We know these statistics by heart: 2.3 million are currently in some form of lockup, and more than 7 million people are under some form of correctional control. There are many causal explanations for the prison boom—the war on drugs being among the most widely cited. Punitive drug policies like mandatory minimums, three-strikes laws, and drug-free school zones, when capacitated through massive expansions in the funding and resourcing of police and other branches of criminal justice, have been undeniably devastating criminalization strategies. However, if the numbers are analyzed, only about one-fifth of people are in prison or awaiting trial on drug-related offenses. Critical prison studies scholars have worked to reorient our vision away from a phenomenology of the tools of criminalization and toward a structural analysis of the persistent histories of economic precarity and social repression in the United States. Most compellingly, they track the scale up of the neoliberal carceral state through parallel increases in prison populations, structural unemployment, concentrated urban poverty, and mass homelessness.[10] And they identify an unlikely catalyst for criminalization. At nearly every juncture, it is the criminalization of liberation movements organized against racial capitalism that spurs the expansion of policing and prosecution strategies—and also helps to solidify an analysis within black and brown communities that criminalization is a tool of repression.[11]

What does this tell us about the *spirit* of American punishment?[12] Certainly, these links between mass criminalization and social repression indicate that we cannot account for the prison boom of the last four decades by cold science alone. However, what is driving this obsession with punishment? And how does today's obsession connect with our nation's carceral beginnings? In the early American penitentiary system, the goal was to produce a penitent citizenry through forced labor and solitude. In the Jim Crow carceral sphere, the goal was to extract black labor, while also eviscerating blackness. The first is a religious genealogy. The second is a materialist one. Each gives us a different way of accounting for the role of religion in American punishment. From the first, we might argue that the religious aspirations of the first prison architects have not gone away; they have just been secularized into modern forms.[13] From the second, we might surmise that the system is best traced by following the evolution of racial capitalism. The spiritual strivings of criminalized communities then get a false consciousness gloss: *God is the sigh of the oppressed yearning for a better life.*

I would like to propose a third explanation: that our rituals of criminalization have an underlying religious logic that is more *blunt* than discipline á la Foucault and more *enchanted* than capital á la Marx. Prisons might be the places where we tell stories about the fall and about sin. But *who* are we telling those stories about? The overlaying of the discourses of sin and crime obscures that the conversation has always been about race. Indeed, the first penitentiaries were also warehouses for free people of color and people fleeing slavery.[14] The theology of slaveholding Christianity was reborn in the theology of the Lost Cause, which provided the former planter class white supremacist religious fodder for imagining and producing the new South through anti-black terror. Common to both was a religious logic of *expulsion* as a means of purifying the body politic. "*We* have God; *They* are not human and dangerous."[15]

Race, religion, and expulsion

This reality of justice by expulsion drove the writing, organizing, and movement of hundreds of thousands of black people across the south immediately following the abolition of slavery. Among them was Ida B. Wells, born in Holly Springs, Mississippi, to enslaved parents just six months before the Emancipation Proclamation was issued. Wells was a journalist, newspaper editor, suffragist, and sociologist. Her deepest cause was documenting lynching in the United States. A pamphlet she produced on the occasion of the 1893 Chicago World's Fair is especially instructive for understanding the religious sensibilities that undergirded the quotidian terror of Jim Crow justice by the chain and the noose.[16]

Black people were poorly represented in all aspects of the 1893 Chicago World's Fair—from underemployment in its running to racist stereotypes that filled the exhibit halls.[17] The pages of Wells' text enumerated "The Reason Why the Colored American Is Not in the World's Columbian Exposition." She outlined the willful erasure of the "progress of the Afro-American since emancipation." She documented the Jim Crow playbook through which black people were first isolated from necessary social supports through "class legislation," second blamed for the abuse they survived through a perverse moral reasoning, and third criminalized for this survival through the convict lease system and the "lynch law."[18] Twenty thousand copies were made available for distribution in the last three months of the fair. Wells set up shop at a desk in the Haitian pavilion where Frederick Douglass (who wrote the pamphlet's introduction) served as official representative. Every day until the fair's end, Wells put copies of "The Reason Why" into the hands of attendees, striking up conversations about race and religion in America with as many as she could.

Wells was writing against a nation that placed blackness in a glaring "religio-racial" frame.[19] Blackness was (and still is) treated alternately as the ecstatic counterpoint to high Protestant "good religion;" as the hyper-religious outlier amid a secularizing nation; as the authentic fix to the iron cage of industrial capitalism; and as the stain so profane that it must be expelled from the "sacred" body public.[20] Wells used her careful observations of the convict lease system and the lynch law to turn this whole religio-racial gaze back upon the White City's architects (and those of the Jim Crow carceral sphere). She gave two interrelated explanations for the "twin infamies" decimating black life. First, "the religious, moral and philanthropic forces of the country—all the agencies which tend to uplift and reclaim the degraded and ignorant, are in the hands of the Anglo-Saxon." In word and deed, they believe that "to have Negro blood in the veins makes one unworthy of consideration, a social outcast, a leper, even in the church." Second, the judges, juries, and court officials "are white men who share these prejudices. They also make the laws."[21]

By publishing "The Reason Why," Wells was determined to make plain how the stringent criminalization and mob murder perpetuated by white judges, juries, officials, and everyday citizens rested on a form of white supremacist Christianity that had legal and political power. This, I argue, is the abiding religious *character* of American punishment: the religious roots of anti-black racism ritualized through terror, murder, and expulsion.

Practicing religion against criminalization
In the decades following Ida B. Wells' action in the "White City," Chicago would become the "Mecca of the Migrant Mob."[22] Thousands of black people traded the twin infamies of the chain gang and the lynch law for the possibility of survival above the Mason-Dixon line. Northern life, however, was not a cake walk. Migrants bore witness daily to how the same old southern racism was dressed up in new northern clothes. Their everyday needs overwhelmed the mainline Protestant churches to which many turned; so, too, did their forms of religious practice. Historian Wallace Best has illuminated how it was precisely these pressures—and migrants' will to survive and thrive—that created a new, and especially *female*, sacred order in Chicago.[23] The mainline denominations that allowed themselves to be were transformed by responding to the needs of the people fleeing the horrors of lynching in the south. And these migrants also built what they needed. The streets of what would become "Bronzeville" on Chicago's South Side were packed with storefront churches and new religious movements that grew out of the endurance of migrants making for themselves what they needed in order to build the world that could be.[24]

That spirit of struggle, survival, and renewal is what Reverend Doris Green so often emphasizes when she explains the pain that birthed MWIPM. Today, Chicago is home to many things: one of the largest jails in the country, a soaring murder rate, gun violence, over-medication, unsupported trauma, overdose deaths... MWIPM's approach is reminiscent of those Great Migration-era mainline pastors who dropped everything to respond to crisis—and of those migrants who made what they needed for themselves after constantly being met with missions designed to fix *them*, not the problems they were facing. Since my first visit to Chicago, Reverend Green has explained it like this: "My people are in pain. At MWIPM, we go to them. We ask what they need. We create programs around those needs. Together, we build something new. It's such a simple formula: 'Ask people what they need and do what they tell you!' But you would be surprised by how many institutions and organizations refuse to do just that. They imagine a problem, imagine a solution, secure millions of dollars to fix it, and haven't even stopped to ask the people what they *need*."

That approach to MWIPM's work is personal for Reverend Green. In 1982, she began to minister to people in prison to save her own life. Fully in the throes of an abusive relationship, isolated from her community and uprooted to Chicago's white suburbs, Reverend Green started going to a church nearby to seek respite. The more she was battered at home, the more she gave to the church. "Hurt people hurt people, the saying goes. For me, it was exactly the opposite. The more pain I had, the more I poured into addressing the pain I saw around me. I did not know what was calling me to go to prison—and I got a lot of push back from church members who wanted me to minister to orphans and other 'innocent' victims. But that was not my calling. As I sat with people behind the walls and heard their stories, I began to find language to express the pain I experienced in my own life. I went in to minister to them, and I was being transformed in the process."

Reverend Green has documented the beginnings of this work in her first book, *Don't Wait Until The Battle Is Over: Shout Victory Now!*[25] In the early 1980s, prison ministries were few and far between. What little support congregations did provide to their brothers and sisters behind bars was usually limited to holiday prayers. The notable exception was Reverend Consuella York (better known as "Mother York") who began her ministry in Cook County Jail in 1952 and founded her own church on the South Side.[26] Inspired by Mother York, Reverend Green found two evangelists to assist her in this spiritual journey. Together with Theresa Washington and Jackie Goss, she began to visit Joliet Prison about thirty miles southwest from Chicago. Their trio was a well-oiled machine. Theresa contributed the gift of organizing: she was the ministry's secretary. Jackie contributed the gift of voice: she led the praise and worship every Sunday. Reverend Green contributed the gift of leadership: she read scriptures and offered messages of hope and guidance. Together, they worked to create a liberatory ministry that grew in step with the needs and visions articulated by those imprisoned at Joliet. At first, Reverend Green thought she was there to help. What stunned her was how every person's story spoke directly to the pain, trauma, and anguish she herself had silently lived through for years. She wrote *Shout* as a collective testimony of her conversion; it is a record of the painstaking process through which she began to walk alongside criminalized people to heal their relationships, their communities, and themselves.[27]

The founding of MWIPM some years later was a love story. After this vibrant start to prison ministry at Joliet Prison, Reverend Doris Green began to also work as a volunteer chaplain at the nearby maximum security Stateville Correctional Center in Crest Hill, Illinois. There she continued to offer her gift of leadership: reading scriptures and providing messages of hope and guidance, in spiritual counseling and in collective worship. It was through her patient presence at Stateville that she met and fell in love with Mike Smith, a brilliant leader and revolutionary who had only begun to run down the years on his decades-long prison sentence. Reverend Green and Mike committed their lives to each other, and through their relationship, they transformed what had been an outside-*into*-prison ministry into a project of social healing that refused the boundaries of prison walls.[28]

Mike began to work with other "old heads" in Stateville and launched the African/African American Cultural Council (AAACC) to teach black history and pride to young people just getting caught up in the drug war carceral boom. Together, the AAACC leadership organized educational sessions, held black religious and cultural events, and built an everyday and patient space for reckoning with the disaster that was ripping their communities apart. But their meetings had a catch. According to prison regulations, the elders of AAACC could only come together if Reverend Green was present as volunteer prison chaplain. She became not only a bridge to support the life-giving connections of people imprisoned ministering to one another; she also became a bridge to their communities outside. In partnership with the men of AAACC, Reverend Green and her sisters on the outside would reach out to parents and children left behind, to girlfriends struggling with addiction. Person by person, inside and out, they built (and often rebuilt) relationships and social networks that were decimated by state rituals of predatory policing, aggressive prosecution, and protracted sentencing. In 1992, they formally incorporated this insurgent community-in-making as *Men & Women* In Prison Ministries.

LAURA MCTIGHE, WITH REVEREND DORIS GREEN

Moving with expulsion to end imprisonment

Today, MWIPM's daily operations are nestled in an eighteen-story tower that overlooks the Green Lie subway stop for "Bronzeville." All of the staff members have spent time in prison or have loved ones in lockup. Those staff members have built a matrix of supports for folks in prison and their families. MWIPM's work has them moving... *constantly*. They reach out to find the people in prison, or those suffering on the outside, often in isolation. They bring them together to provide community, care, and uplift to one another. They do that through the monthly family support meetings; through their quarterly newsletter mailed to more than 1,000 people in prison; and through their prison ministry training program to transform churches into safe houses.[29]

What does MWIPM teach us about religion in a time of mass criminalization? Reverend Green and I have been working to answer that question since we first met in 2008. In late 2009, she invited me to Chicago to spend several days moving with her and the MWIPM staff. We went to churches, to community centers, to food pantries, and to a long-standing black radical basement meeting on Chicago's South Side. That evening, Reverend Green launched into a presentation on HIV prevention in the black community by asking: "How are you going to be a revolutionary when you're so sick you can't get out of bed to fight?" This was a hermeneutic for Reverend Green—to sidestep the shame and stigma and conspiracy theories that swirled around HIV, and to figure out what to do about it. I watched as Reverend Green grasped the sides of the podium adorned with red, black, and green streamers to steady herself. She then began to speak on the modes of HIV transmission, chiding herself for being a minister and talking about sex, before segueing into MWIPM's work to get harm reduction tools into the Illinois prison system. When she concluded, she physically braced herself again for the storm of questions she knew was coming. Hands were up. And the comments were biting, bubbling with the anger of people who live in the shadows of America's "hoods" and with the precision of self-taught scholars who can connect statistical bias, funding disparities, and the destruction of the black family in a single breath. As we were driving home that night, Reverend Green explained to me that the basement meeting happens every week, that "those brothers *really need that space*." She knew most of them through Mike. Coming to this meeting was part of her enduring work to stretch across prison walls and to keep people connected in community when they came home. "I'm just trying to instill love for my people."

To instill love for your people, you have to *be with* your people. You have to be, as Reverend Green has been for more than thirty years, on the move. Moving with Reverend Green has oriented me to a very different way of thinking about religion. MWIPM is not approaching religion as a thing that be found in an institution or a creed or a sacred text; MWIPM is *practicing* religion as living, embodied, and everyday process.[30] The MWIPM family is living through a crisis not unlike the times that Ida B. Wells wrote about. It was the lynching of three of her friends in Memphis that pushed Ida B. Wells to *do* something: to research, to write, to travel the world, and to get up to Chicago. The same is true for Reverend Green and the prison ministry she founded. Moving-with is a methodology that the MWIPM family have taught me for understanding the prophetic and liberatory practice of religion in a time of mass criminalization. When we are moving, we are not keyed in to looking for things in boxes. We are *following* the people.

By following the people, we can also begin to see how the forces that keep MWIPM moving are no less religiously driven. A logic of expulsion —that abiding religious *character* of American punishment ritualized through terror, murder, and confinement—drives mass criminalization. This is a wholly different way of analyzing criminalization. Too often, analyses of "mass incarceration" are produced in statistical terms: the number of people in jails, state prisons, federal prisons, immigration detention, and juvenile facilities. Emphasis is placed on the trends in policing, prosecution, and imprisonment rates and duration. However, what a story of bodies-in-beds obscures is the homes and families from which those people were taken.[31] By obscuring the processes through which people were forcibly ripped from their neighborhoods and scattered in facilities two, five, eight, eighteen hours away, "mass incarceration" seems to be a fact; and it seems to extend indefinitely into the future.[32]

This searing analysis of the rituals of anti-black racism through ritualized expulsion is one that was first pioneered, unsurprisingly, behind the walls. In 1979, a group of incarcerated men called "The Think Tank" devised a research study to test the commonsense of criminalization and

Expulsion from Brooklyn to Upstate New York Prisons

In/Out Flows as People are Expelled to Upstate New York Prisons and Released to Brooklyn

targeted expulsion circulating on the housing blocks of New York's Green Haven prison. Through careful analysis of prison admission statistics and census records accessed in partnership with allies on the outside, this group of incarcerated scholars discovered that seventy-five percent of the state's black and Latino prison population came from (and returned) to just seven neighborhoods in New York City. These two Brooklyn maps attempt to visualize the community-crippling impacts of this level and scale of concentrated city-to-prison and prison-to-city forced migration.[33]

Like their comrades in New York, the AAACC elders knew the Illinois version of the "Million Dollar Blocks" story the second they arrived on the housing blocks in Stateville.[34] Everyone incarcerated there was from the Chicago neighborhoods where they grew up. Mike and the other AAACC members could stitch together community behind bars and work with Reverend Green through MWIPM to connect with loved ones outside, in part, because everybody knew *everybody.*

The people that AAACC engaged behind the walls rarely "maxed out" their full sentences; they were most often released with the diffused supervision of parole or probation. That meant that when these elders and the younger generation they organized ran down the clock on their prison sentences, they would go from being forcibly *expelled* to prisons to being forcibly *stuck* in so-called free society. The crippling burden of post-imprisonment restrictions on housing, benefits, employment options, and the like made it nearly impossible for them to make ends meet. Add in swarms of police squads and surveillance cameras that have turned many neighborhoods into open air prisons, and you got a form of social death —and sometimes literal death—that felt intractable. Too often this system would then set people forcibly moving again. Two-thirds of people will be rearrested within three years of their release.

The work of MWIPM also adds another interpretive layer to this system of mass criminalization as forced migration. When the MWIPM family talks about prisons, they are not just talking about the expulsion of the individuals who are sentenced. They are talking about the disruption —the *severing*—of social ties with everyone who loves them. They are talking about the *death* of entire communities. It is a violent process. Mindy Fullilove calls it "root shock"—that "traumatic stress reaction to the destruction of all or part of one's emotional ecosystem."[35] Fullilove was writing about decades of urban renewal projects starting in 1949, through which 1,600 black districts in cities across the United States were bulldozed and destroyed. However, her analysis maps onto MWIPM's own. Reading across psychiatry, public health, and urban planning, Fullilove insisted that urban renewal did not just disrupt black communities; it ruined their economic health and social cohesion, stripping displaced residents of their sense of place. Likewise, mass criminalization (often waged on the very peoples who were displaced just decades before) did not merely disrupt communities; it left life-threatening gashes—gashes that MWIPM, in partnership with AAACC, was founded to heal.

Reassembling the social

"When the legal system fails, the entire family is incarcerated." This simple truth has guided the bone-deep work of Chicago's MWIPM for more than three decades. By speaking this truth, they bear witness to the contemporary (and historic) destruction of black families through the brutal "magic of the state" ritualized through expulsion.[36] They also affirm the sacred texture of reparative labors to preserve (and defend) their families and communities.[37] Their work on race and religion in American unfolds in the intimacies of relational bonds, quotidian terror, and freedom dreams. By practicing religion in time of mass criminalization, they both refuse and evade their subjection—even while they are transformed in the process.

This is the work: reach into the prisons; make way for those coming home; support our loved ones; and reunite our families. In these ways, the MWIPM family works to bring healing to the Chicago communities targeted by mass criminalization. That is no small task. In fact, it is THE task. The abiding religious *character* of mass criminalization is manifest in a racist practice of justice by expulsion. The whole rotten system works by ripping people from community in order to destroy the relationships that sustain life. Traveling across prison walls, pulling people back into the fold, actively stitching together the severed threads of community. These are no mere pastoral exercises to help people cope better. Cultivating relationships dismembered by criminalization as sites of truth-telling and resistance is deeply prophetic work. Put another way, MWIPM teaches us a different sort of prison politics. Their success is not measured in the tactile closing of prisons—though this is important. They are actively "reassembling the social."[38] And by reassembling the social, they are attacking mass criminalization at the roots.

How do they do that? What materials do they use? Where do they find these materials? Where do they anchor their work? How do they keep making the journey? How do they carry their histories with them? How are they practicing religion along the way? How do they make way for others to come along? What do they learn while they are on the move? And how do these lessons help them to build new and more livable futures?

My work with MWIPM and alongside Reverend Green has given me a glimpse into how currently and formerly imprisoned people and their families are reassembling the social in Chicago. Reverend Green followed up her visit to that South Side revolutionary basement meeting by presenting on a panel at the annual Nation of Islam's Savior's Day entitled "There no such thing as a no-good woman." The Harm Reduction in Prison Coalition that Reverend Green mentioned at the basement meeting has since worked with the Illinois Department of Corrections and the State Legislature to enact twenty-one unique policies on a matrix of life-sustaining and abolitionist-oriented issues ranging from conditions of confinement to family restoration to community health and thriving.[39] For each, MWIPM brought all of the formerly imprisoned members of the coalition to educate the Illinois state legislature in Springfield. That momentum of formerly imprisoned leaders realizing government accountability through their advocacy and presence in the legislative process has opened further possibilities for working on voting rights, identification restoration, and overdose prevention statewide. And the method has remained as it always has been: "Taking it to the Streets" to connect with the people, to bring them into the fold, and to ensure that their needs and visions for change are leading the movement.[40]

What comes into view here are the dynamic religious lifeworlds that Chicago's "Transcendent Third" are ever in the process of assembling *amidst* the structural challenges they confront daily and *through* the religious visions they put to prophetic ends. That is how MWIPM works, in Reverend Green's words, "to instill love for my people." Through their presence, the MWIPM family brings healing to the Chicago communities most burdened by mass criminalization and cultivates relationships divided by prison walls as sites of truth-telling and transformation. In so doing, MWIPM has been able to mobilize community networks to advance the decarcerating policy changes needed to bring *and keep* their family members home and realize a world beyond prisons.

Reverend Green always reminds me, "The people are the catalysts for change. Their relationships carry the movement." By living religion, the MWIPM family has set their hands to dismantling the very systems that were designed to destroy them. They are on the move. And they are enduring. Through their labors, they are bringing into being a world in which the next generation can know freedom. Together, they are building their own Promised Lands.

Acknowledgment

I would like to thank Reverend Doris Green for the decade of collaboration and spiritual mentorship that makes this article possible. Our work has been undertaken every step of the way in partnership with the Men & Women In Prison Ministries family, most especially Kimberly Wallace, Richard Wallace, Russell Jackson, and the late Dawn Kindred. I would also like to thank my academic community for your invaluable insights and suggestions on various incarnations of this article—Courtney Bender, Josef Sorett, Bethany Moreton, Pamela Voekel, Yui Hashimoto, Yana Stainova, Golnar Nikpour, Becky Clark, Vaughn Booker, and my colleagues in the Dartmouth College Department of Religion. Finally, to James Logan: thank you for the vision of justice and healing that guides this whole special issue and for the invitation to join you in writing, speaking, and living it out loud.

Notes

1. The conceptual frame "mass criminalization as forced migration" has two distinct genealogies in the scholarly literature. In 2006, North Carolina-based public health researchers posited a structural root for the coincidence of sexually transmitted infections (STIs) and incarceration. By their analysis, the court-mandated movement of unprecedented numbers of people through incarceration had disrupted families and social networks thereby degrading social cohesion that might otherwise have prevented STIs. See Thomas, James C. and Elizabeth Torrone, 2006, "Incarceration as forced migration: effects on selected community health outcomes," *American Journal of Public Health*, 96 (10), pp. 1762-5. Others, however, have read the criminalization-forced migration connection more historically as the afterlife of slavery. Narratives linking the Middle Passage to modern-day prison overcrowding, or the shackles of the transatlantic slave trade and the shackles of prison transport, have long been used by scholars and activists alike to underline the continuous legacy of racial oppression meted out against people of African descent living on U.S. soil. In each of these examples, the line between the metaphorical and the literal is blurred, such that what is signified is a historical weight of forced migration that is both of another time and immanently being carried forward in the present.
2. I use the term "mass criminalization" in the tradition of indigenous feminist and black feminist critiques of U.S. and Canadian carceral and settler contexts. Black feminist and activist-scholar Mariame Kaba has argued that because incarceration in prisons, jails, and detention centers is only facet of community-wide criminalization, especially for women and gender nonconforming people, a more effective concept for abolitionist feminisms is that of "mass criminalization." This critical reframing maps onto the "transcarceral continuum" framework developed by Indigenous feminist activist-scholars in Canada to name the intrusive reach of punitive carceral controls into the everyday lives and onto the marked bodies of perpetually criminalized and disabled indigenous women, black women, and other women of color (including queer, trans, and gender nonconforming people). In the context of MWIPM's work, "mass criminalization" is a specifically resonate framework for connecting the sentencing and detention of individuals to the effective criminalization of the families and communities who "do time" along with them. Thus, for MWIPM, "mass criminalization" is a total-system, family-centered analysis of the system's socially destructive intent.
3. See, for example, Lewis, W. David, 1965, *From Newgate to Dannemora: The Rise of The Penitentiary in New York, 1796–1848*, Ithaca: Cornell University Press; Rothman, David J., 1971, *The Discovery of the Asylum: Social Order and Disorder in the New Republic*, Boston: Little, Brown, and Company; Dumm, Thomas L., 1987, *Democracy and Punishment: Disciplinary Origins of the United States*, Madison: University of Wisconsin Press; and Hirsch, Adam Jay, 1992, *The Rise of the Penitentiary: Prisons and Punishment in Early America*, New Haven: Yale University Press.
4. See Graber, Jennifer, 2011, *The Furnace of Affliction: Prisons and Religion in Antebellum America*, Chapel Hill: University of North Carolina Press; and Smith, Caleb, 2009, *The Prison and the American Imagination*, New Haven: Yale University Press.
5. I use "mass incarceration" in quotes here to not only signal its specificity as a term initially intended to name the dramatic expansion of the carceral state since the 1970s, but also how this term introduced a sense that the problem with incarceration was simply the

"mass," not the incarceration. Here, I follow the work of black feminist abolitionists on prisons and racial capitalism, most especially Gilmore, Ruth Wilson, 2007, *Golden Gulag: Prisons, Surplus, Crisis, and Opposition in Globalizing California*, Berkeley: University of California Press; and Davis, Angela, 2003, *Are Prisons Obsolete?*, New York: Seven Stories Press. Editors Deborah E. McDowell, Claudrena N. Harold, and Juan Battle provide essential historical, political, economic, and sociocultural roots of "mass incarceration" in their collected work, 2013, *The Punitive Turn: New Approaches to Race and Incarceration*, Charlottesville: University of Virginia Press. Michelle Alexander offered what remains the most popular and widely disseminated framing on how "mass incarceration" and post-prison restrictions have created a racial caste in America in 2010, *The New Jim Crow: Mass Incarceration in the Age of Color Blindness*, New York: New Press

6. The phrase "worse than slavery" comes from a cartoon by Thomas Nast in 1874, "The Union as it was/The Lost Cause, worse than slavery," *Harper's Weekly* 18(930), October 24, p. 878. See also Oshinsky, David M., 1996, *"Worse than Slavery": Parchman Farm and the Ordeal of Jim Crow Justice*, New York: Free Press; Blackmon, Douglas A., 2008, *Slavery by Another Name: The Re-Enslavement of Black Americans from the Civil War to World War II*, New York: Doubleday; and McLennan, Rebecca M., 2008, *The Crisis of Imprisonment*, Cambridge: Cambridge University Press. In the postbellum North, black people were also incarcerated at disproportionate rates, though proportions would not reach Jim Crow-era racial disparities until the explosion of the incarcerated population through the war on drugs. Still, to take Illinois as one example: Between 1890 and 1930, African American women averaged only 2.4 percent of the state's female population, but they represented two-thirds of the daily population at Joliet women's prison. See Dodge, L. Mara, 2006, *"Whores and Thieves of the Worst Kind": A Study of Women, Crime and Prisons, 1835-2000*, Dekalb: Northern Illinois University Press, pp. 72-3, 84.

7. In her work on terror, slavery, and self-making in nineteenth-century America, Saidiya Hartman proposes the term "burdened individuality" to capture how "the disembodied equality of liberal individuality" is inseparable from "the dominated, regulated, and disciplined embodiment of blackness." Hartman points to the separate-but-equal doctrine of *Plessy v. Ferguson* to explain how "the double bind of equality and exclusion...distinguishes modern state racism from its antebellum predecessor." See Hartman, Saidiya, 1997, *Scenes of Subjection: Terror, Slavery, and Self-Making in Nineteenth-Century America*, New York: Oxford University Press, pp. 121,115, 10.

8. In her work on gender and race in Jim Crow Georgia, Sarah Haley theorizes how the carceral complex—most specifically through Black women's sentencing to the chain gang—became a key infrastructure for producing and reinforcing the impossibility of the postbellum black female subject. As Haley documents, even when state law specifically prohibited sending *women* to work on chain gangs, white women were diverted, while black women were still sent by the thousands. Haley, Sarah, 2016, *No Mercy Here: Gender, Punishment, and the Making of Jim Crow Modernity*, Chapel Hill: University of North Carolina Press.

9. The Prison Policy Initiative's "Whole Pie" reports have become among the most systematic analyses of incarceration and court supervision. Through careful analysis of pre-trial detention, state and federal incarceration, parole, probation, immigration detention, territorial prisons, and involuntary commitment, these reports interrogate many tried and true

myths of the prison reform movement, including "Can it really be true that most people in jail are being held before trial? And how much of mass incarceration is a result of the war on drugs?" See Wagner, Peter and Wendy Sawyer, 2018, "Mass Incarceration: The Whole Pie 2018," *Prison Policy Initiative*, https://www.prisonpolicy.org/reports/pie2018.html, accessed February 11, 2019.

10. See especially Gilmore, *Golden Gulag*; Jordan T. Camp, 2016, *Incarcerating the Crisis: Freedom Struggles and the Rise of the Neoliberal State*, Berkeley: University of California Press; and Hinton, Elizabeth, 2016, *From the War on Poverty to the War on Crime: The Making of Mass Incarceration in America*, Cambridge: Harvard University Press. See also Wang, Jackie, 2018, *Carceral Capitalism*, South Pasadena, CA: Semiotext(e); Herivel, Tara and Paul Wright, eds., 2003, *Prison Nation: the Warehousing of America's Poor,* New York: Routledge; Parenti, Christian, 2008, *Lockdown America*, London: Verso; and Sudbury, Julia, ed., 2005, *Global Lockdown: Race, Gender, and the Prison-Industrial Complex*, New York: Routledge.

11. See Berger, Dan, 2016, *Captive Nation: Black Prison Organizing in the Civil Rights Era*, Chapel Hill: University of North Carolina Press. On the enduring and global analysis of racial capitalism in the black radical tradition, see Robinson, Cedric J., 1983, *Black Marxism: The Making of the Black Radical Tradition*, Chapel Hill: University of North Carolina Press.

12. See Foucault, Michel, 1995, *Discipline and Punish*, New York: Vintage; and Modern, John Lardas, 2007, "Ghosts of Sing Sing, or the Metaphysics of Secularism," *Journal of the Academy of American Religion* 75(3), September, pp. 615–50.

13. See Sullivan, Winnifred Fallers, 2009, *Prison Religion: Faith-Based Reform and the Constitution*, Princeton: Princeton University Press; and Erzen, Tanya, 2017, *God in Captivity: The Rise of Faith-Based Prison Ministries in the Age of Mass Incarceration*, Boston: Beacon Press, especially pp. 38-58.

14. More recent critical prison studies scholarship is increasingly exploding the myth of prisons as penitent experiments in early America. For example, Jen Manion's groundbreaking research on carceral culture in early America demonstrates that black women—not black men—who quickly outnumbered their white counterparts in the nation's first penitentiary. Black women were more heavily policed than other women, and often received much longer sentences for simple property and nuisance crimes. Manion argues that this targeted criminalization was inextricably linked with black women's freedom: black women and children seeking to live, work, survive, and thrive were criminalized from the moment they broke free from the chattels of slavery. See Manion, Jen, 2015, *Liberty's Prisoners: Carceral Culture in Early America*, University of Pennsylvania Press.

15. To theorize expulsion, I draw on Mary Douglas, specifically her discussion of ritualized approaches to "the problem of evil." See Douglas, Mary, 2003, *Natural Symbols: Explorations in Cosmology*, New York: Routledge, especially Chapter 7.

16. Wells, Ida B., 1893, *The Reason Why the Colored American Is Not in the World's Columbian Exposition: The Afro-American's contribution to Columbian literature*, http://digital.library.upenn.edu/women/wells/exposition/exposition.html, accessed February 11, 2019.

17. I developed portions of this analysis for "Many Hands Make Light Work," my contribution to the 2017-2018 "Is This All There Is?" forum on *The Immanent Frame*, https://tif.ssrc.org/2018/03/09/many-hands-make-light-work/, accessed February 11, 2019. There, I use Simone Browne's concept "dark sousveillance" to connect Ida B. Wells' pamphlet for the 1893

Chicago World's Fair to black women's long-running actions of *theorizing* religion and race in America. See Browne, Simone, 2015, *Dark Matters: On the Surveillance of Blackness*, Durham: Duke University Press.

18. In outlining these three interlocking layers as a "Jim Crow playbook," I draw on Beth Richie's analysis of how black women are isolated, blamed, and criminalized for violence they survive through the intersection of intimate, communal, and structural forces, which she calls "the violence matrix." Richie, Beth, 2012, *Arrested Justice: Black Women, Violence, and America's Prison Nation*, New York: New York University Press, p. 133.

19. In her award-winning book *New World A-Coming: Black Religion and Racial Identity in the Great Migration*, Judith Weisenfeld develops the term "religio-racial identity" to characterize early twentieth-century Black religious communities that challenged U.S. racial hierarchy by fashioning their own new identities; she employs the term as an historical descriptor. More than a shorthand for religion and race being "co-constituted categories," I argue that Weisenfeld's concept "religio-racial" demands methodical and theoretical attention to the place of white agency and white taxonomies of race within religious studies. See Weisenfeld, Judith, 2017, *New World A-Coming: Black Religion and Racial Identity in the Great Migration*, New York: New York University Press.

20. My attention to blackness as foil for secularizing white America is informed by Josef Sorett's analysis and critique of the idea of black sacred-secular fluidity in 2016, "Secular Compared to What?" in Race and Secularism in America, edited by Kahn, Jonathon S. and Vincent W. Lloyd, New York: Columbia University Press, pp. 43–73. See also Lofton, Kathryn. 2009, "The perpetual primitive in African American religious historiography" in The New Black Gods: Arthur Huff Fauset and The Study of African American Religions, edited by Edward E Curtis IV and Danielle Sigler, Bloomington: Indiana University Press, pp. 171–91. I also draw on Curtis Evans' work on how a presumed connection between blackness and religiosity bolstered abolitionists' claims of black capacity for freedom, and later became proof of black people's incompatibility with modernity. Furthermore, I follow Khalil Muhammad in appreciating that appeals to religiosity were often one of the only tools that black people had for troubling Progressive Era equations of blackness with criminality. See Evans, Curtis J., 2008, *The Burden of Black Religion*, Oxford: Oxford University Press; Muhammad, Khalil Gibran, 2010, *The Condemnation of Blackness: Race, Crime, and the Making of Modern Urban America*, Cambridge: Harvard University Press.

21. Wells, Ida B., "The Convict Lease System," in *The Reason Why the Colored American Is Not in the World's Columbian Exposition*.

22. Johnson, Charles S., 1923, "These Colored United States, Chicago: Mecca of the Migrant Mob," *Messenger*, December, p. 5.

23. See especially "Chapter 3: Southern Migrants and the New Social Order" and "Chapter 6: A Woman's Work, an Urban World" in Best, Wallace D., 2013, *Passionately Human, No Less Divine: Religion and Culture in Black Chicago, 1915–1952*, Princeton, Princeton University Press.

24. The sociological transformation of Chicago was most meticulously mapped by St. Clair Drake and Horace R. Cayton. See Drake, St. Clair and Horace R. Cayton, 1993 [1945], *Black Metropolis: A Study of Negro Life in a Northern City*, Chicago: University of Chicago Press. Arthur Fauset's work was also foundational for understanding the Great Migration-era new religious

movements. See Fauset, Arthur, 2002 [1944], *Black Gods of the Metropolis: Negro Cults of the Urban North*, Philadelphia: University of Pennsylvania Press.

25. Green, Reverend Doris, 2017, *Don't Wait Until the Battle Is Over: Shout Victory Now!*, Meadville, PA: Christian Faith Publishing, Inc.

26. Reverend Consuella York, known as "Mother York," is believed to be the first black woman to be ordained into the clergy in Chicago by the Baptist denomination. From 1952 until her death in 1995, she visited Cook County Jail at least three times each week. She also made visits to state prisons. She was pastor of Christ Way Missionary Baptist Church, 1210 E. 62nd St., in Woodlawn, which she founded. This church, which has 300 members, began as a Bible study class that met in the basement of a South Side home, evolved into a storefront mission, and moved to its present location in 1976. Her obituary from the *Chicago Tribune* is available online at http://articles.chicagotribune.com/1995-12-13/news/9512130367_1_jail-minister-cook-county-jail-mother-teresa, accessed Febrary 11, 2019. Her papers are available online at http://www2.wheaton.edu/bgc/archives/GUIDES/397.htm, accessed Febrary 11, 2019.

27. One of the first times Reverend Green publically shared her own history of abuse was for a story by Vazquez, Enid, 2009, "The Reverend Doris Green: A Prison Minister Shares the Peace of Her Own Survival," *Positively Aware*, http://www.thebody.com/content/art54824.html, accessed February 11, 2019.

28. Reverend Green and Mike Smith had a personal commitment ceremony at Stateville, and were officially married when Mike was transferred to Dixon prison.

29. Men and Women In Prison Ministries, "Events," http://www.mwipm.com/news—events.html, accessed February 11, 2019.

30. See Bender, Courtney, 2012, "Practicing Religion," in *Cambridge Companion to Religious Studies*, Cambridge: Cambridge University Press, pp. 273, 274, 285–288; and de Certeau, Michel, 1984, "Walking in the City," in *The Practice of Everyday Life*, Berkeley: University of California Press, pp. 91–111. On this point, I am reminded of Bruno Latour's dismay that "social" has come to mean "a type of material, as if the adjective was roughly comparable to other terms like 'wooden,' 'steely,' 'biological,' 'economical,' 'mental,' 'organizational,' or 'linguistic.'" He advances instead a conception of social as "a movement during a process of assembling." See Latour, Bruno, 2005, *Reassembling the Social: An Introduction to Actor-Network-Theory*, Oxford: Oxford University Press, p. 1.

31. Saskia Sassen's analysis of the making of international migrations offers a much-needed re-complication. She sets aside the usual push-pull explanations of migrations, and instead focuses our attention on the mechanisms by which push and pull conditions can become factors significant enough to spur—and, more importantly, *support*—movement. Under every migrant's feet, there is a path: a *bridge*. In Sassen's research, migration bridges include former colonial bonds, the intentional recruitment of workers, and connections with family members living overseas. In my own, prison migrants travel across bridges that have been constructed out of policies like mandatory minimum drug sentencing laws, citizen lobbying efforts to create jobs in former factory towns by turning them into "prison towns," and kickbacks that private prison corporations give to judges and state governments to increase convictions and prolong sentences. See Sassen, Saskia, 2007, "The Making of International Migrations," in *A Sociology of Globalization*, New York: W. W. Norton & Company, pp. 129–63.

32. In her research on prisons and public life in Iran, Golnar Nikpour has powerfully argued for the need for a critical, abolitionist historical method that insists on excavating the prison's origins as a necessary precondition for being able to imagine its ends. During a February 11, 2019 talk at Dartmouth College on "Dreaming Beyond the Incarcerated Modern," she explained: "The history of the modern prison — like that of all seemingly entrenched structures and struggles — provides students of that history with an essential insight. That is, to understand the historical origins of the modern prison is to be able to imagine a world beyond the prison as well. In other words, when a story has a beginning, it may very well also have an end. In the Middle East, where so many conflicts and crises are described as timeless battles stretching back beyond memory, this insight is especially crucial."

33. The "Seven Neighborhood Study" was first published in 1979 and then again in 1990; both times it received little attention. In 1992, it was sent to the *New York Times* and published as a front-page story. In 2013, the study was revisited by the then-released members of The Think Tank who went on to found the Center for NuLeadership: https://www.nuleadership.org/s/seven-neighborhood-revisited-rpt.pdf, accessed February 11, 2019. These findings were the inspiration for a joint project of Laura Kurgan of the Spatial Information Design Lab and Eric Cadora of the Justice Mapping Center, who together used the term "Million Dollar Blocks" to map the government resources spent to incarcerate people by their home zip codes, thereby illuminating the city-prison-city-prison migration flow of people and resources: http://spatialinformationdesignlab.org/projects/million-dollar-blocks, accessed February 11, 2019.

34. Chicago's Million Dollar Blocks project is available online at https://chicagosmilliondollarblocks.com/, accessed February 11, 2019.

35. Fullilove, Mindy Thompson, 2004, *Root Shock: How Tearing Up City Neighborhoods Hurts America, And What We Can Do About It*, New York: New Village Press, p. 11.

36. Taussig, Michael, 1997, *The Magic of the State*, New York: Routledge.

37. On this idea of the reparative work and the sacred, I am especially indebted to James Logan's careful development of "ontological intimacy" as an expression of radical human bondedness through difference—in and through which we can address the problem of racism and imprisonment. See Logan, James, 2008, *Good Punishment?: Christian Moral Practice and U.S. Imprisonment*, Grand Rapids, MI: William B. Eerdmans Publishing Company, especially Chapter 6. Logan's work dovetails nicely with Ruth Wilson Gilmore's probing of the ways in which power and difference might couple non-fatally in her essay 2002, "Fatal Couplings of Power and Difference: Notes on Racism and Geography," *The Professional Geographer* 54(1), pp. 15-24.

38. See Latour, *Reassembling the Social*.

39. See Men & Women In Prison Ministries, "Harm Reduction in Prison and Jail Coalition" PowerPoint presentation.

40. The name "Taking it to the Streets" was first coined by Reverend Green's son Richard Wallace. He organized community block parties on the themes of sexual health, HIV/AIDS prevention, and testing to literally "Taking it to the Streets." Now, MWIPM has adapted this event concept for their work in the Austin neighborhood of Chicago to "Taking it to the Streets" to address gun violence and overdose deaths by walking and working with the people returning from jail and prison.

CROSSCURRENTS
CONTRIBUTORS

Keri Day is Associate Professor of Constructive Theology and African American Religion at Princeton Theological Seminary in Princeton, NJ. Her teaching and research interests are in womanist/feminist theologies, social critical theory, cultural studies, economics, and Afro-Pentecostalism. Her first academic book, *Unfinished Business: Black Women, The Black Church, and the Struggle to Thrive in America*, was published in November of 2012. Her second book, *Religious Resistance to Neoliberalism: Womanist and Black Feminist Perspectives*, was published in December of 2015. In 2017, she was recognized by ABC News as one of six black women at the center of gravity in theological education in America. She has written for the Dallas Morning News, The Feminist Wire, and The Huffington Post.

Keri.Day@ptsem.edu

Antonia Michelle Daymond is a constructive theologian working in the areas of systematic and contemporary models of theology as well as critical theory and black studies. Her research interests engage in the intersectionalities of theology, race, gender, sexuality, and power.

amdaymond@gmail.com

Gary Dorrien teaches social ethics, theology, and philosophy of religion as the Reinhold Niebuhr Professor of Social Ethics at Union Theological Seminary and Professor of Religion at Columbia University. He was previously the Parfet Distinguished Professor at Kalamazoo College, where he taught for 18 years and also served as Dean of Stetson Chapel and Director of the Liberal Arts Colloquium. Professor Dorrien is the author of 19 books and more than 300 articles that range across the fields of social ethics, philosophy, theology, political economics, social and political theory, religious history, cultural criticism, and intellectual history.

gdorrien@uts.columbia.edu

Rev. **Doris J. Green** is the Founder/CEO of Men & Women in Prison Ministries in Chicago. She has worked with the incarcerated population for more than thirty-six years. In her work as the Director of Correctional Health & Community Affairs at the AIDS Foundation of Chicago, she developed and implemented innovative strategies to assist highly impacted communities to respond to the HIV/AIDS epidemic. Additionally, she has served as Prisoners Representative to the Cook County Bureau of Health Services Institutional Review Board; Commissioner for the Illinois Torture Inquiry and Relief Commission; Advisory Board Member to the NAACP's National HIV Faith & Social Justice; and Master Ambassador to Gilead Sciences' "The Black Church & HIV: The Social Justice Imperative" initiative. Her first book, *Don't Wait Until the Battle is Over: Shout Victory Now!*, showcases the stories of five incarcerated individuals, each of which parallels her life journey.

queenmakeda11@gmail.com

Rev. Dr. **Jennifer Harvey** is a writer, speaker, and professor of religion and ethics at Drake University. She has a Ph.D. in Christian Ethics from Union Theological Seminary in the city of New York. Her work focuses primarily on racial justice and white anti-racism. Dr. Harvey's most recent books include *Raising White Kids: Bringing Up Children in Racially Unjust America* (Abingdon Press) and *Dear White Christians: For Those Still Longing for Racial Reconciliation* (Wm. B. Eerdmans). Dr. Harvey has contributed to the *New York Times, CNN* nd been a guest on both Iowa and National Public Radio (including NPR's "It's Been a Minute with Sam Sanders"). She is a widely sought-after public speaker and is ordained in the American Baptist Churches (USA).

jennifer.harvey@drake.edu

Stanley Hauerwas is the Gilbert T. Rowe Professor emeritus in Duke Divinity School. His most recent book is The Character of Virtue.

hauerwass@gmail.com

Terrence L. Johnson is Associate Professor of Religion and Government at Georgetown University. Johnson is the author of *Tragic Soul-Life: W.E.B. Du Bois and the Moral Crisis Facing American Democracy* (Oxford 2012) and serves as co-editor of the Duke University Press Series *Religious Cultures of African and African Diaspora People*. His essays have appeared in a number of edited volumes and journals, including the *Journal of Religious Ethics, Journal of Africana Religions*, and the *Journal of the Society Christian Ethics*.

Johnson is completing a manuscript tentatively titled *We Testify with Our Lives: Black Power and the Ethical Turn in Politics,* which explores the decline of Afro-Christianity in the post-civil rights era and the increasing efforts among African American leftists to imagine ethics and human rights activism as necessary extensions of, and possibly challenges to, liberal public philosophies rooted in individualism, neutrality, and exceptionalism.

tlj44@georgetown.edu

Vincent Lloyd is Associate Professor at Villanova University, affiliated with the Theology and Religious Studies Department and the Africana Studies Program. He has held fellowships from the American Council of Learned Societies, the James Weldon Johnson Institute for the Study of Race and Difference at Emory University, and the Notre Dame Institute for Advanced Study. His books include *Black Natural Law* (Oxford, 2016), *Religion of the Field Negro* (Fordham, 2017), *In Defense of Charisma* (Columbia, 2018), and the co-edited volume *Anti-Blackness and Christian Ethics* (Orbis, 2017). Lloyd co-edits the journal *Political Theology*. His current research focuses on the theological background of the political vocabulary that circulates in the Movement for Black Lives.

vincent.lloyd@villanova.edu

James Logan holds the *National Endowment for the Humanities Endowed Chair in Interdisciplinary Studies* at Earlham College. He teaches in the Religion department, and teaches in and directs the Program in African and African American Studies. Logan's areas of teaching and research cover religious, philosophical and social ethics; religion and law; constructive Christian theologies; Black religion; theories of religion; and the relationships between religion, ethics and politics in civil/public life.

jlogan@earlham.edu

Laura McTighe is a Postdoctoral Fellow in the Dartmouth College Society of Fellows. She comes to the academy through twenty years of organizing in movements to end AIDS and prisons. Building on her published work in *Signs: Journal of Women and Culture in Society* (2018) and *Souls: A Critical Journal of Black Politics, Culture, and Society* (2017), her first book project, "Fire Dreams: Terror, Resistance, and Rebirth," is a collaborative ethnography of activist persistence undertaken in partnership with the Black feminist leaders of Women With A Vision in New Orleans after their offices were firebombed and destroyed in a still-uninvestigated arson attack. Her second project, "A Wall is just a Wall," moves with Chicago's Rev. Doris Green throughout her more than three decades of work to reassemble the communities decimated by mass criminalization. This research has been supported by the Woodrow Wilson National Fellowship Foundation and the Wenner-Gren Foundation for Anthropological Research.

Laura.McTighe@dartmouth.edu

The Rev. Dr. **Rubén Rosario Rodríguez**, a graduate of the College of William and Mary in Virginia, Union Theological Seminary in New York, and Princeton Theological Seminary, is Associate Professor of Systematic Theology in the Department of Theological Studies at Saint Louis University. An ordained Presbyterian minister, Dr. Rosario's first book, *Racism and God-Talk: A Latino/a Perspective* (NYU Press, 2008), won the 2011 Alpha Sigma Nu Book Award for Theology. Last year he published *Christian Martyrdom and Political Violence: A Conversation with Judaism and Islam* (Cambridge University Press, 2017); next month his next book, *Dogmatics After Babel: Beyond the Theologies of Word and Culture* (Westminster John Knox Press, 2018), will be released; and he is currently editing the multi-author *T&T Clark Companion to Political Theology* (Bloomsbury/T&T Clark, forthcoming 2019). Dr. Rosario has served as Director of the Mev Puleo Scholarship in Latin American Theology, Politics, and Culture since 2010, a ten-week immersion experience focusing on liberation theology and social justice, and he is also a symposium editor for the Political Theology Network.

ruben.rosariorodriguez@slu.edu

www.ingramcontent.com/pod-product-compliance
Lightning Source LLC
Chambersburg PA
CBHW040259170426
43193CB00020B/2940